My eLab | Efficient teaching, effective learning

High Intermediate Level

Brent Davis Reid

PERSPECTIVES

English Skills with Grammar

PEARSON Longman

My eLab is the interactive environment that gives you access to self-graded exercises and additional study resources related to your textbook. Be sure to register for **My eLab** to ensure your success!

TO REGISTER

❶ Go to **http://mybookshelf.pearsonerpi.com**

❷ Follow the instructions. When asked for your access code, please type the code provided underneath the blue sticker.

❸ To access **My eLab** at any time, go to http://mybookshelf.pearsonerpi.com. **Bookmark this page for quicker access.**

Access to My eLab is valid for 12 months from the date of registration.

login: 1734058

Account ID: 88847053

STUDENT ACCESS CODE

PEGRST-SETUP-BONNE-BIVVY-HIGHS-FLEES

WARNING! This book CANNOT BE RETURNED if the access code has been uncovered.

Note: Once you have registered, you will need to join your online class. Ask your teacher to provide you with the class ID.

TEACHER Access Code

To obtain an access code for My eLab, please contact your Pearson ELT consultant.

1 800 263-3678, ext. 2
pearsonerpi.com/help

133287W (A33287)

High Intermediate Level

Brent Davis Reid

English Skills
with Grammar

PERSPECTIVES

High Intermediate Level

Brent Davis Reid

English Skills
with Grammar

PERSPECTIVES

Acknowledgements

To paraphrase a well-known proverb, "it takes a team to make a book." And what a team we had! Many thanks to Sharnee Chait, Lucie Turcotte, Julie Hough, Katya Epstein, Mairi MacKinnon and Linda Barton for all their hard work. Thanks also to Keith Boeckner for his contribution to the grammar.

I would also like to express my gratitude to the following colleagues for their invaluable input:

Suzie Dufresne, Cégep régional de Lanaudière
Christine Lalonde, Cégep de Sainte-Foy
Laura McGee, Collège de Maisonneuve
Gerald Vallée, Collège de L'Assomption
Derek White, Cégep de Lévis-Lauzon
Brenda Young, Collège François-Xavier-Garneau

In honour of Murray and Max

Managing Editor
Sharnee Chait

Editor
Lucie Turcotte

Copy Editors
Katya Epstein
Linda Barton

Proofreader
Mairi MacKinnon

Photo Research
Marie-Chantal Masson
Amy Paradis

Permissions
Marie-Chantal Masson

Art Director
Hélène Cousineau

Graphic Design Coordinator
Karole Bourgon

Book and Cover Design / Layout
Claire Senneville

Registration of copyright: Bibliothèque et Archives nationales du Québec, 2010
Registration of copyright: Library and Archives Canada, 2010

Printed in Canada   456789   SO   20 19 18 17
ISBN 978-2-7613-3287-3   133287 ABCD   OF10

Credits

Unit 1 p. 1 Photograph © Tiago Estima / iStockphoto. pp. 3–4 "The Red Pants" by Malka Zipora. Copyright © Malka Zipora 2007. Reprinted with permission. p. 4 Photograph © Denis Potapov / iStockphoto. p. 17 Photograph © Viorika Prikhodko / iStockphoto.

Unit 2 p. 21 Photograph © iStockphoto. p. 24 "Did I Miss Anything?" by Tom Wayman reprinted with permission. pp. 26–28 "Single-Sex Classes: Equality or Gender Apartheid?" by Elsie Hambrook reprinted with permission from the author. p. 27 Photograph © Steve Stone / iStockphoto. p. 30 Audio text "Single-Sex Classes" © Canadian Broadcasting Corporation. pp. 35–36 "Humbled by a Real Fight for Women's Rights" by Naomi Lakritz reprinted by permission of the Victoria Times Colonist Group Inc., a CanWest Partnership. p. 38 Video segment "Little Women, Big Hearts" © Canadian Broadcasting Corporation. p. 39 Photograph © Alison Wright / Corbis.

Unit 3 p. 46 Photograph © iStockphoto. p. 50 "Smart" by Shel Silverstein © 1974, renewed 2002 Evil Eye Music, LLC. Reprinted with permission from the Estate of Shel Silverstein and HarperCollins Children's Books. pp. 52–54 "Financial Health Is a Part of Overall Health" by Jane Claxton-Oldfield reprinted with permission from the author. p. 53 Photograph © iStockphoto. p. 56 Video segment "Frugal Shopping" © Canadian Broadcasting Corporation. pp. 60–62 "The Gift of Thrift" reprinted with the express permission of The National Post Company, a CanWest Partnership. p. 61 Photograph © National Post / Laura Leyshon. p. 65 Audio text "Radical Thrift" © Canadian Broadcasting Corporation.

Unit 4 p. 74 Photograph © Tobias Helbig / iStockphoto. p. 77 "If I Had My Life to Live Over" by Erma Bombeck reprinted with permission from The Aaron M. Priest Literary Agency, 2009. p. 79 Photograph © Pablo Scapinachis Armstrong, arquiplay / BigStock. pp. 79–80 "Relics of a Former Life" by Gail Kerbel reprinted with permission. p. 82 Video segment "Send in the Robots" © Canadian Broadcasting Corporation. pp. 87–88 " 'Too Old' or 'Too Young'" by Brett Anningson reprinted with permission from the author. p. 90 Audio text "Designing for Seniors" © Canadian Broadcasting Corporation. p. 93 Photograph © Glen Hougan.

Unit 5 p. 101 Photograph © Alex Potemkin / iStockphoto. p. 105 "Obsessive Me" by Lennard J. Davis © 2008 by Lennard J. Davis. Reprinted with permission. pp. 108–110 "Exploring Inner Space" by Jim Withers reprinted with the express permission of CanWest News Service, a CanWest Partnership. p. 113 Video segment "Positively Autistic" © Canadian Broadcasting Corporation; photograph © KS ART, New York. pp. 118–120 "Awakening in a Twilight Zone Not to Be Feared" by Davidicus Wong reprinted with permission from the author. p. 122 Audio text "Mental Health Stand-up" © Canadian Broadcasting Corporation; photograph © David Granirer.

Unit 6 p. 131 Photograph © Michal Szota / iStockphoto. pp. 133–136 "In the Waiting Room" by David Sedaris © 2008 by David Sedaris. Reprinted by permission of Little, Brown & Company. pp. 139–141 "Sometimes You Have to Just Jump" by Sarah Regan reprinted with permission. p. 140 Photograph © Eduardo Leite / iStockPhoto. p. 142 Audio text "Risk-Takers: Boon or Burden?" © Canadian Broadcasting Corporation. p. 143 Map of Grouse Mountain area © 2007. Her Majesty the Queen in Right of Canada, Natural Resources Canada; map of Sarnia area © 2002. Her Majesty the Queen in Right of Canada, Natural Resources Canada. pp. 147–148 "Self-Indulgent Risks Reflect Larger Issues" by Brett Anningson reprinted with permission from the author. p. 150 Video segment "Binge Drinking" © Canadian Broadcasting Corporation.

Unit 7 p. 157 Photograph © Fernando Alonso Herrero / iStockphoto. p. 158 Photograph © iStockphoto. p. 159 Photograph © Mary Marin / iStockphoto. pp. 159–161 "Finding a Nationality That Fits" by Isabel Vincent reprinted with permission from the author. pp. 163–164 "Hallway Culture Clash" by Matthew Coutts © 2009 The National Post Company. All rights reserved. Unauthorized distribution, transmission or republication strictly prohibited. Reprinted with permission. p. 164 Photograph © Graça Victoria / iStockphoto. p. 166 Audio text "Neighbours: When to Say No to Nice?" © Canadian Broadcasting Corporation.

Cover photograph © Murat Giray Kaya / iStockphoto.

Introduction

Perspectives is an integrated four-skills college-level textbook with a print and online grammar component designed for high intermediate students of English as a Second Language (ESL).

In *Perspectives*, students consider a variety of opinions and the influences that shape opinions, with a view to fostering social responsibility, cultural awareness and openness.

Unit 1 is recommended for all students as it presents the underlying concept of the textbook and explains the suggested structures for written and spoken productions. Units 2 to 6 explore topics such as gender differences and unequal rights (Unit 2); financial health and thrift (Unit 3); aging and ageism (Unit 4); autism and mental health (Unit 5); and risk-taking, risk-takers and risky behaviours (Unit 6). Unit 7 concludes with a look at multiculturalism.

Reading, listening and watching activities not only allow students to develop their comprehension and vocabulary skills, but also provide material for writing and speaking activities that can be done individually or in groups. In addition, various joint writing and speaking projects encourage students to express their creativity. Two appendices provide useful information on researching, referencing and revising, as well as techniques for effective reading and active listening.

An important component of *Perspectives* is the Grammar Guide, also available as an eText on My eLab. As students review essential grammar notions in their books, they are reminded to practise their grammar skills in My eLab. Those using the electronic version have direct access to automatically graded exercises and instant feedback.

Apart from the grammar eText and eighty grammar exercises, My eLab offers a variety of reading, listening and vocabulary exercises that are also automatically graded. Teachers can assess their students' progress by using the gradebook, where results are automatically compiled.

To conclude, it is hoped that students will enjoy reading and hearing about other people's opinions from a variety of perspectives and that they in turn will readily and respectfully share their own opinions from their unique perspectives, for the benefit of all.

Brent Davis Reid

Highlights

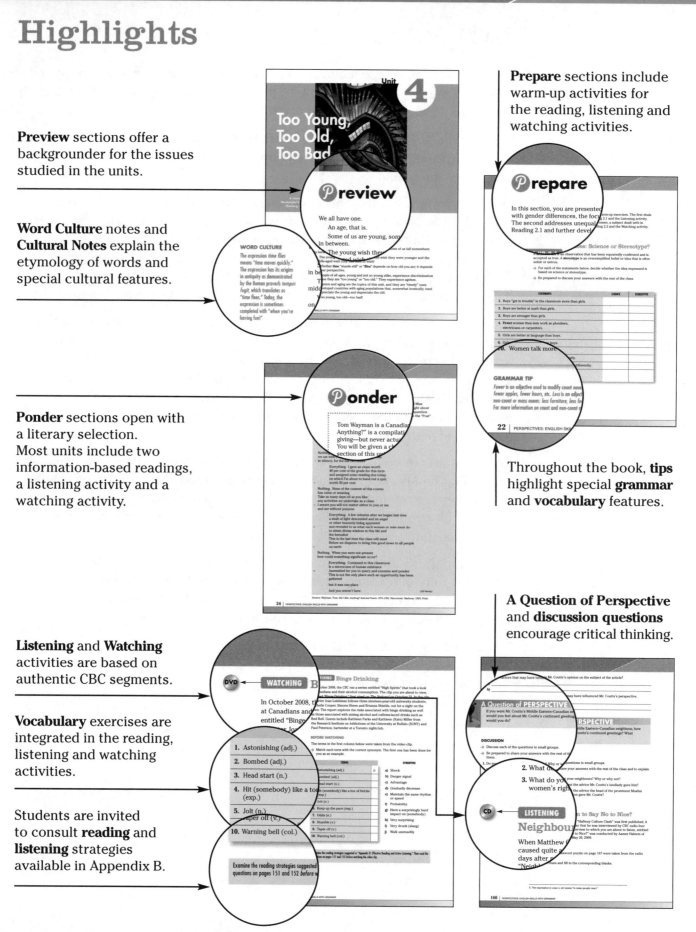

Preview sections offer a backgrounder for the issues studied in the units.

Word Culture notes and **Cultural Notes** explain the etymology of words and special cultural features.

Ponder sections open with a literary selection. Most units include two information-based readings, a listening activity and a watching activity.

Listening and **Watching** activities are based on authentic CBC segments.

Vocabulary exercises are integrated in the reading, listening and watching activities.

Students are invited to consult **reading** and **listening** strategies available in Appendix B.

Prepare sections include warm-up activities for the reading, listening and watching activities.

Throughout the book, **tips** highlight special **grammar** and **vocabulary** features.

A Question of Perspective and **discussion questions** encourage critical thinking.

© PEARSON LONGMAN • REPRODUCTION PROHIBITED

Present sections provide topics for group discussions and individual presentations.

In the **Post** sections, students are asked to produce various types of texts, from paragraphs to essays.

Participate sections include joint writing and speaking projects that allow students to express their creativity.

Works to further explore the topics studied are listed in the **Pursue** sections.

My eLab offers additional reading, listening and vocabulary exercises with automatic grading and feedback.

Two appendices contain guidelines for researching, referencing and revising, and strategies for effective reading and active listening.

The **Grammar Guide**, also available as an eText on My eLab, reviews ten essential grammar notions. Eighty online exercises with automatic grading provide students with appropriate practice.

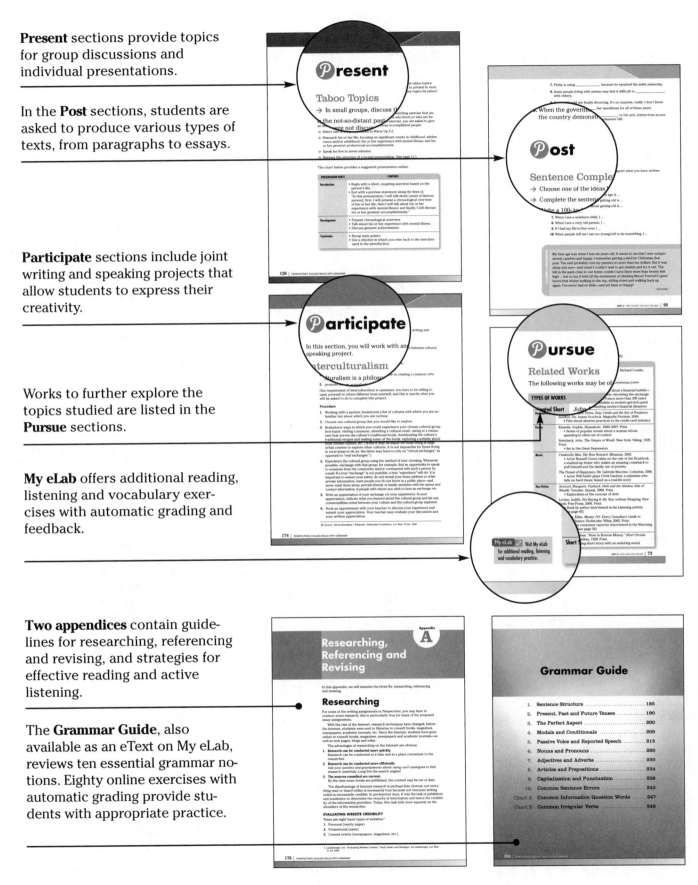

Scope and Sequence

	UNIT 1 Understanding Perspectives	UNIT 2 Worlds Apart	UNIT 3 Dollars and Sense
Reading	• Identify factors influencing opinion • Identify controlling ideas and supporting details • Recognize single, significant, specific and supportable topics • Identify preview statements, controlling ideas and transition terms, types of evidence, grabber and clincher techniques, summary statements • Read a novel	• Identify main ideas, supporting details and opinions	• Identify main ideas, supporting details and opinions
Writing	• Write a 125-word paragraph • Group activity: write a four- or five-paragraph essay • Write a report on a novel	• Paraphrase • Create a free-verse poem • Write a 400- to 450-word persuasive essay • Use statistics and expert opinions as evidence • Refute opposite opinions	• Paraphrase • Write a 100- to 125-word rhyming poem • Write a 400- to 450-word process essay • Write a fable
Listening	• Listen to a speech • Identify preview statements, controlling ideas and transition terms, types of evidence, grabber and clincher techniques, summary statements	• Understand a discussion of study results • Identify main ideas, supporting details and opinions	• Identify main ideas, supporting details and opinions
Speaking	• Express and share opinions • Adopt a different opinion / perspective • Brainstorm ideas • Practise the basic structure of a formal speech in a five- to seven-minute presentation • Prepare a speech outline • Discuss a novel	• Discuss questions in small groups • Participate in a single-sex discussion • Present a five- to seven-minute speech with a partner, expressing opposite opinions • Make a video clip	• Discuss questions in small groups • Analyze case studies and offer advice • Present a five- to seven-minute speech on a proverb
Vocabulary	• Identify phrasal verbs • Define words from context • Find synonyms	• Match words with their definitions • Define words from context • Find synonyms	• Match words with their definitions • Define words from context
Critical Thinking	• Consider influences on opinions • Identify and apply the elements of formal discourse	• Classify statements • Create a literary work • Prepare and defend arguments	• Self-evaluate • Distinguish wants from needs • Create literary works • Explain a process

© PEARSON LONGMAN • REPRODUCTION PROHIBITED

UNIT 4 Too Young, Too Old, Too Bad	UNIT 5 Mind Matters	UNIT 6 All or Nothing	UNIT 7 One Last Look
• Identify main ideas, supporting details and opinions	• Identify main ideas, supporting details and opinions • Proofread one's work	• Identify main ideas, supporting details and opinions	• Identify main ideas, supporting details and opinions • Proofread one's work
• Support an idea with a 100- to 125-word paragraph • Write a 400- to 450-word informative essay • Use credible sources, paraphrase and quote • Support ideas with expert opinion, facts and statistics • Produce a report on an interview segment	• Paraphrase • Narrate a funny moment in a 100- to 150-word text • Write a 400- to 450-word definition essay • Write blogs to stamp out social stigma	• Paraphrase • Write about a time when one dared being different in a 100- to 150-word text • Write a 400- to 450-word personal essay • Prepare interview questions • Prepare a report outline	• Paraphrase • Write a 100- to 150-word paragraph about a custom • Write a 400- to 450-word compare and contrast essay • Exchange with a different cultural group • Write an appreciation of one's intercultural experience
• Identify main ideas, supporting details and opinions	• Identify main ideas, supporting details and opinions	• Identify main ideas, supporting details and opinions	• Identify main ideas, supporting details and opinions
• Explain an opinion • Participate in a seminar • Make a five- to seven-minute formal presentation • Run a discussion • Conduct an interview	• Discuss questions in small groups • Participate in a discussion about taboo topics • Make a five- to seven-minute formal presentation	• Discuss questions in small groups • Participate in a discussion to rank and recommend escapist activities • Make a five- to seven-minute formal presentation • Conduct an interview • Give an oral report	• Discuss questions in small groups • Participate in a discussion about customary clothing • Take a position for or against a dress code in a five- to seven-minute presentation • Brainstorm • Exchange with a different cultural group • Express an appreciation of one's intercultural experience
• Match words with their definitions • Define words from context	• Define words from context • Find synonyms	• Define words from context • Match terms with synonyms • Create sentences using studied vocabulary	• Define words from context • Do a crossword puzzle • Identify words from synonyms
• Apply a definition • Complete sentences • Collect and organize information	• Connect facts • Construct a personal definition • Relate historical details	• Categorize and evaluate actions • Relate a life lesson • Interpret personal data	• Identify differences in meaning • Analyze similarities and differences • Discover a new culture

Table of Contents

Understanding Perspectives

Vasco de Gama Tower, Lisbon, Portugal. View from the ground

Preview

I am a very old man, or at least that's what my five-year-old daughter tells me.

I am a very young man, or at least that's what my eighty-five-year-old mother tells me.

I am forty-five years old.

So who's right?

From the perspective of a five-year-old, I am old—very old. From the perspective of an eighty-five-year-old, I am young—very young. From my perspective, I am neither very young nor very old.

When understanding the opinions of others, especially opinions that differ from our own, it is important to consider what has shaped their opinions. It is important to understand their perspectives.

GRAMMAR TIP

Verbs like *can* and *will* are called **modals**. These are auxiliary verbs used with the base form of other verbs to express a particular mood: "you **will** learn"; "a singular object **can** be viewed"; etc. For more information on modals, turn to page 209.

Who we are and *what we have experienced* **will** influence our opinions. Factors such as age, gender, health, wealth, race and sexual orientation will have an impact upon our opinions, as will significant life experiences such as the death of a loved one or recovery from a life-threatening disease.

So, do you think I am very young or very old? Well, your answer likely depends on your age as well as the forty-five-year-olds you have met.

As you work through *Perspectives*, you will be asked to identify opinions and the influences on these opinions with a view to broadening your own.

In this introductory unit, you will read a short story that serves as a metaphor for the concept underlying this textbook: A singular object or idea **can** be viewed from more than one perspective, generating very different opinions. And these opinions, even if opposing, can be "right," or, at the very least, valid. In the rest of the unit, you will learn the basics of essay writing and public speaking in order to prepare you to share your perspectives with others in an academic context.

I hope you will enjoy the experience.

 **repare**

WARM UP What's Your Opinion?

Below is a list of statements based on subjects that this textbook deals with, directly or indirectly.

→ In the space provided, indicate your level of disagreement or agreement with each of the statements.

→ Be prepared to discuss your answers.

1	**2**	**3**	**4**	**5**
Strongly disagree	Disagree	Undecided	Agree	Strongly agree

1. Having siblings[1] is better than being an only child. _____5_____

2. Studying in a single-sex classroom improves student grades. _____1_____

3. Education is a right, not a privilege. _____4_____

4. It is the school's responsibility to teach students how to budget. _____3_____

5. Young people today are spoiled.[2] _____4_____

6. Old people are beautiful. _____5_____

7. Women should be allowed to drive after they turn sixteen; men, after they turn eighteen. _____2_____

---

1. Siblings are brothers and/or sisters.
2. *Spoiled* means "overindulged."

8. It is possible to make the most of any situation.   *4*

9. Extreme sports should be outlawed.   *2*

10. Racism, sexism and ageism can be eliminated from North American society.   *3*

DISCUSSION

→ Gather into small groups to respond to each of the questions.

1. Were you and your classmates of one opinion, or did your perspectives differ?

2. Were any differences in perspective influenced by gender? If so, for which statement(s) did you notice this influence?

$\mathcal{P}$onder

CULTURAL NOTE

Hasidic Judaism (or Hasidism) is a Jewish religious movement that originated in eastern Europe in the eighteenth century.

Malka Zipora is the pseudonym of a Hasidic woman living in Outremont, Quebec. She is a mother and an author who considers her twelve children to be her life's achievement. Her book *Rather Laugh Than Cry* is a collection of writings about her daily life in a Hasidic community. The story you are about to read was taken from this collection.

The Red Pants

By Malka Zipora

1 I sit on the floor, surrounded by a mountain of boxes. The snow outside has melted. Passover[3] (*Pesach*) is approaching, and with it comes the new season,
5 which means preparing the children's winter wardrobe. I wade into the contents of the boxes to sort out the clothing accumulated over the years. I must decide the fate of each item; which child will in-
10 herit it this year, or put it aside to review again next season, or get rid of it altogether. It is an emotionally exhausting occupation, for these clothes are saturated with vivid and sentimental memories.

15 I stare lovingly at the little red pants at the top of the pile. They have outlived the store where I purchased them over twenty years ago. I remember how the little outfit taunts me for three days begging me from
20 the window—"Buy me! Buy me!" The price is marked just above the fancy European label. Never before have I spent the exorbitant price of *sixteen dollars* on a child's outfit. My conscience and I are at war.

25 "Just this once!" I reason with myself. "Little Moishy will look royal. His black hair against the red fabric."

---

3. Passover is a Jewish holiday in spring when Jews remember the escape from Egypt described in Exodus.

Yes, it is obvious that the outfit is destined for me ... or is it? Why not?

30 "Can I justify spending so much, when my budget is so tight?" I ask myself. "Maybe if I save on diapers by changing them less often? No? Okay, I won't spend on treats for a half a year ... Of course I 35 can afford it! I deserve it ... I can ... I will! ... And before the next objection can arise I run into the store, leaving my conscience outside to watch the carriage. This is how the little red pants come to be intertwined 40 with the history of my family.

Moishy is irresistible. I walk him, wheel him and parade him, strutting proudly, confident that crowds are lining up to see the remarkable Moisheleh (little Moishy) 45 in his red pants. I try to stifle my disdain for anyone who does not dress his or her children as well as I do.

I hem the pants up one season and down the next, so that the next child can 50 use them. Sheindl, unlike Moishy, is chubby and blond. Her blue eyes sparkle and she fills the red pants to the maximum—plus. Her natural bulges are advertised by the contour-hugging double knit. 55 She is adorable and I have long forgotten the price. The compliments keep coming despite the evident hemlines.

And it comes to pass that Avromeleh (little Avraham) is heir to the outfit. He 60 does not share my respect for it, and his persistent crawling thins out the knees of the red pants. The thread I use to mend it is so close in colour that one really has to make an effort to notice it. My favourite 65 picture of Benyamin (the next in line) shows him smiling happily in the exact same red pants in all their glory.

It may have been somewhere between Leah and Yoel—I do not remember which 70 child wore the outfit—when one of the eyes of the embroidered giraffe disappears. It does not matter, for the charm remains. I think it is cute when I change the matching knit shirt for one that is less frayed, 75 though not quite so perfectly matched. For Yoel I add fancy patches at the knees and fool the whole world into thinking that they belong to the original design of the pants. I do not notice that the compliments 80 stopped long ago. Nevertheless, I am sure that this is exactly the finery that every mother would wish for her child.

As I sort through the winter clothes, I sit reflecting for fifteen minutes, debating 85 whether the time is ripe[4] to hand the pants down to Lipa. The truth is, I am not so desperate, because over the years I have sporadically bought quite a few more "memories," which I will get to as 90 soon as I have decided on the destiny of these red pants.

---

4. *The time is ripe* means "it is a suitable moment."

The door opens and I am **caught red-handed** (or red-pantsed) by my daughter Sheindl, now all grown up, who has
95 accomplished quite a bit of Passover (*Pesach*) cleaning while I am meditating. She stares at the red pants.

WORD CULTURE

The expression *to be caught red-handed* means "to be caught doing something wrong." The expression originally referred to murder alone, alluding to the blood found on a murderer's hands.

"Mummy, you're not keeping that rag (*shmatte*) … or are you?" she bursts out in
100 disbelief. "Half those boxes should have been dumped long ago," she says pointing to the stack that almost reaches the ceiling.

"A *rag*? What heresy!" I think to myself, but I know I am defeated. Without the
105 memories, that is exactly what the red pants are—rags!

I cannot bear to part so abruptly with this emotional treasure, so I suggest giving it away to charity (*gemach*).

110 "Oh please, Mummy! They would be embarrassed to wear this in Rwanda. Anyway, I need a good rag to wipe the top of the china cabinet."

I stare at her wordlessly, feeling misun-
115 derstood. How could she be so disloyal to something that had served her so well eighteen years ago? So, this is what is meant by the generation gap!

Sheindl rips the pants apart and
120 marches off with two limp red cloths that had once been full and bursting with little Sheindl herself. Dutifully, with one goal in mind, she hurries to polish the furniture with my precious memories.

(895 Words)

Source: Zipora, Malka. *Rather Laugh Than Cry*. Montreal: Véhicule, 2007. 21–25. Print.

VOCABULARY AND COMPREHENSION

You may have to do research to find some of the answers to the questions below.

1. **Phrasal verbs** are two- or three-word verbs consisting of a verb followed by an adverb or a preposition, functioning as a single unit of meaning. In line 6, the author uses the phrasal verb *wade into*. What does this verb mean? What image does the verb create in the context in which it is used?

   _____

   _____

   _____

   _____

2. What is the author doing?

   _____

3. **Personification** is a figure of speech in which inanimate objects are given human qualities. What two objects are personified in the second and fifth paragraphs (lines 15–25 and 30–40)?

   a) _____

   b) _____

4. Why does the author struggle over buying the outfit?

   _____

5. Define the words that follow according to the context used in the sixth paragraph (lines 41–47):

    a) strutting: _____

    b) stifle: _____

    c) disdain: _____

6. Why does the author hem the pants up and down?

_____

_____

7. Why does the author mend the knees of the pants?

_____

_____

8. Which word in the ninth paragraph (lines 68–82) means "worn" or "threadbare"? _____

9. What does the author hope to achieve by patching the pants?

_____

_____

10. The author jokingly writes that she is caught "red-handed" (or "red-pantsed") by her daughter. What "crime" was the author committing when her daughter walked in on her? (See the Word Culture note on page 5.)

_____

_____

_____

11. What allows the author to see the red pants as something other than rags?

_____

12. Why do the author and her daughter not share the same perspective with respect to the little red pants? List two possibilities.

    a) _____

    b) _____

DISCUSSION

→ Gather into small groups to respond to each of the questions.

1. Why did the author write the short story? List two possibilities.

2. Whose perspective do you share? The mother's or the daughter's? (Are the red pants precious or practically worthless?) From whose perspective is the story told?

3. Did you enjoy reading "The Red Pants"? Why or why not? Which of the following factors may have had an influence on your appreciation of the short story: gender, age, social role (being a mother, father, daughter, son, etc.), ethnicity?

Post

In this section, activities focus on writing paragraphs and then essays, two skills that you will develop as you work through this textbook. The basic structure of the paragraph and the academic essay are presented in this unit. In later units, you will be given an opportunity to write different types of academic essays: the argumentative essay (Unit 2), the process essay (Unit 3), the informative essay (Unit 4), the definition essay (Unit 5), the personal essay (Unit 6) and the compare and contrast essay (Unit 7).

The Paragraph

The short story "The Red Pants" is made up of seventeen "units of writing," more commonly referred to as paragraphs. A paragraph deals with one particular idea. In non-fiction writing, the main idea of a paragraph is often referred to as the **controlling idea**, and the controlling idea is always accompanied by supporting details (or evidence). A paragraph typically moves from the general to the specific in order to advance a particular point of view.

The Paragraph

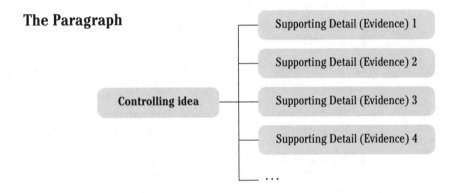

Controlling idea

Supporting Detail (Evidence) 1

Supporting Detail (Evidence) 2

Supporting Detail (Evidence) 3

Supporting Detail (Evidence) 4

...

EXAMPLE PARAGRAPH

First impressions can be deceiving. The first time I met Gwyneth, it wasn't exactly love at first sight. She was really into the goth rock scene and dressed accordingly. Her outfits were all black, and she had dyed her naturally blond hair to match. Her eyes were always heavily made up with dark eyeliner and even her fingernails were painted black. Now I can imagine I wasn't her type either! She immediately nicknamed me "Mr. Preppy" due to my "boring" clothes: a button-down shirt, an argyle sweater, cuffed chinos and boat shoes. (In my defence, while my attire may indeed have been boring, at least it had some colour!) Fortunately, we quickly got beyond these deceptive first impressions and will shortly be celebrating our twentieth wedding anniversary with our two daughters, who are both, perhaps not surprisingly, rather fond of goth culture.

EXERCISE 1.1

→ Referring to the example paragraph, respond to the questions below.

1. What is the controlling idea of the example paragraph?

_____

2. What details support the controlling idea?

_____

_____

_____

3. The first sentence is a general statement; the second, a specific statement.

☐ True   ☐ False

WRITING ACTIVITY: THE PARAGRAPH

→ Write a paragraph of approximately 125 words in response to one of the questions below.

→ Begin your paragraph by presenting your point of view and then support it with pertinent details (i.e., move from the general to the specific).

1. Who has most influenced your perspective on life? Name the person and indicate his or her relationship to you. Explain why that person has had the greatest influence.

2. Write about a time when you influenced someone's opinion. Indicate how and why you influenced that person.

3. Write about an experience that caused you to change your mind about something. Indicate what happened and how your opinion changed.

4. How are you similar to your parents? How are you dissimilar? Are you more alike than you are different? Explain.

5. Have you gotten wiser as you have gotten older? Illustrate your point of view with a real-life example.

The Academic Essay

The academic essay is a formal, structured piece of writing consisting of an introductory paragraph, a two- or three-paragraph development and a concluding paragraph. Due to its formality, you may be asked not to use first- and second-person pronouns (*I, you, we, my, your, our*, etc.) or contractions (*he's, they're, we're*, etc.) when writing an academic essay. A title page, research and referencing may also be required. (For more information on research and giving references, see "Appendix A: Researching, Referencing and Revising.")

Academic Essay

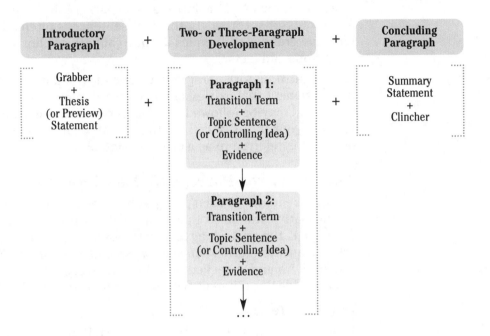

An effective essay is based on a subject that passes the 4-S test.[5]

The subject must be:

1. Single
An academic essay deals with one, and only one, subject. As a consequence, the thesis statement—upon which the entire essay is constructed—must express the writer's opinion on one, and only one, subject.

2. Significant
An academic essay is written to be read. In an educational setting, the reader is typically your teacher and perhaps one or more of your classmates. Your teacher and your classmates deserve to read essays on meaningful subjects.

3. Specific
Academic essays are brief. The more specific your thesis statement, the more justice you can do to the topic selected; for example, instead of writing about war, write about the internment of Japanese-Canadian citizens during World War II.

4. Supportable
An academic essay requires that you prove your point (your thesis). If you can't support your thesis statement, change it.

Even when assigned a subject, you will likely have to refine it so that it passes this very important test.

---

5. For more information on the 4-S test, see Norton, Sarah, and Brian Green. *Essay Essentials with Readings.* Montreal: Harcourt, 1997. 24, 29, 31, 113. Print.

The Introductory Paragraph

The first sentence of the introductory paragraph should grab the reader's attention. Not surprisingly, this first sentence is often referred to as a **grabber**. Effective grabber techniques include (but are not limited to) using quotations, definitions and facts.

The introductory paragraph must end with a **thesis statement**, an affirmative statement that expresses the writer's opinion about the subject of the essay, and may be followed by a list of two or three main points to be used to support your thesis. When the thesis statement is followed by a list of main points, it is referred to as a **preview statement**.

Two- or Three-Paragraph Development

The first sentence of each paragraph in the development is a **topic sentence**, an affirmative statement that supports the thesis statement. The topic sentence is the controlling idea of the paragraph. Each topic sentence begins with a transition term such as *First*, *Second* and *Third* or *To begin*, ~~*To continue*~~ and ~~*To finish*~~ and is backed up with evidence: statistics, expert opinion or example. Ideally, different types of evidence are used in the development.

finally

Transition Terms

Transition terms lend coherence to a text, indicating relationships between ideas. The list below provides examples of commonly-used transition terms and the functions of these terms.

FUNCTIONS	EXAMPLES
To add an idea	additionally, also, furthermore, in addition (to), in the same way, moreover
To emphasize an idea	indeed, in fact
To provide an example	for example, for instance, to illustrate
To show a result	as a result, therefore, consequently
To show a contrast	however, nevertheless, on the contrary, on the other hand, otherwise
To conclude	briefly, hence, in brief, in conclusion, in summary, to conclude

Concluding Paragraph

The first sentence of the concluding paragraph is a **summary statement**, a paraphrase of the thesis statement and topic sentences. The summary statement begins with a transition term such as *To sum up*, *In summary*, *To conclude* or *In conclusion*.

The last sentence of the concluding paragraph is the **clincher**, a technique used to encourage the reader to reflect upon the essay. Effective clincher techniques include (but are not limited to) connecting with the introduction, asking a rhetorical question (question for which no answer is expected) or offering a suggestion.

The Importance of Pondering

By Brent Davis Reid

Ponder means "spend time thinking carefully and seriously about a problem, question or occurrence." In a world where chatting, texting and twittering have supplanted cultured conversation, meticulously handwritten messages and small talk over a leisurely cup of coffee, few people ponder nowadays— and more's the pity.[6] This paucity in pondering may well explain why so many people have difficulty putting pen to paper, for pondering is indispensable to the essay-writing process, occurring before the essay is written, while the essay is being written and after the essay has been written.

Before the essay is written, the writer must first select a subject. This subject must pass the 4-S test; that is, the subject must be single, significant, specific and supportable. The writer must then formulate an opinion on the subject. At this stage in the process, some preliminary research is required: the writer must consider what others think about the subject—and why they think as they do. Once the writer has processed the research and arrived at a personal opinion on the subject, a preview statement must be constructed: this statement expresses the writer's opinion on the subject as well as the main points to be discussed. From the time the writer was given the task of writing an essay to the construction of a preview statement, it is obvious that a fair amount of pondering has taken place.

While the essay is being written, the writer must carefully consider all required structural elements, choosing the best techniques to communicate his or her message. Should the grabber be a quotation, a definition or a fact? Should the topic sentence be backed up by statistics, expert opinion or example? What clincher technique should be employed: connecting with the introduction, asking a rhetorical question or offering a suggestion? By the time each of the structural elements has been selected, a plan outlined and a first draft written, even more time has been spent pondering.

After the essay has been written, the writer must revise the essay. Ideally, the first draft of the essay is put aside for a while, allowing the writer the time needed to read the essay objectively. While reading, the writer must evaluate the essay with respect to the five Cs: creativity, cohesion, clarity, cogency and correctness.[7] The essay must be read and reread many times— forward *and* backwards! (Reading the essay backwards is a proven proofreading technique for spotting spelling errors.) Once again, much pondering has taken place.

To conclude, pondering is requisite to essay-writing, occurring throughout the process. While more challenging than chatting, texting and twittering, essay-writing is also more satisfying in that what is produced on paper will likely be around long after the digital blips on a screen have disappeared.

(457 words)

6. *More's the pity* means "that's a shame."
7. For more information on revising, see "Appendix A: Researching, Referencing and Revising" (p. 176).

EXERCISE 1.2

Part A

→ Indicate with checkmarks whether each of the following subjects passes the 4-S test.

1. The generation and gender gaps

   Single ☐   Significant ☒   Specific ☐   Supportable ☒

   in my opinion

2. My dog Max

   Single ☒   Significant ♡   Specific ☒   Supportable ☐

3. Charity

   Single ☒   Significant ☒   Specific ☐   Supportable ☒

4. The impact of a poor economy on charitable giving in 2009

   Single ☒   Significant ☒   Specific ☒   Supportable ☒

5. The future of humanity

   Single ☒   Significant ☒   Specific ☒   Supportable ☐

Part B

1. What is the subject of the essay, "The Importance of Pondering"?

   ___The academic essay___

EXERCISE 1.3

Part A

→ For each of the following grabbers, circle the technique used.

1. German philosopher Arthur Schopenhauer made the following comment with respect to individual perspective: "Every man takes the limits of his own field of vision for the limits of the world."

   (a) Quotation   **b)** Definition   **c)** Fact

2. More people speak English in China than in Canada and the United States combined. This fact helps put China's population in perspective.

   a) Quotation   **b)** Definition   **(c)** Fact

Part B

1. What type of grabber was used in the essay, "The Importance of Pondering"?

   ___definition___

EXERCISE 1.4

Part A

→ Circle the letters of the correct answers. More than one answer is possible.

1. Which of the following are not thesis statements?

   a) Many Hasidic families live in Outremont, Quebec.

   b) North American couples should be given financial incentives to have more children.

   c) Should children be forced to wear hand-me-downs?

   d) The gender gap cannot be bridged.

2. A thesis statement is:

   a) always followed by a list of main ideas.

   b) a synonym of "a preview statement."

   c) located at the end of the introductory paragraph.

   d) located at the start of the introductory paragraph.

3. A topic sentence:

   a) is located at the end of each paragraph in the development.

   b) is located at the start of each paragraph in the development.

   c) is preceded by evidence.

   d) is followed by evidence.

   e) supports the thesis statement.

   f) is a controlling idea.

4. A summary statement is:

   a) identical in wording to the thesis statement.

   b) located at the start of the concluding paragraph.

   c) located at the end of the concluding paragraph.

   d) introduced by a transition term.

Part B

→ Referring to "The Importance of Pondering," respond to the questions below.

1. Copy out the preview statement. (Write only the words that express the thesis statement and main ideas.)

   pondering is indispensable to the essay-writing process
   -before   -while   -after

2. List the three transition terms that introduce each of the three topic sentences.

   before   _while_   _after_

EXERCISE 1.5

Part A

→ For each of the following statements, circle the type of evidence used.

1. Computer scientist and respected educator Seymour Papert concurs, calling upon teachers to "… create the conditions of invention rather than provide ready-made knowledge."

   a) Statistics   **(b)** Expert opinion   **c)** Example

2. Education pays! In 2004, the unemployment rate for twenty-five- to forty-four-year-olds without a high school diploma was almost twice that for the same age group with a high school diploma.

   (a) Statistics   **b)** Expert opinion   **c)** Example

3. By way of illustration, some teachers see the class as half empty; others, as half full.

   a) Statistics   **b)** Expert opinion   **(c)** Example

Part B

1. Which type of evidence is used in each of the developing paragraphs in "The Importance of Pondering"?

   Expert opinion   example

EXERCISE 1.6

Part A

→ For each of the following, circle the type of clincher used.

1. Who can claim with any credibility that their perspective is the "right" perspective? Nobody!

   a) Connecting with the introduction

   (b) Asking a rhetorical question

   c) Offering a suggestion

2. The next time you find yourself in a conflict, remember to listen more and talk less!

   a) Connecting with the introduction

   b) Asking a rhetorical question

   (c) Offering a suggestion

Part B

→ Referring to "The Importance of Pondering," respond to the questions below.

1. Which transition term introduces the summary statement?

   to conclude

2. Copy out the summary statement.

to conclude, ponderin is requisite to essay-writing

3. How does the summary statement differ from the preview statement?

it is a summary of the preview (not really but stfu)

4. What type of clincher is used?

connection w/ intro

WRITING ACTIVITY: THE ACADEMIC ESSAY

→ In small groups of two or three, write an academic essay of approximately 450 words in which you explain the importance of understanding perspectives different from your own.

→ If working in a group of two, write a four-paragraph essay; if working in a group of three, write a five-paragraph essay.

Procedure

1. Brainstorm as many reasons as you can why it is important to understand different perspectives.

2. Choose the best two (if working in a group of two) or three (if working in a group of three) reasons.

3. Working together, write the introductory paragraph.

4. Working individually, write a development paragraph. (Each person in the group is responsible for one paragraph of the development.)

5. Working together, write the concluding paragraph.

6. Turn to Appendix A and read the section on revising (p. 180); then revise your essay.

7. Write a clean copy of your revised essay, being sure to doublespace your work.

8. Add a title page, following the format suggested opposite. (Add a note on the other side of the title page, indicating who was responsible for writing the first, second and, for groups of three, third paragraph of the development.)

9. Submit your work to your teacher for evaluation.

Sample Title Page

Essay Title

By
(Students' names)

Presented to
(Teacher's name)

For the course
(Course name and code)

(Academic institution)
(Date submitted)

resent

In this section, you will be given the opportunity to do small-group and individual speaking activities. The individual speaking activity in this unit provides the basic structure of a formal speech. In later units, you will be asked to apply this structure to a variety of individual speaking activities: "He Said, She Said," a debate-like activity (Unit 2); "Proverbially Speaking" (Unit 3); "Running a Seminar" (Unit 4); "Accomplished People" (Unit 5); "The Adventurers" (Unit 6); and "You Can't Wear That!" (Unit 7).

SPEAKING ACTIVITY: "ON THE OTHER HAND …"

In the warm-up exercise of this unit (p. 2), you shared your opinions on ten different subjects expressed as statements. For this speaking activity, you will discuss the subjects again—only this time, you must express opinions different from those expressed during the warm-up.

Procedure

1. Form small groups.

2. Turn to page 2 in your textbook.

3. Discuss each of the subjects again, this time expressing an opinion opposite to what you previously expressed. (For example, if you indicated that you strongly disagree with statement 1 during the warm-up exercise, discuss statement 1 as if you strongly agree with it during this activity. Note: If you indicated "Undecided," it is now time to get off the fence! You must take a stand one way or the other.)

POST-MORTEM CLASS DISCUSSION

In this context, *post-mortem* refers to an analysis of a finished event. After having participated in the activity "On the Other Hand …" discuss the following questions:

1. Did your opinions on any of the subjects change?

2. If so, how did your opinions change?

3. Why did your opinions change? Did they change a great deal—or only slightly?

The Formal Speech

The structure of a formal speech is identical to that of an academic essay: an introduction (with grabber and preview statement), development (with transition terms, main ideas and evidence) and conclusion (with summary statement and clincher) are all required. (See page 9.) However, different grabber and clincher techniques better suited to oral expression are often used. Contrary to the academic essay, first and second person pronouns are freely used (*I, you, we, my, your, our*, etc.) as are contractions (*he's, they're, we're*, etc.). Like the academic essay, a formal speech may require doing some research, and the subject of the speech should pass the 4-S Test.

Introduction

The opening line of a formal speech is the grabber. Grabber techniques suggested for oral expression are rhetorical questions, provocative statements and short anecdotes. At the end of the introduction, a preview statement is required.

Development

Typically, two or three main points are presented during a formal speech. Each main point should be introduced with an appropriate transition term. Each main (or controlling) idea should be supported with evidence: statistics, expert opinion or example. Ideally, different types of evidence are used in the development.

Conclusion

The conclusion begins with an appropriate transition term followed by a brief summary statement. The conclusion ends with a clincher. Clincher techniques suggested for oral expression are connecting with the introduction (a technique also recommended for written expression), demonstrating the importance of the thesis statement and offering a solution.

EXERCISE 1.7

In this exercise, you will listen to a speech about giving a speech! Before listening, read the questions below; as you are listening, answer the questions in the space provided.

1. What grabber technique is used? More than one grabber technique may be used.

    _____

    _____

2. What is the preview statement?

    _____

    _____

3. What transition term introduces the first main (or controlling) idea?

    _____

4. Which of the three types of evidence is not used during the presentation?

    _____

5. What transition term introduces the summary statement?

    _____

6. What clincher technique is used? More than one clincher technique may be used.

    _____

    _____

    _____

SPEAKING ACTIVITY: THE FORMAL SPEECH

→ In small groups of two or three, prepare a five- to seven-minute oral presentation in which you explain the influence of one of the following factors on perspective: age, gender, health, race, sexual orientation or wealth.

Procedure

1. Brainstorm as many reasons as you can as to how age, gender, health, race, sexual orientation or wealth influences perspective.

2. Choose the best two or three reasons.

3. Outline the presentation by completing the chart on page 19. You may wish to photocopy that page and to complete your outline on the copy as you may need to use the chart to complete subsequent speaking assignments.

4. Make copies of the outline for your teacher and you.

5. Give your presentation, referring to your outline as necessary. If working in groups of two, divide the speech in two. If working in groups of three, one member presents the introduction; one member, the development; and one member, the conclusion.

Oral Presentation Outline

Title	
Introduction	Grabber:
	Preview Statement:
Development	First Main (or Controlling) Idea and Supporting Evidence:
	Second Main (or Controlling) Idea and Supporting Evidence:
	Third Main (or Controlling) Idea and Supporting Evidence (if required):
Conclusion	Summary Statement:
	Clincher:

A Novel Experience

VOCABULARY TIP

Used as an adjective, the word *novel* means "new or original"; used as a noun, it means "a work of fiction."

Teachers typically assign a novel at the start of the academic session in order to allow students time to read the novel before participating in a discussion or completing an assignment later in the course. They may choose to assign one novel to the entire class, or they may decide to create small groups and assign a different novel to each group. Novels are assigned to enrich vocabulary, raise cultural awareness and provide students with an enjoyable literary experience. (Yes, reading can be fun.) This activity has two parts.

Part A: Writing a Report

→ Read the English-language novel assigned by your teacher.

→ Write a three-paragraph report.

The first paragraph is the introduction. In the introduction, indicate the title of the book, the author's name and publishing details; present the main idea (thesis) of the book.

The second paragraph is a summary. In the summary, indicate the main parts of the book, summarizing the important points of each part; explain how these parts are related to the main idea.

The third paragraph is the conclusion. In the conclusion, give your appreciation of the book, referring to elements discussed in the introduction and summary.

→ Submit your report to your teacher for evaluation.

Part B: Participating in a Discussion

→ Discuss the novel in a small group of four or five students, respecting the procedure outlined below.

Procedure

1. Working individually, write a list of ten discussion questions about the novel.

2. Working together, create a common list of twenty discussion questions working from your individual lists. Eliminate redundant or uninteresting questions. Proofread the list and submit it to your teacher for evaluation.

3. Working together, discuss the novel, using the twenty questions as the basis of your discussion. Your teacher may evaluate your discussion.

My eLab ✎ Visit My eLab for additional reading practice.

Worlds Apart

Converging perspectives: view from the bottom of a staircase in a modern building (location unknown)

review

Those who live *worlds apart* live in very different places, metaphorically speaking; they experience a shared reality in very different ways.

Teachers and students share the same classroom, yet they do not share the same academic experience.

Male and female students share the same school, yet they do not share the same learning experience.

Women in a developed country share the same planet as those in a developing country, yet they do not share in the same right to an education.

This unit is about the world of education and the men and women who inhabit this world. It is about those who have a part in this world and about those who remain apart from this world.

repare

In this section, you are presented with two warm-up exercises. The first deals with gender differences, the focus of Reading 2.1 and the Listening activity. The second addresses unequal rights for women, a subject dealt with in Reading 2.1 and further developed in Reading 2.2 and the Watching activity.

WARM UP 2.1
Gender Differences: Science or Stereotype?

A **scientific fact** is an observation that has been repeatedly confirmed and is accepted as true. A **stereotype** is an oversimplified belief or idea that is often unfair or untrue.

→ For each of the statements below, decide whether the idea expressed is based on science or stereotype.

→ Be prepared to discuss your answers with the rest of the class.

STATEMENTS	SCIENCE	STEREOTYPE
1. Boys "get in trouble" in the classroom more than girls.		✓
2. Boys are better at math than girls.		✓
3. Boys are stronger than girls.	✓	
4. **Fewer** women than men work as plumbers, electricians or carpenters.	✓	
5. Girls are better at language than boys.		✓
6. Girls are less competitive than boys.		✓
7. Girls and boys learn differently.	✓	
8. The brains of girls and boys develop differently.	✓	
9. The sensory systems of boys and girls develop differently.		
10. Women talk more than men.		✓

GRAMMAR TIP

Fewer is an adjective used to modify count nouns: *fewer chairs, fewer apples, fewer hours*, etc. *Less* is an adjective used to modify non-count or mass nouns: *less furniture, less food, less time*, etc. For more information on count and non-count nouns, turn to page 221.

Gender Discrimination or Gender Diversity?

Gender discrimination is the practice of treating men and women differently and unfairly. **Gender diversity** is the practice of treating men and women equitably, while appreciating their differences.

→ Decide whether each of the facts below is an example of gender discrimination or gender diversity.

→ Be prepared to discuss your answers with the rest of the class.

FACTS	DISCRIMINATION	DIVERSITY
1. For many years, Quebec women were prohibited from drinking in taverns.	✓	
2. In some parts of the world, girls have been denied a formal education.	✓	
3. Many fitness clubs only accept women.		✓
4. Most public buildings have separate restrooms for men and women.		✓
5. No women play in the National Hockey League.	✓	
6. Prior to 1918, Canadian women were not allowed to vote in federal elections.	✓	
7. The American Academy of Motion Picture Arts and Sciences hands out best actor and best actress awards.		✓
8. The Correctional Service of Canada separates male and female prisoners.		✓
9. The Yale Club of New York City, a private club for Yale University alumni, did not admit women prior to 1969.	✓	
10. Upper Canada College in Toronto only admits boys; Havergal College in Toronto only admits girls.		✓

𝒫onder

Tom Wayman is a Canadian poet and academic. His poem "Did I Miss Anything?" is a compilation of responses that Mr. Wayman thought about giving—but never actually gave—students who asked him this question. You will be given a chance to respond to Mr. Wayman's poem in the "Post" section of this unit in an activity on free verse.

"Did I Miss Anything?"

By Tom Wayman

> Question frequently asked by
> students after missing a class

Nothing. When we realized you weren't here
we sat with our hands folded on our desks
5 in silence, for the full two hours

> Everything. I gave an exam worth
> 40 per cent of the grade for this term
> and assigned some reading due today
> on which I'm about to hand out a quiz
10 worth 50 per cent

Nothing. None of the content of this course
has value or meaning
Take as many days off as you like:
any activities we undertake as a class
15 I assure you will not matter either to you or me
and are without purpose

> Everything. A few minutes after we began last time
> a shaft of light descended and an angel
> or other heavenly being appeared
20 and revealed to us what each woman or man must do
> to attain divine wisdom in this life and
> the hereafter
> This is the last time the class will meet
> Before we disperse to bring this good news to all people
25 on earth

Nothing. When you were not present
how could something significant occur?

> Everything. Contained in this classroom
> Is a microcosm of human existence
30 Assembled for you to query and examine and ponder
> This is not the only place such an opportunity has been
> gathered

> but it was one place

> And you weren't here

(229 Words)

Source: Wayman, Tom. *Did I Miss Anything? Selected Poems 1973–1993.* Vancouver: Harbour, 1993. Print.

VOCABULARY AND COMPREHENSION

You may wish to work with a partner as you answer the questions below.

1. Which words from the poem have the following meanings?
   a) Agree to do: _undertake_
   b) Next world: _hereafter_
   c) To ask questions of: _to query_
   d) Consider thoughtfully: _Ponder_
   e) Brought together: _gathered_

2. Is the poem written in the first or third person? From whose perspective is the poem written?

   the teacher

3. The **tone** of a poem or other written work refers to the general feeling or attitude expressed. Indicate which adjective best describes the tone of "Did I Miss Anything?"

   PETTY AF

4. Why does the author use a recurring indented stanza?

   Contrast

5. **Poetic licence** is the freedom taken by poets and other artists to deviate from convention by changing facts, ignoring grammar rules, etc. Which grammar rules does the author ignore?

   Ponctuation

6. The question "Did I miss anything?" reveals a certain assumption on the student's part. What is the assumption?

   that they didn't miss anything

DISCUSSION

→ Discuss each of the questions below in small groups.

→ Be prepared to share your answers with the rest of the class and to explain them

1. Most teachers like the poem, and most students don't. Why do you think this is so?

2. After missing a class, have you ever asked your teacher, "Did I miss anything?" How did the teacher respond? How did you find the teacher's response?

3. Did you like the poem? Do you like poetry in general? Do you read poetry on your own? Why or why not?

"Single-Sex Classes: Equality or Gender Apartheid?"

Elsie Hambrook is chairperson of the New Brunswick Advisory Council on the Status of Women. Ms. Hambrook writes a weekly column on women's issues for the *Times & Transcript*, a New Brunswick newspaper. Her article "Single-Sex Classes: Equality or Gender Apartheid" was published in June of 2009.

BEFORE READING

→ Scan the article, circling the vocabulary terms listed below.

→ Define these terms according to the context in which each is used.

1. apartheid (n.): _discrimination_
2. coed (adj.): _mixed education (boys/girls)_
3. short-changed (v.): _stopped/blocked_
4. woes (n.): _problems_
5. flounder (v.): _fail_

Examine the reading strategies suggested in "Appendix B: Effective Reading and Active Listening." Then read the questions on pages 28 and 29 *before* reading the article itself.

Single-Sex Classes: Equality or Gender Apartheid?

By Elsie Hambrook

Does education have to be coed or should we have single-sex classes?

Is "separate" discriminatory or is it failure to recognize the different needs and ways of learning by girls and boys that is discriminatory?

The topic of single-sex education is a polarizing one: adamant opposition or support is more likely than indifference.

Some are for or against the idea even before the science behind it is known, some are against gathering scientific facts about it, and some believe that the one consistent finding of single-sex education—girls' self-esteem benefits from it—is reason enough to do it.

In recent history, single-sex classes have largely existed in religious and private schools. That does not mean public schools haven't grappled with these issues. In the 1960s and 1970s, concern grew over female students, who still gravitated toward courses that prepared them for unstable and low paying careers. Into the 1990s, there were declarations of girls being <u>short-changed</u> in their education, overlooked and undermined in the classrooms.

More recently, a "boy crisis" has become a focus of concern, wherein it is suggested that boys are struggling in classes because the standard expected from students (sitting quietly, raising your hand, reading) is more traditional behaviour for females than males. Some retort the "crisis" is a media fabrication and a backlash against women's gains.

We know that boys are diagnosed more frequently with behaviour disorders, face disciplinary action more often and drop out at higher rates. Is that related to "natural" tendencies, learned behaviour, male role models, female teachers or teaching methods, or something else?

We also know that it is not a new phenomenon. Neither is girls' faltering self-esteem and continued under-representation in non-traditional subject areas (and non-traditional careers) such as the trades and engineering.

Single-sex schooling is increasingly heralded as a potential solution to these woes.

The theory behind single-sex schooling is that there are differences between boys and girls that must be taken into account.

There is no difference in what boys and girls can learn, but in how and when they learn best. It isn't clear why this is so: some argue that the sexes are fundamentally hard-wired differently and therefore learn differently. Others claim that boys and girls are not so different, but their social experiences are distinct—so we should separate classes, if not schools, according to sex.

Stereotypes break down, and boys and girls in single-sex settings become unafraid to try activities typically associated with the opposite sex, because the opposite sex is not there to assert their dominance. Also, test scores and behaviours supposedly improve if boys are taught in hands-on classes, exposed to math and spatial relations earlier, and allowed to express their energy and talk about actions rather than emotions. Girls would do better if taught in quiet, non-competitive settings, allowed to master language earlier and to express themselves.

What proof backs this up? The research to date is not rigorous enough: the studies are obscure or compare private single-sex schools with public coed schools, or they fail to take into account that parents who place their children in single-sex schools are demonstrating an active interest in their child's education and so their child's chance of success may be higher in any case.

Are the arguments for single-sex classrooms just stereotypes dressed-up as science? Does treating girls like passive emotional creatures and boys as rambunctious go-getters create a self-fulfilling prophecy or acknowledge a hard-wired disposition? How do you educate boys who identify more with typically female traits, and vice versa?

There are differences between today's boys and girls, whether hard-wired or socially constructed. The question is whether educating children in gender-segregated classrooms is the best way to address that reality.

105   Consider the future of these students in the work world—would time in sex-segregated classrooms help them to be the best version of themselves they can be, empowering them to easily adapt to
110 new challenges? Or, to give one example, would women who've been educated in low pressure environments <u>flounder</u> in a world of deadline-based male-influenced employment?

115   Is single-sex education a step toward acknowledging diversity, or a step backwards toward separate and unequal?

It is likely that the answer contains nuances which we don't appreciate fully:
120 simply separating boys from girls is no guarantee of anything good happening. You need teachers who are trained in gender specific strategies, you need attention to learning styles and a flexible
125 student-centred curriculum.

If you have that, does it still matter if the setting is single-sex or coed?

(757 words)

Source: Hambrook, Elsie. "Single-Sex Classes: Equality or Gender Apartheid?" *Times & Transcript* [Moncton], 11 June 2009. Web. 15 Jan. 2010.

VOCABULARY AND COMPREHENSION

You may have to use external sources (dictionary, website, etc.) to find some of the answers to the following questions.

1. Paraphrase the following sentence: "The topic of single-sex education is a polarizing one: adamant opposition or support is more likely than indifference." (Line 7)

    _____

    _____

2. Which of the following statements about the history of single-sex education is(are) false? Circle the letter(s) of the correct answer(s). More than one answer is possible.

    a) In recent times, public schools have had more single-sex classrooms than private schools.

    b) In the '60s and '70s, there was increasing concern in public schools over the career paths for which female students were preparing.

    c) In the '90s, some claimed that girls were being treated inequitably in the classroom.

    d) As of late, some are of the opinion that male students are having difficulty because classroom behavioural "norms" are based on traditional female, as opposed to traditional male, standards of behaviour.

3. Which of the following statements is true? More than one answer is possible. According to the author,

    a) boys misbehave more frequently than girls and are more likely to leave school.

b) girls lack confidence in their abilities and tend to avoid non-traditional careers.

c) supporters of single-sex schooling claim it lowers the male student dropout rate and gives female students the confidence to pursue non-traditional careers.

4. Which of the following statements is(are) false? More than one answer is possible.

   a) Single-sex schooling is based on the theory that boys and girls learn differently.

   b) Single-sex schooling is based on the theory that boys and girls differ in what they can learn.

   c) Proponents of single-sex schooling disagree on why boys and girls learn differently; some proponents attribute differences to nature (genes) and others, to nurture (environment).

5. Underline the correct answers.

   According to supporters of single-sex education, (<u>boys</u> / girls) learn best in (<u>an active</u> / a non-competitive) environment and should be exposed to math early on; (boys / <u>girls</u>) learn best in (an active / <u>a non-competitive</u>) environment and should be exposed to language early on.

6. The scientific evidence supporting single-sex education is solid.

   ☐ True   ☒ False

7. Paraphrase the following sentence: "Does treating girls like passive emotional creatures and boys as rambunctious go-getters create a self-fulfilling prophecy or acknowledge a hard-wired disposition?"

   _____
   _____
   _____

8. What is the subject of the article?

   <u>coed education</u>

9. What is the author's opinion on the subject of the article?

   <u>it shouldn't happen</u>

   _____

A Question of PERSPECTIVE

If you were of the opposite sex, would your career goals change? Why or why not? Would they have been different twenty-five years ago? Fifty years ago?

DISCUSSION

→ Discuss each of the questions in small groups.

→ Be prepared to share your answers with the rest of the class and to explain them.

1. Is support for single-sex education based on science or stereotype? (See Warm Up 2.1 on page 22.)

2. Is single-sex education discriminatory, or is it an acknowledgement of gender diversity? (See Warm Up 2.2 on page 23.)

3. From your experience in the classroom, are boys better at some subjects and girls better at others?

LISTENING Single-Sex Classes

Anna Maria Tremonti is host of *The Current*, a weekday program on CBC Radio. On March 7, 2005, Ms. Tremonti interviewed Dr. Leonard Sax, a family doctor, psychologist and founder of the National Association for Single-Sex Public Education in the United States. Dr. Sax is the author of *Why Gender Matters: What Parents and Teachers Need to Know about the Emerging Science of Sex Differences.*

BEFORE LISTENING

The terms listed below are used in the audio clip.

→ Working alone or with a partner, write the letter of the correct term beside each definition. The first one has been done for you as an example.

DEFINITIONS		TERMS
1. Accommodate; meet the specific needs of someone or something	e	a) Avail yourself of something (exp.)
2. Act; conduct yourself	c	b) Be aware of something (exp.)
3. Be conscious of something	b	c) Behave (v.)
4. Be important / influential	d	d) Carry weight (exp.)
5. Group of animals whose members are similar and can breed together	h	e) Cater to someone or something (v.)
6. Having a lot of money	j	f) Non-starter (n.)
7. Idea or plan having no chance of success	f	g) Op-ed piece (n.)
8. Newspaper article in which a personal opinion is expressed	g	h) Species (n.)
9. University student working for his or her first degree	i	i) Undergraduate (n.)
10. Use to your advantage	a	j) Wealthy (adj.)

COMPREHENSION

The questions below are in sequence. You will hear the answer to question 1, then question 2, then question 3, etc. If you miss an answer, do not worry about it; simply move on to the next question.

1. Fill in the blanks. "There was a time when boys were boys and girls were girls, and that's just the way things were when it came to how children __behaved__ . But after the '40s and '50s, educators, doctors and parents started to become skeptical of the role gender played in a child's development. Other psychological aspects such as social pressure and role-modelling started to __carry weight__ ." (Anna Maria Tremonti)

2. Fill in the blanks: "Now there's a return in old-fashioned gender thinking, a hearkening back to [reminder of] the days when boys and girls were considered different and treated and taught differently. And that's leading to a change in the way children are being schooled. More courses are attempting to __cater__ to the gender of the students." (Anna Maria Tremonti)

3. According to Dr. Sax, how big a role does the gender of a child play in his or her development?

    a) A small role

    b) A big role

    c) A larger role than previously thought

4. Dr. Sax refers to a study done at Cambridge University in the United Kingdom, focusing on newborn babies. On one side of the crib, there was a woman's face; on the other, a mobile decoration. What were the findings of the study?

    girls look at face
    boys look at mobile

5. How does Dr. Sax interpret the findings of the Cambridge study on newborns?

    _____

    _____

6. Dr. Sax refers to a series of studies done on premature babies to test music therapy (the playing of "soft music" in a baby's crib). What were the general findings of these studies?

    girls → more related/ate better/leave earlier

    boys → no value

7. How does Dr. Sax explain the findings of the music therapy studies?

the baby boys can't hear the music because men hearing is not as strong.

8. Adult men hear better than adult women.

☐ True   ☒ False

9. Dr. Sax began working on the issue of single-sex education due in part to the large number of young boys sent to see him who had been erroneously diagnosed with attention deficit disorder.

☒ True   ☐ False

10. Dr. Sax advocates separating girls from boys in the classroom. How does Dr. Sax defend his position?

_____

_____

_____

_____

11. Dr. Sax claims that single-sex schools are "a must."

☐ True   ☒ False

12. According to Dr. Sax, what type of question does not work for middle school and high school boys when studying English literature? What type of question should be used instead?

"what would you do" instead of 'how would you feel"

13. Which of the following statements is(are) false? More than one answer is possible. According to Dr. Sax,

a) as compared to female students, a smaller proportion of boys are finishing high school and going on to college studies.

b) in Canada, female undergraduates represent nearly fifty percent of the student body.

c) scholars agree on why boys are increasingly disengaged from school.

d) teachers are not aware of how fundamentally differently girls and boys learn.

e) books assigned in middle school and high school do not appeal to boys; as a result, fewer boys are reading.

f) girls who go to single-sex schools are six times more likely to major in computer science, physics or engineering in college than are girls of comparable ability who go to coed schools.

g) the brains of girls and boys develop in a different sequence.

14. What is the subject of the interview?

the diff. dev. of boys and girls

15. What opinion does Dr. Sax have on the subject of the interview?

teachers should accomedate

A Question of PERSPECTIVE

If you had a daughter with a keen interest in science, would you prefer her to be educated in a single-sex or a coed school? Explain your preference.

DISCUSSION

→ Discuss each of the questions in small groups.

→ Be prepared to share your answers with the rest of the class and to explain them.

1. Would you allow your son to play with dolls? Your daughter to play with trucks? Why or why not?

2. How would you feel if you were sent to a single-sex school?

3. What would you do if you were sent to a single-sex school?

VOCABULARY REVIEW

→ Without looking back at the terms and definitions provided on page 30, correctly fill in the blanks with the words from the chart below.

→ Pluralize nouns and conjugate verbs as required. The first one has been done for you as an example.

ADJECTIVE	EXPRESSIONS	NOUNS	VERBS
wealthy	avail yourself of (something) be aware of (something) carry weight	non-starter op-ed piece ~~species~~ undergraduate	behave cater to someone or something

1. According to the Canadian Biodiversity Web Site, there are between 1.5 and 1.8 million named _____species_____ in the world, about half of which are insects.

2. Benjamin Franklin coined the proverb, "Early to bed, early to rise makes a man healthy, _____ and wise."

3. Did you read that great _____ on education reform in *The Globe and Mail*? The writer was really quite convincing.

4. Do you think that students _____ how long it takes teachers to prepare a class?

5. For many Americans, government-run health care is a _____ ; they simply don't believe the public sector can provide health care as well as the private sector.

6. I'm afraid that your opinion doesn't _____ much _____ around here; you lack the expertise to make an informed suggestion!

7. If you don't _____ , you will be asked to leave.

8. Jeremiah _____ to his wife's every demand; he has never refused her anything.

9. They met when they were _____ at McGill University.

10. When applying for a job, _____ of all the information on the company's website: the more you know about the company, the more likely you are to be hired.

READING 2.2

Humbled by a Real Fight for Women's Rights

Naomi Lakritz has worked as a staff writer, reporter and columnist. Her column "Humbled by a Real Fight for Women's Rights" appeared in the *Victoria Times Colonist* on April 5, 2009.

BEFORE READING

→ Scan the article, circling the vocabulary terms listed below.

→ Define these terms according to the context in which each is used.

1. jumble (n.): ___mixed up in an untidy way___
2. unbearable (adj.): ___not tolerable___
3. pay lip service (exp.): ___?___
4. blithely (adv.): ___~~happily~~ thoughlessly___
5. boo hoo (n.): ___fake sadness___

> Examine the reading strategies suggested in "Appendix B: Effective Reading and Active Listening." Then read the questions on pages 36 and 37 *before* reading the article itself.

Humbled by a Real Fight for Women's Rights

By Naomi Lakritz

There are a number of sentiments that Canadian women **ought to** feel upon learning of the repressive new law[1] that women in Afghanistan could soon begin
5 living under.

VOCABULARY TIP

The modal *ought to* is a synonym of *should* when used to express expectation: They *ought to* (*should*) be arriving soon!

Among the jumble of emotions that of course include shock, outrage and disgust, there should be room for things like gratitude, humility and shame.

10 Gratitude because we women here in Canada are so rich in precious freedoms that we don't even realize it until something like this comes along.

And even then, we can't begin to imag-
15 ine what it must be like to live in a country where you can't go to school, can't leave the house without your husband's permission, can't say "no" to your husband when you're not in the mood and whatever else
20 is in this law, the precise wording of which remains unknown.

Afghan feminists describe the human rights violations of the law that President Hamid Karzai[2] supposedly signed a month
25 ago, as due to make conditions for women more unbearable than they were under the Taliban.

WORD CULTURE

Originally coined during the Cold War, the *Third World* referred to countries not allied with capitalist or communist countries. Today it refers to poor, industrially undeveloped countries. Some find the term offensive and use *developing world* instead.

Karzai is thought to be supporting the law because it will make him more popular
30 with a group of Shia[3] Muslims whose votes could swing the next election in his favour. He must have been paying lip service all this time to the advancement of women's rights in his country—otherwise, he would
35 not have so blithely sacrificed them to advance his own interests.

People who genuinely care about human rights do not abandon these basic principles for anything.

40 We should also feel humility. How lucky we are that we won the crapshoot of birth or immigration. That kind of lottery win means we have an absolute, inescapable obligation to speak up against injustices
45 being done to women who struggle in far less fortunate circumstances.

These are women whose daily lives we can only guess at, but never really know, except for those among us who were for-
50 tunate enough to escape these places and come to Canada.

But there's also the matter of shame. How do we face these women and tell them that while they struggle under soul-
55 killing laws that dictate the most mundane of their daily comings and goings, we here in Canada are so rich and so spoiled that we can afford to spend time arguing over something as trivial as whether the word
60 "alderman" is sexist and should be changed to "councillor"?

Not only that, the debate is framed in language that is obscene when you think how the same words are used to describe
65 the oppression of women who suffer in despotic **Third World** regimes. ···········>

---

1. Shia Family Law or Shiite Personal Status Law.
2. President of Afghanistan (December 7, 2004–).
3. The second largest denomination of Islam after Sunni.

The last time that the alderman versus councillor debate raised its silly head in my hometown of Calgary, I heard it said
70 that "alderman" is damaging to women's self-esteem, that it makes them feel excluded, and that it will discourage girls from growing up to run for city council. Oh, boo hoo.

75 You want to see "excluded" and "damaging to self-esteem"?

Try going to school in a country where men throw acid in your face because you dare to claim the right to an education.
80 Or try living in a place where you need a man's permission to step outside the front door of your home. Or where you risk being the victim of an honour killing at the hands of your father and brothers if you
85 make the slightest misstep in your relations with individuals of the opposite sex, or have the misfortune of being a rape victim.

Tell these women that the word "alderman" causes soul injury because it
90 contains the suffix "man" and they'd look at you in amazement. They'd think you were crazy.

The Fourth World Conference on Women in Beijing in 1995 highlighted this gaping
95 chasm between the First and Third Worlds. The representatives from the Third World sat open-mouthed as Western women debated trendy questions of gender-neutral language—such as, is it sexist for a street
100 sign to read "Men at work"?

What the women from Western countries considered to be hot-button topics were not even on the radar screen for their counterparts from the Third World, who
105 had come to discuss things like malaria, clean water and the perennial shortage of nourishing food for their children.

How fortunate we are here in Canada, fortunate beyond the wildest dreams of
110 millions of women elsewhere in the world.

Shame on us every time we take it for granted. More than a little perspective is in order.

(741 words)

Source: Lakritz, Naomi. "Humbled by a Real Fight for Women's Rights." *Times Colonist* [Victoria] 5 April 2009. Web. 30 June 2009.

VOCABULARY AND COMPREHENSION

You may have to use external sources (dictionary, website, etc.) to find some of the answers to the questions below.

1. To whom does the author address her article?
   Women

2. Afghan feminists oppose the new law.
   [X] True   [ ] False

3. Some think the Afghan president's support for the new law shows a disregard for human rights.
   [X] True   [ ] False

4. Paraphrase the following: "How lucky we are that we won the crapshoot of birth or immigration. That kind of lottery win means we have an absolute, inescapable obligation to speak up against injustices being done to women who struggle in far less fortunate circumstances." (Line 40)

5. Which of the following statements is(are) false? More than one answer is possible. According to the author,

    a) most Canadian women are able to understand the struggle of Shia women in Afghanistan. *(selected)*

    b) given the Shia women's struggle in Afghanistan, Canadian women should be ashamed of participating in debates on gender-neutral language. *(selected)*

    c) the use of sexist language makes her feel sad.

6. In the fourteenth paragraph (lines 77–87) , the author provides three examples of what she considers to be "excluding of" and "damaging to" women. List these examples.

    a) _men throwing acid because they claim their right to education_

    b) _needing a mans permission to go outside_

    c) _risk being an honour killing victim_

7. a) From the example provided in the fifteenth paragraph (lines 88–92), what is a "suffix"?

    the end of a word that has a meaning on its own

    b) By inference, what is a prefix?

    the begining of the word that has a meaning on its own

8. At the Fourth World Conference on Women, why did women from the Third World not actively participate in debates over gender-neutral language?

    they were scared

9. What is the subject of the article?

    sexism

10. What is the author's opinion on the subject of the article?

    We take our freedom for granted and we should do something

A Question of PERSPECTIVE

If you lived in a country in which some of its citizens were violently opposed to your obtaining an education due to your gender, would you risk a physical attack to attend school?

DISCUSSION

→ Discuss each of the questions in small groups.

→ Be prepared to share your answers with the rest of the class and to explain them.

1. Should Western nations intervene when human rights are abused in the developing world? How should they intervene? Militarily? Financially? Explain.

2. Is it impossible to understand human rights abuses if you've never had your rights removed or infringed upon? Justify your response.

3. Is it important to use gender-neutral language in North America? Why or why not?

DVD ← **WATCHING** Little Women, Big Hearts

In a brief report from the CBC's *The National*, reporter Bonnie Allen profiles Alaina Podmorow, a ten-year-old student and women's rights activist from the Okanagan Valley in British Columbia who established Little Women for Little Women in Afghanistan, an organization that raises money to help Afghan schoolgirls. The piece was first broadcast on November 9, 2007.

BEFORE WATCHING

The terms listed below are used in the video clip.

→ Working alone or with a partner, write the letter of the correct term beside each definition. The first one has been done for you as an example.

DEFINITIONS		TERMS
1. Be preoccupied by something; keep thinking about something	e	a) Be moved by something (exp.)
2. Child (informal)	f	b) Entice someone to do something (v.)
3. Deal with a situation	d	c) Forbid someone from doing something (v.)
4. Imprison someone in their home	g	d) Handle something (v.)
5. Insufficient number or amount of something	h	e) Have something on one's mind (exp.)
6. Leader of unofficial military group fighting against a government	j	f) Kid (n.)
7. Made to feel strong emotions	a	g) Put someone under house arrest (v.)
8. Necessary objects (plural)	i	h) Shortage (n.)
9. Persuade someone to do something, often by offering something in exchange	b	i) Supplies (n.)
10. Prohibit someone from doing something	c	j) Warlord (n.)

Examine the listening strategies suggested in "Appendix B: Effective Reading and Active Listening." Then read the listening comprehension questions below *before* watching the clip.

COMPREHENSION

The questions are in sequence. You will hear the answer to question 1, then question 2, then question 3, etc. If you miss an answer, do not worry about it; simply move on to the next question.

1. Why did Alaina's mother, Jamie, question taking her daughter to hear Canadian journalist Sally Armstrong speak on women in Afghanistan?

   the information could've been a little heavy for her

2. Why did Jamie finally decide to take her daughter?

   She's mature enough / can handle it

3. Fill in the blanks. "Armstrong described how the Taliban government enforced an extreme form of Islamic law, *put* women *under house arrest* and *forbade* them from showing their faces. Girls were not allowed to attend school." (Bonnie Allen)

4. According to Armstrong, many Afghan girls have gone back to school since the fall of the Taliban in 2001; however, other girls are afraid to do so. Who does Armstrong specify is keeping these girls out of school?

   the warlords that come in classes

5. How did Alaina come up with the idea of establishing Little Women for Little Women in Afghanistan?

   She saw a presentation about it and was moved by it.

   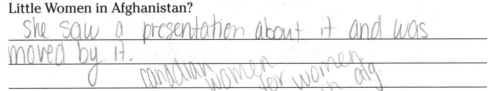

   canadian women for women in afg.

6. Which of the following statements is(are) true? More than one answer is possible.

   a) Little Women for Little Women in Afghanistan focuses its efforts on raising money to build schools in Afghanistan.

   b) In many areas of Afghanistan, parents believe their daughters must be taught by female teachers.

   c) There is a shortage of female teachers in Afghanistan.

   d) The girls of Little Women for Little Women in Afghanistan have a solid understanding of Afghan politics and religious law.

7. How much money has Little Women for Little Women in Afghanistan raised?

enough for 5 teachers (750×5)

8. People from other parts of Canada have indicated an interest in starting their own chapters of Little Women for Little Women in Afghanistan.

☒ True ☐ False

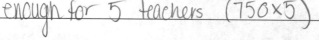

A Question of PERSPECTIVE

If you were a school-aged girl in Afghanistan, would you expect non-Afghans to defend your right to an education? Explain.

DISCUSSION

→ Discuss each of the questions in small groups.

→ Be prepared to share your answers with the rest of the class and to explain them.

1. List five adjectives that you would use to describe Alaina. Justify your choices.

2. Name three famous people who "made a difference" when they were young. Explain how they made a difference.

3. Should North American men and women be concerned about the right of Afghan girls to attend school? Why or why not?

VOCABULARY REVIEW

→ Without looking back at the terms and definitions provided on page 38, replace each of the terms in italics by one of the terms in the box below.

→ Pluralize nouns and conjugate verbs as required. The first one has been done for you as an example.

EXPRESSIONS	NOUNS	VERBS
be moved by (something)	kid	entice (someone to do something)
have (something) on one's mind	shortage	forbid (someone from doing something)
~~put someone under house arrest~~	supplies	handle (something)
	warlord	

1. Burmese authorities *have imprisoned* _____have put_____ Nobel Prize winner Aung San Suu Kyi *in her home* ____under house arrest____.

2. Have they bought the *objects they will need* _____ for their trip?

3. Many American *were made to feel strong emotions* _____ listening to Martin Luther King.

4. Mrs. Feodor Vassilyev, an eighteenth-century Russian peasant, gave birth to sixty-nine *children* _____: sixteen pairs of twins, seven sets of triplets and four sets of quadruplets.

5. Parents with children in the military *are preoccupied with thoughts of war* _____.

6. The deposed dictatorship *prohibited* _____ girls from attending school.

7. Are politicians truly concerned about the *insufficient number* _____ of doctors in Canada?

8. They *persuaded* _____ him to come to the party with offers of cheap beer!

9. *Unofficial military leaders* _____ ruled throughout China in the years following the Chinese Revolution of 1911.

10. You study full time and work part time. Are you sure you can *deal with* _____ both at the same time?

𝒫ost

Free Verse

Free verse is poetry that does not have a fixed structure and does not rhyme. The poem "Did I Miss Anything?" (p. 24) by Tom Wayman is written in free verse. Respond to Mr. Wayman's poem with a free verse poem of your own entitled "Did You Do Anything?" Write between 100 and 125 words.

The Argumentative Essay

In an argumentative (or persuasive) essay, the author attempts to persuade the reader through argumentation that his or her opinion on a contentious issue is the right one. As mentioned in "Single-Sex Classes: Equality or Gender Apartheid?" (p. 26), the topic of single-sex education is a polarizing one; it is also the topic of this assignment.

→ Write an essay of 400 to 450 words, based on the academic essay outlined in Unit 1 on page 9. You will need an introduction, a development and a conclusion.

→ Take a position in support of or in opposition to single-sex education. The position you take constitutes your claim (thesis).

→ Present two or three main ideas to support your claim. These supporting ideas are known as arguments.

→ Support each argument with solid evidence.

When writing your persuasive essay, remember to

→ take a strong stand;

→ rely on statistics and expert opinion rather than example to support your arguments;

→ vary the sources used;

→ place your weakest argument in the second paragraph of the development (paragraph 3) if you are writing a five-paragraph essay, as the first and third arguments conceal the weakness of the second;

→ discuss viewpoints opposite to your own, and then refute these viewpoints.

To increase reader interest, exaggerate your position *slightly*. Compare the following two thesis statements:

1. Single-sex education helps students succeed.

2. Single-sex education guarantees student success.

The second thesis, though an obvious exaggeration, would make for much better reading.

The chart below provides a structural overview, detailing elements to consider. Remember to always proofread your work prior to submission.

ESSAY SECTIONS	PARAGRAPHS	STRUCTURAL ELEMENTS
Introduction	1	• Begin with a grabber technique: a pertinent quotation, definition or fact. • End with your claim (thesis) followed by a list of the two or three arguments you will use to support your claim.
Development	2 3 4 (optional)	• Use transition terms for each of the paragraphs in the development. • Include hard evidence from varied sources (statistics and expert opinion). • Discuss opposing viewpoints and then refute.
Conclusion	5	• Begin with a transition term, a brief recapping of your claim and two or three arguments. • End with a clincher technique: connecting to the introduction, asking a rhetorical question or offering a suggestion.

Sharing is stronger

Present

Single-Sex Discussions

→ Create small "all-male" and "all-female" discussion groups.

→ In your groups, discuss the questions below, taking brief notes as you go.

→ Once you have discussed all the questions, pair up with a discussion group of the opposite sex and compare your answers.

1. How are women and men similar? Other than the obvious physical differences, how are they different?

2. Do you prefer male or female teachers? Explain.

3. Do you prefer to talk about your thoughts or your feelings? Explain.

4. Would you describe your learning style as collaborative or competitive?

5. How is participating in single-sex discussion different from participating in a discussion that includes both males and females?

"He Said, She Said"

→ Choose a partner of the opposite sex.

→ Select one of the subjects below.

→ One partner prepares a speech as to why he or she "loves" something, and the other, as to why he or she "hates" that thing.

→ Both speakers must respect the structure of a formal speech (see page 17).

→ Each speaker should speak for approximately five to seven minutes.

→ Flip a coin to decide who speaks first.

1. Why I Love/Hate Driving All-Terrain Vehicles

2. Why I Love/Hate Getting Dressed Up

3. Why I Love/Hate Languages

4. Why I Love/Hate Math

5. Why I Love/Hate Playing Computer Games

6. Why I Love/Hate Playing Contact Sports

7. Why I Love/Hate Reading

8. Why I Love/Hate Shopping

9. Why I Love/Hate Talking about My Feelings

10. Why I Love/Hate Watching Romantic Movies

Participate

In this section, you will work with another student on a joint writing and speaking project.

Making a Video Clip

In this project, you and your partner will research a gender-related human rights issue and make a short video clip to be uploaded to a course management system (CMS) or worldwide video community (such as YouTube).

Procedure

1. Type "gender-related human rights issues" or "human rights issues" into a search engine.

2. Working with your partner, determine which issue you would like to learn and talk about.

3. Make a research portfolio on the selected issue. Include printouts of website articles in which you have highlighted important information.

4. Decide what particular aspect of the issue you would like to address.

5. Take a position on the issue.

6. Find three ideas that support your position.

7. Write up cue cards containing relevant information. Your presentation should last approximately ten minutes.

8. Make a video recording of your joint presentation.

9. Upload your video clip to your CMS or worldwide video community. (If uploading to a video community, protect your identity.)

10. Submit your research portfolio and cue cards to your teacher. Provide your teacher with the Web location (URL) of your video clip.

Your teacher will grade your work and may or may not have other students watch your clip.

Related Works

The works listed on page 45 may be of interest for continued study.

TYPES OF WORKS	TITLES
Documentary	*Afghanistan: Between Hope and Fear.* Dir. Dominic Morissette, Julian Sher, Andrea Thiel. CBC Learning, 2008. • Watch online at the CBC website: http://www.cbc.ca/doczone/afghanistan/video.html *Afghanistan: The Lost Truth [Haghighat-e Gomshodeh].* Dir. Yassamin Maleknasr. Women Make Movies, 2003. • A woman filmmaker travels across Afghanistan (subtitled)
Fiction	Carter, Angela. *The Bloody Chamber.* Toronto: Penguin (Canada), 1979. Print. • A feminist retelling of fairy tales and legends (Some of the stories are rather dark: reader discretion is advised!) Hosseini, Khaled. *The Kite Runner.* New York: Riverhead, 2003. Print. • First Afghan novel written in English Smiley, Jane. *A Thousand Acres.* New York: Knopf, 1991. Print. • A modern-day King Lear, told from a daughter's point of view
Movie	*Dead Poets Society.* Dir. Peter Weir. Buena Vista, 1989. • Story of an inspiring English teacher who challenges students at a boys' prep school to change their lives of conformity *He Said, She Said.* Dir. Ken Kwapis, Marisa Silver. Paramount, 1991. • A romantic story told twice: once from the man's perspective, once from the woman's *Yentl.* Dir. Barbra Streisand. MGM, 1983. • Film adaptation of a play based on the short story "Yentl the Yeshiva Boy," by Isaac Bashevis Singer
Non-Fiction	Gray, John. *Men Are from Mars, Women Are from Venus.* New York: HarperCollins, 1992. Print. • Suggestions for improving relationships between men and women through a better understanding of gender-specific communication styles and emotional needs Sax, Leonard. *Why Gender Matters: What Parents and Teachers Need to Know about the Emerging Science of Sex Differences.* New York: Doubleday, 2005. Print. • Book on gender differences in learning, by the doctor interviewed in the Listening section of this unit

My eLab ✎ Visit My eLab for additional reading, listening and vocabulary practice.

3

Dollars and Sense

Low-angle view of different corporate buildings in New York City

review

VOCABULARY TIP

The nouns *tightwad*, *cheapskate* and *skinflint* are synonyms as are *parsimonious*, *provident* and *prudent*. Enlarge your vocabulary by using a thesaurus to help you find new synonyms for words you already know.

Does money burn a hole in your pocket? Or do you need to dust off your wallet when the time comes to pay for something?

The world can be divided into two very different groups of people: spendthrifts and savers.

With recent downturns in world economies, much of the world has converted to saving—if not out of choice, then out of necessity.

Saving money and being thrifty go hand in hand—and they also go in and out of fashion with upturns and downturns in the stock market.

When money is tight, people stop spending; when it is not, many start spending like there is no tomorrow.

Are thrifty people **tightwads**, **cheapskates** or **skinflints**? Or are they **parsimonious**, **provident** or **prudent**?

$\mathcal{P}$repare

In this section, two warm-up exercises are proposed: the first deals with financial health, the focus of Reading 3.1 and the Watching activity; the second with thrift, the focus of Reading 3.2 and the Listening activity.

How Financially Healthy Are You?

How financially healthy are you? Take the following pop quiz to find out.

→ Circle the letter of the most appropriate answer.

→ Be prepared to share your score with the rest of the class.

1. Which of the following statements best describes your relationship with money?

   a) I know the value of a dollar, and I spend each dollar wisely.

   b) I am pretty good with my money, but every once in a while I like to splurge.

   c) Money burns a hole in my pocket.

   d) Money? What money?

2. Which of the following statements is true for you?

   a) I follow a budget, writing down what I earn and what I spend.

   b) I live within my means, but I don't record my expenditures.

   c) I have tried living on a budget, but after a couple of days I give up!

   d) A budget? You must be kidding!

3. When I want to buy something, I

   a) ask myself whether I really need it before putting money aside to buy it.

   b) save the money and buy it.

   c) buy it—and worry about whether I can afford it later.

   d) buy it—and everything else I can lay my hands on.

4. Which of the following statements would you be most likely to make?

   a) Waste not, want not.

   b) Neither a borrower nor a lender be.

   c) "Money can't buy happiness, but it can make you awfully comfortable while you're being miserable."[1]

   d) "Whoever said money can't buy happiness simply didn't know where to go shopping."[2]

5. I can tell you

   a) exactly how much money I spent yesterday.

   b) approximately how much money I spent yesterday.

   c) approximately how much money I spent yesterday, if I think about it for a while.

   d) that I spent money yesterday.

1. Quote by Clare Booth Luce (American diplomat and playwright, 1903-1987).
2. Quote by Bo Derek (American actress, 1956-).

6. I know
   a) how much money is in my bank account.
   b) approximately how much money is in my bank account.
   c) that there is money in my bank account.
   d) that I have a bank account.

7. How do you feel about saving money?
   a) Love it!
   b) Like it!
   c) Don't hate it!
   d) Don't know; never done it!

8. Which of the following statements best describes how you feel about the future?
   a) I am optimistic about the future.
   b) I am cautiously optimistic about the future.
   c) I am a bit pessimistic about the future.
   d) Future? There is no future.

9. Waiting to buy something
   a) builds character.

   b) is difficult, but sometimes necessary.
   c) is frustrating.
   d) is to be avoided at all costs.

10. Debt
   a) is to be avoided.
   b) is sometimes a necessary evil.
   c) is necessary.
   d) is something I'd rather not think about.

Scoring

Each time you answered (a), give yourself 3 points; (b), 2 points; (c), 1 point; and (d), 0 points.

Interpretation

21–30 points: Your finances are healthy. Just keep doing what you're doing.

11–20 points: You get to the end of the money before you get to the end of the month. You might consider changing some of your ways.

0–10 points: Run, do not walk, to your nearest library and borrow a copy of "The Ant and the Grasshopper." Read it; reread it; and then read it again!

© PEARSON LONGMAN • REPRODUCTION PROHIBITED

CULTURAL NOTE

"The Ant and the Grasshopper" is a fable by Aesop. In the story, the grasshopper spends all day lying about, while the ant works hard storing up food; come winter, the grasshopper is starving and the ant is doing just fine. The moral of the story? Work hard and save for the future.

GRAMMAR TIP

Relative pronouns join clauses to form complex sentences. Examples of relative pronouns include *who, whom, which, whose* and *that*. For more information on relative pronouns, see page 227.

WARM UP 3.2 Want or Need?

People **who** are thrifty know the difference between "want" and "need." Many people choose to cultivate thrift of their own accord; others have it thrust upon them by circumstances beyond their control (loss of a job, poor economy, unforeseen medical expenses, etc.). In this warm-up exercise, you and some of your classmates are asked to participate in a small-group activity in which you will have to agree on what is a need and what is merely a want.

Description of the Activity

You are exiled to Cyberia, a virtual world in which your virtual survival depends on the choices you make. Cyberia is a cold place, resembling its name-sake, (northern) Siberia, in both climate and geography: temperatures range from −50°C (−58°F) in January to 15°C (59°F) in July and the landscape is barren. You must survive a full year in Cyberia before being allowed to return home. On page 49, you will find a list of items available to have with you during your exile. You are only allowed to take fifteen of the items in addition to the clothes you have on your backs. Ironically, there is no electricity in Cyberia.

Procedure

Decide which items are essential for your survival and which are not.

1. Prioritize the items by writing a number from 1 to 15 beside each of the essential items, where 1 indicates the most essential item and 15 indicates the least essential item.

2. Compare your answers with those from other groups.

Rules

1. You have thirty minutes in which to complete the exercise.

2. Team members must arrive at a consensus when choosing and prioritizing essential items.

LIST OF AVAILABLE ITEMS

ITEMS	PRIORITY	ITEMS	PRIORITY
1. Books		16. Matches	
2. Boots		17. Mattresses	
3. Bullets		18. Money	
4. Candy		19. Oil lamp	
5. Can opener		20. Laptop computer with 9-hour charged battery	
6. Canned foods		21. Portable toilet	
7. Charged iPod loaded with favourite songs		22. Radio	
8. Cigarettes		23. Radio batteries	
9. Coats		24. Sleeping bags	
10. Cooking pot		25. Small brick dwelling with no bathroom or kitchen	
11. Deodorant		26. Toothpaste	
12. Gloves and scarves		27. Utensils	
13. Guitar		28. Water	
14. Gun		29. Wood (logs and twigs)	
15. Lamp oil		30. Wood stove	

ⓟonder

Shel Silverstein (1930–1999) was an American poet, musician, cartoonist and author of children's books. The poem you are about to read was published in *Where the Sidewalk Ends*.

Smart

By Shel Silverstein

My dad gave me one dollar bill
'Cause I'm his smartest son,
And I swapped it for two shiny quarters
'Cause two is more than one!

And then I took the quarters
And traded them to Lou
For three dimes—I guess he don't know
That three is more than two!

Just then, along came old blind Bates
And just 'cause he can't see
He gave me four nickels for my three dimes,
And four is more than three!

And I took the nickels to Hiram Coombs
Down at the seed-feed store,
And the fool gave me five pennies for them,
And five is more than four!

And then I went and showed my dad,
And he got red in the cheeks
And closed his eyes and shook his head—
Too proud of me to speak!

(229 Words)

Source: Silverstein, Shel. "Smart." *Where the Sidewalk Ends*. New York: HarperCollins, 1974. 35. Print.

VOCABULARY AND COMPREHENSION

You may wish to work with a partner as you answer the questions below.

1. Which words from the poem have the following meanings?

    a) Exchanged: _____

    b) Got angry: _____

2. From whose perspective is the poem written?

   _____

3. Why does the author use the grammatically incorrect structure "he don't know"?

   _____

4. An **ironic situation** is one that is unusual or amusing because something strange happens, or the opposite of what is expected happens or is true. Working from this definition, how is the poem's ending (fifth stanza) ironic?

   _____

   _____

   _____

5. **Style** refers to the way a literary work is written. When analyzing style, consider the author's word choice and level of language. With this definition in mind, how would you describe the author's writing style?

   _____

DISCUSSION

→ Discuss each of the questions in small groups.

→ Be prepared to share your answers with the rest of the class and to explain them.

1. How would you characterize "old blind Bates" and "Hiram Coombs"?

2. How do you feel about the poem? What do you think of the poem?

3. "A fool and his money are soon parted" is a well-known English proverb. Do you feel sympathetic toward the foolish child? Why or why not?

READING 3.1

Financial Health Is a Part of Overall Health

Jane Claxton-Oldfield is a natural nutrition coach who writes a monthly column for the *Times & Transcript* health page. Her article "Financial Health Is a Part of Overall Health" appeared in the *Times* on January 15, 2009.

BEFORE READING

→ Scan the article, circling the vocabulary terms listed below.

→ Define these terms according to the context in which each is used.

1. overall (adj.): _____

2. crux of the matter (exp.): _____

3. going to hell in a hand-basket (exp.): _____

4. well off (adj.): _____

5. bombarded with (v.): _____

6. creeping up (v.): _____

7. beyond a shadow of a doubt (exp.): _____

   _____

8. doom and gloom (exp.): _____

Examine the reading strategies suggested in "Appendix B: Effective Reading and Active Listening." Then read the questions on pages 54 and 55 *before* reading the article itself.

Financial Health Is a Part of Overall Health

By Jane Claxton-Oldfield

Whenever we hear the word *health*, most of us think immediately about physical health. Many of us also think about emotional/psychosocial/mental health and some of us will no doubt think about spiritual health.

These are all, undeniably, very important elements that contribute toward the overall picture that makes up our "health" —good or otherwise. In other words, if any of these elements are missing/out of balance, then our "health" is automatically compromised. I wonder, however, how many of us would include financial health as an integral part of our overall health? After all, it certainly has the ability to impact our lives—either positively or negatively.

Let me start by saying that I am not suggesting that in order to be "financially healthy," we have to be rich or even comfortably well off. Instead, I am talking about the ability to handle our finances in a healthy way. For example, there are many people who have been "rich" in the conventional sense (i.e., had a lot of money), but ended up losing it all or filing for bankruptcy. My own definition of financial health is the ability to "manage well" whatever amount of money/wealth that one does possess. Some of the most financially healthy people I know are, ironically, those who have the least amount of money coming in, but know how to budget and live "within their means." This is very different from having a good/great salary, but constantly living in the overdraft or putting everything on credit cards. Sadly, it seems that too many of us fall into this latter category these days.

It appears that we have become a society that has to have "things," have them now, and have them at any cost— even when that cost is as high as 28 percent (or higher) in interest rates! Those of us who had grandparents who lived in the early 1900s know that they would be absolutely horrified at the way that many of us waste money today and purchase material things like there is no tomorrow. And, for a few people this may be the crux of the matter. They have convinced themselves that there likely will be no tomorrow. To them, "the world is going to hell in a hand-basket any day now, so what's the point of saving money or waiting for what you want?"

I find it particularly disturbing how many people (especially young people) have expressed this sentiment to me. You can almost feel the cloud of gloom descend around them when they are talking about money ("What's the point of saving?").

65 We are bombarded with media stories of wars, scares of disease epidemics, famine, environmental crises, future lack of resources, etc., every day. For some, these stories serve to validate and further 70 feed into their fears of "everything going wrong in this world."

But is it really? Are we really on the verge of annihilation?

After all, wars have been in existence 75 since groups of humans have lived together. Plagues, epidemics and famine are part of the world's history, yet we have always survived as a species. Yes, we do need to be concerned. We certainly need to take 80 better care of the environment, but this requires our diligent action—not the continued purchasing (on plastic) of even more "material things" (packaged in plastic) to contribute even further to the 85 problem—not to mention the fumes released from our vehicles on the drive to and from the mall to make the purchase!

There are many other reasons why people get into debt. Some of us have 90 quite simply never been shown how to budget. Sometimes it is necessary to get into debt to purchase a house or business, pay for necessary medical treatments, etc. Sometimes debt comes through being 95 frivolous (see it, like it, buy it). Whatever the reason, many of us start to feel the

stress creeping up within us as we see the negative balance creeping up on the credit card bill or bank statements!

100 Stress is a major contributor to ill health and ultimately disease. What we have always known on an intuitive level has now been proven beyond a shadow of a doubt. Indeed, scientists can now meas-105 ure the negative effects that stress has on us physiologically. The stress of worrying about world affairs is one thing, but the fact that too many of us bring on unnecessary financial stress as a result of that fear 110 is quite another. Because there is a chance that "the world might end tomorrow" or because we just "want" the latest big screen TV/computer/clothes, does this really justify us getting deeper and deeper 115 into debt?

If you are someone who finds yourself thinking "doom and gloom" or you find yourself buying "material things" to "self-comfort" or purely for pleasure, then I 120 encourage you to think about this: statistically speaking, the odds of the world ending are extremely low. Realistically speaking, it is much more likely that we will all still be here in twenty, thirty, 125 forty years from now—with huge credit card bills to pay.

Now, that is scary!

So, when you are thinking about what you want for yourself this year I hope, 130 like me, you are going to spend some time working on your financial health.

Ironically, what serves us best in the other areas of good healthy habits would also make good budgetary sense too. 135 For example, our physical health would be helped tremendously by eating more whole foods. Whole foods prepared from scratch are arguably much cheaper than packaged foods. Eating less packaged food 140 helps to cut back on packaging and, therefore, garbage. We would also be eating a lot less refined food—white sugar, white flour, white oils and white salt, which many packaged foods are "loaded" with. If we walked instead of taking the car, the exercise would do us good, plus we would save money on gas.

If we turned off the TV and avoided the "bad news" even a couple of times a week and prayed or meditated for world peace instead, we can raise our spirits. If we committed a random act of kindness to help lift us out of our "woe is me and the world" mode, we will have made a big difference to our mental health and helped someone else into the bargain.

If we decided that we would only spend what money we have coming in, we would get one step closer to financial health. If we lived more consciously in all these matters, the world would have no choice but to become a better place—even if only in our own little corner of it!

It was Mahatma Gandhi who said: "The future depends on what we do in the present." Let's live today as if we have a wonderful future ahead of us. Let's take care of our bodies as if we intend to still be alive and vibrant when we are a hundred and let's budget as if we don't want to leave debt to our children! In good health—until next time.

(1185 words)

Source: Claxton-Oldfield, Jane. "Financial Health Is a Part of Overall Health." *Times & Transcript*. CanadaEast Interactive, 15 Jan. 2009. Web. 1 Dec. 2009.

VOCABULARY AND COMPREHENSION

You may have to use external sources (a dictionary or a web search, for example) to find some of the answers to the questions below.

1. According to the author, what jeopardizes our health?

   _____

   _____

   _____

2. How does the author define *financial health*?

   _____

3. What does the author find ironic? (Lines 19–40)

   _____

   _____

4. List the two types of people the author describes as financially unhealthy in the fourth paragraph (lines 41–57).

   a) _____

   b) _____

   _____

5. What does the author blame for many people's pessimistic outlook on the future?

   _____

   _____

6. Why is the author's outlook on the future cautiously optimistic?

_____

_____

_____

7. List three reasons why people get into debt.

a) _____

b) _____

c) _____

8. It is an established fact that the stress caused by debt contributes to poor health and disease.

☐ True ☐ False

9. Eating food that is good for our bodies is perhaps also good for our pocketbooks and and is certainly good for the environment.

☐ True ☐ False

10. List three things people can do to improve their mental health.

a) _____

b) _____

c) _____

11. What must people do to attain financial health?

_____

12. What is the subject of the article?

_____

13. What is the author's opinion on the subject?

_____

A Question of PERSPECTIVE

How would your perspective on the future differ if you were extremely wealthy? Extremely poor?

DISCUSSION

→ Discuss each of the questions in small groups.

→ Be prepared to share your answers with the rest of the class and to explain them.

1. Provide your own definitions for each of the following terms:

a) Emotional health   **c)** Mental health

b) Psychosocial health   **d)** Financial health

2. Do you budget? Why or why not?

3. As a rule do you buy what you need, or do you "need to buy"? Explain.

WATCHING Frugal Shopping

On December 12, 2008, CBC's *The National* aired "Frugal Shopping." In the segment, reporter Kas Roussy interviews Canadians of various ages about their spending habits during an economic recession. Featured in the report are a young Toronto family, Michael Szabo, Tara Tucker and their infant daughter Julia; twenty-seven-year-old Brian Burgio; and retiree Gilles Legault. Ms. Roussy also interviews Ellen Roseman, a consumer reporter and *Toronto Star* columnist, who offers some advice on personal finance.

BEFORE WATCHING

The following quotes were taken directly from the segment:

1. "They've discovered *slashing your budget* doesn't need to be painful."

2. "A *sluggish* economy ..."

3. "... they are *hunkering down* for Christmas."

4. "... spending money on *frivolous* things."

5. "It's a *wake-up call* all right; you can't just keep opening your wallet every time you want something."

6. "... a generation that hasn't known the *hardship* of a recession."

7. "... the economic turmoil has forced him to *rein in* his spending habits."

8. "... you still want to be able to do some of the things you did before; you still want to be able to shop and *not* have it *strain your wallet* so much."

9. "Gilles Legault won't let credit crunches and *plunges* in the stock market spoil his holiday mood."

10. "... it's just not cool to, you know, *overdo* it."

→ Rewrite the terms in *italics* and write a synonym for each in the chart below. You may wish to use a thesaurus.

→ The first one has been done for you as an example.

ITALICIZED TERMS	SYNONYMS
1. *slashing your budget*	cutting expenses
2.	
3.	
4.	
5.	

ITALICIZED TERMS	SYNONYMS
6.	
7.	
8.	
9.	
10.	

Examine the listening strategies suggested in "Appendix B: Effective Reading and Active Listening." Then read the comprehension questions below *before* watching the clip.

COMPREHENSION

The questions below are in sequence: you will hear the answer to question 1, then question 2, then question 3, etc. If you miss an answer, do not worry about it; simply move on to the next question.

1. What do Michael and his wife plan to do with some of the gifts their daughter Julia received for her first birthday?

   _____

2. List two ways in which the Szabos have changed their plans for the coming holiday season?

   a) _____

   _____

   _____

   b) _____

3. Fill in the blanks. Ellen Roseman states, "I think that it's [the recession has] already changed people's thinking about consumption. They don't want to look as if they're into _____; they don't want to look as if they're _____ or spending money on frivolous things."

4. Circle the letter of the correct answer(s). More than one answer is possible. Brian Burgio maintains that his generation

   a) has never lacked for anything.

   b) has not had to work for what it has.

   c) will be devastated by the recession.

5. List two ways in which Brian has reduced his expenses.

   a) _____

   b) _____

   _____

6. What advice does Ellen Roseman offer to people living on a budget?

_____

7. Gilles Legault will not alter his holiday tradition of putting up Christmas lights.
☐ True ☐ False

WORD CULTURE

A *buck* is American slang for a dollar. *Buck* likely comes from "buckskin," as deerskins were used by Amerindians and frontiersmen as trade items with merchants.

8. What is the subject of the segment?

_____

9. What is the main opinion presented?

_____

A Question of PERSPECTIVE

The expression *feast* or *famine* refers to periods of overabundance or shortage. How does a period of feast affect your perspective? A period of famine? List a minimum of three ways for each.

DISCUSSION

→ Discuss each of the questions in small groups.

→ Be prepared to share your answers with the rest of the class and to explain them.

1. Brian Burgio claims he has been happier since he reduced his spending. Why would this be so?

2. Can frugality be fun? Explain.

3. Is your generation a generation of excess or moderation? Justify your position.

VOCABULARY REVIEW

→ Without looking back at the synonyms that you found for the terms in italics on pages 56 and 57, correctly fill in the blanks with the words from the chart below.

→ Pluralize nouns and conjugate verbs as required.

ADJECTIVES	EXPRESSIONS	NOUN	VERBS
frivolous sluggish	not strain (one's) wallet wake-up call	hardship	hunker down overdo plunge rein in slash

Like many young people, I received my first credit card during my first term at university. Even though I didn't have a job, the company gave me a $2000 spending limit. I was so proud: having a credit card made me feel like a real adult. I went right out and made my first purchase: a ninety-nine-dollar poster. What a (1) _____ thing to buy! I convinced myself that it was a necessary purchase—that my dorm room needed something to brighten up the dingy walls. As the weeks progressed, I bought more and more things, (2) _____ deeper and deeper into debt. Within a couple of weeks, I had reached my spending limit—and I can tell you that my first credit card bill was a real (3) _____ ! When I opened the bill, I felt sick. My first reaction was to (4) _____ expenses: I stopped going out with my friends and (5) _____ my food budget in half. I wasn't getting enough to eat, and felt (6) _____ most of the time. Unfortunately, spending less was not enough to pay off my debt: I had to get a job. I soon found myself studying full-time and working full-time: what a (7) _____ that proved to be! I was really (8) _____ it, trying to pay off everything I had bought as quickly as I could. Strangely enough, the more money I made, the more I wanted to spend. I put some money on the debt, making sure to pay the minimum balance every month, but I always found some little "necessity" that I was convinced (9) _____ my wallet too much! But ten dollars here and twenty dollars there—it all adds up! When I had finally had enough of living to work instead of working to live, I cut up my credit card and paid off my bill; I quit my job, (10) _____ and started studying (and living!) full-time once again.

READING 3.2 The Gift of Thrift

Jane Macdougall writes a regular column for the *National Post*. Her article "The Gift of Thrift" was published on July 10, 2009.

BEFORE READING

→ Scan the article, circling the vocabulary terms listed below.

→ Define these terms according to the context in which each is used.

1. immutable (adj.): _____

2. steady pace (exp.): _____

3. woozy (adj.): _____

4. ad-hoc (adj.): _____

5. discards (n.): _____

6. leafing through (v.): _____

7. forebears (n.): _____

8. herd (n.): _____

9. lay waste (exp.): _____

10. scope (n.): _____

Examine the reading strategies suggested in "Appendix B: Effective Reading and Active Listening." Then read the questions on pages 62 to 64 *before* reading the article itself.

The Gift of Thrift

By Jane Macdougall

When did it change?

My guess is somewhere between Swatch watches,[3] Beanie Babies,[4] billion dollar handbags, pre-ripped jeans and
5 spinning rims.[5]

Our grandparents lived by a different set of rules than we do today. And the rules were based on immutable truths:
* Use it up, make it last, make it do.
10 • A penny saved is a penny earned.
* A stitch in time saves nine.
* Waste not, want not.

WORD CULTURE

The proverb *a stitch in time saves nine* means "it's easier to solve a small problem before it becomes a big problem." The expression is based on the analogy of repairing a small rip before having to sew an entirely new seam.

The merit of these values was self-evident. Everybody from Aesop's "Ant and
15 the Grasshopper" to the "Little Red Hen" —who asked, "Who will help me bake my bread?"—understood them.[6] Time-tested, they had advanced individuals and nations at a steady pace. Virtually all gratification
20 was delayed, but its arrival was assured.

Calvin Coolidge famously remarked: "Industry, thrift and self-control are not sought after because they create wealth, but because they create character."

25 Yup, thrift held a place of honour in the hierarchy of values. Profligacy[7] was a red flag, perhaps even a sign of degeneracy.

Speaking of degeneracy, I'm going to confess something: A few years back I
30 noticed I had three dozen pairs of shoes, not including boots. I had more sweaters than I had drawer space. I had enough lipsticks to paint a fire truck.

It made me woozy.

35 One day, a neighbour gave me a bucket-load of black bamboo. I planted it, but it splayed out like a newborn colt trying to stand.

Driving down my alley one night, I spied
40 a black wrought iron chair set out in anticipation of garbage day. The rush seat[8]

3. Swatch watches are a brand of wrist watches introduced in the 1980s.
4. Beanie Babies are small stuffed animals that began to be marketed in the 1980s.
5. A spinning rim is a type of hubcap that spins independently inside the wheel itself.
6. Both of these well-known children's stories emphasize the importance of hard work and personal initiative.
7. *Profligacy* means "wastefulness" (formal).
8. A *rush seat* is a chair seat made of rushes (grass-like plants).

had given way and it was being junked. Uncollected, it remained in the alley for weeks.

As I tried to discipline the flailing bamboo, it occurred to me that the chair frame might corral the spindly shoots. I dragged the chair back to my Vancouver home, hacked out the remaining seating and, like an ad-hoc tomato cage, lowered the frame over the bamboo. The black bamboo canes supported by a sculptural frame of black metal looked grand.

I was enchanted. This wasn't some mere purchase. This was ... ingenuity. Unique. Personal. It was also free. I liked that part, too.

In the weeks ahead, I kept my eyes open for another chair and—here's the funny thing—I discovered I had dozens of discards to choose from. I started to envision lots of innovative uses for them. And each came at the same cost: free. Free.

It made me woozy.

Soon, I had an exotic landscape of river rock and black chair skeletons encircling black bamboo. I can't tell you the immense pleasure it gave me to show it off. I felt like ... like an explorer or an artist.

My bamboo garden was now secure, but the habit of searching was ingrained.

Jane Macdougall posing in front of brightly painted satellite dishes displayed as outdoor artwork

My eye had become accustomed to seeing what others did not. An abandoned chimney pot became a planter, the glass from a kicked in TV set transformed in the hands of a jeweller friend, and wait till you see what I did with discarded satellite dishes!

This was exciting! I was creating stuff rather than just buying stuff. I was shrinking my carbon footprint while saving money, and it was fun.

While leafing through a fashion magazine, my imagination was ignited by the challenge of recreating couture pieces using stuff I already owned. And man, did I already own stuff!

Every peel went into the compost; potted plants got watered from a bucket tucked inside my shower; I unplugged all appliances when not in use; I hung dry virtually all my laundry; I grazed organic sheep on my roof and, by candle light, spun their wool.

I'm lying about that last part, but I did put in a vegetable garden.

The point is that my life got cooler for all this. Instead of a dirty '30s sense of deprivation, I felt energized by the engagedness of the whole process. It had become a sort of game. The second best part of it was keeping score by adding up my savings.

There's an inverse relationship between the history of shopping and the decline of personal savings indexes. These days, you can part with your money around the clock. Perceived and planned obsolescence have ensured that we spend it faster than we make it.

In my estimation, eBay, the modern trading post, has replaced banking. Instead of actual money put aside, we now have an inventory of excess stuff to sell via the Internet. Despite the miracles of the millennia, we're back to trading wampum and pelts. All hail PayPal!

The toll this is taking on the earth's limited resources is well documented but largely ignored. We furrow our brows, saying, "All very sad about the ozone hole, but great gobs of shaving foam in a highly decorative metal and plastic can are a necessity, right? How did our forebears cope?"

Maybe I don't understand Thing One about all this [...] but I do know that there are too many people taking too many liberties with the earth and, on a personal level, counting on the lottery to bail them out financially.

Acting like everything is limitless is as bad for the planet as it is for your wallet. What's more, it costs a lot of money to run with the herd ... and who wants to look like part of a herd?

We down vitamins, log hours on treadmills, and pray that socialized medicine will be there when it's our knee that needs an arthroscopic[9] tune-up. We want our individuality acknowledged but we mask ourselves in costly uniformity. And we lay waste to the earth in the process.

"Waste," according to Thomas Edison, "is worse than loss. The time is coming when every person who lays claim to ability will keep the question of waste before him constantly. The scope of thrift is limitless."

And by scope of thrift, I'm sure Edison is referring to creativity, ingenuity, resourcefulness, not watering down the milk.

So, why be one of a million, when you can be one in a million?

And speaking of millions, every fortune starts with a single dollar.

Welcome back to the Age of Thrift.

Our grandparents are expecting us.

(1037 words)

Source: Macdougall, Jane. "The Gift of Thrift." *National Post* 10 Jul. 2009. Web. 1 Dec. 2009.

VOCABULARY AND COMPREHENSION

You may have to use external sources (a dictionary or a web search, for example) to find some of the answers to the questions below.

1. The author begins her article with the question, "When did it change?" What is she referring to? (What is the "it"?)

    _____

2. Paraphrase the following idiom: a penny saved is a penny earned. (Line 10)

    _____

3. Paraphrase the following sentence: "Virtually all gratification was delayed, but its arrival was assured." (Lines 19 and 20)

    _____

4. The author uses the following sentence twice: "It made me woozy." (Lines 34 and 64) What made her woozy the first time she employs the sentence? The second time?

    a) _____

    b) _____

9. Surgery performed with an arthroscope, a small tube-like instrument that uses fibre optics to examine and treat a joint.

5. A **simile** is an expression that describes something by comparing it with something else, using the words "as" or "like." What is the simile the author uses to describe the bamboo she planted?

_____

6. In your own words, briefly explain why the author took the iron chair out of the garbage.

_____

_____

_____

7. If an object is *repurposed*, it is used in a new way that is different from its original use. List three items the author repurposed, indicating how each item was used in a new way.

a) _____

b) _____

c) _____

8. Which of the following statements is(are) true? More than one answer is possible.

The author

a) composted.

b) watered plants with water from her shower.

c) unplugged appliances not in use.

d) hung her laundry out to dry.

e) spun the wool from her own herd of sheep.

9. Being thrifty made the author feel deprived.

☐ True   ☐ False

10. Paraphrase the following: "There's an inverse relationship between the history of shopping and the decline of personal savings indexes ... Perceived and planned obsolescence have ensured that we spend it faster than we make it." (Lines 104–110)

_____

_____

_____

11. What does the author mean when she writes, "... we're back to trading wampum and pelts"? (Lines 117 and 118)

_____

_____

_____

_____

12. Sarcasm is a way of expressing yourself that involves saying or writing the opposite of what you mean in order to make an unkind joke or show annoyance. Explain the sarcasm of the following statement: "How did our forebears cope?" (Line 124)

_____

_____

_____

_____

_____

13. The author claims that our desire to have what everybody else has is ruining the earth.

☐ True   ☐ False

14. According to the author, what was Thomas Edison referring to when he wrote of "the scope of thrift"?

_____

15. What is the subject of the article?

_____

16. What is the author's opinion on the subject?

_____

_____

A Question of PERSPECTIVE

How would your perspective on thrift and wastefulness be different if you were fifty years older than your current age?

DISCUSSION

→ Discuss each of the questions in small groups.

→ Be prepared to share your answers with the rest of the class and to explain them.

1. Do industry, thrift and self-control create character? Explain.

2. Why is waste worse than loss?

3. An English proverb states that, "Necessity is the mother of invention." Explain this proverb in your own words and provide real-life examples where this proverb has proven itself true.

LISTENING Radical Thrift

CULTURAL NOTE

In Canada, April Fool's Day jokes only last until noon; this is not the case in countries such as France and the United States. The origins of April Fool's Day are uncertain.

On April 1, 2009, the CBC program *The Current* aired "Radical Thrift," a radio segment that, unbeknownst to listeners, was an April Fool's Day joke. You will hear the first nine-and-a-half minutes of the segment, during which host Anna Maria Tremonti interviews journalist Judith Levine, author of *Not Buying It: My Year without Shopping* (a real book), entrepreneur Gretel Meyer Odell, who runs a community listserv, and politician Elizabeth May, leader of the Green Party of Canada.

BEFORE LISTENING

The following quotes were taken directly from the segment:

1. "The economic downturn has left a lot of people looking for ways to *cut corners*."
2. "This morning, we're talking about the many ways people *are pinching pennies*, from the simplest and most obvious to ones that require a bit more dedication. Some call it 'Radical Thrift' ..."
3. "... the places that you *hang out*."
4. "Now personally, you tried to be *frugal*."
5. People have used the listserv "... to borrow an item that they just need for one-time use that when you're *in a pinch*, you end up going out and buying."
6. "There's a group in New York called 'freegans'—I guess they're all over the United States—and they make their entire lifestyle on *bartering* and getting stuff for free."
7. "I will do all of my travel ... by *hitchhiking*."
8. "... there are some *glitches*, but overall I think we can pull off an entire tour ..."
9. "... One must be gregarious and friendly and also, of course, willing to trust in *the milk of human kindness* and put thoughts of repeat sex offenders out of your mind as you stick your thumb out on the road."
10. "... just how important is social grace when you're trying to *mooch* off someone?"

→ Rewrite the terms in *italics* and write a synonym for each in the chart below. You may wish to use a thesaurus.

→ The first one has been done for you as an example.

ITALICIZED TERMS	SYNONYMS
1. *cut corners*	reduce costs
2.	
3.	
4.	
5.	

	ITALICIZED TERMS	SYNONYMS
6.		
7.		
8.		
9.		
10.		

Examine the listening strategies suggested in "Appendix B: Effective Reading and Active Listening." Then read the comprehension questions below *before* listening to the clip.

COMPREHENSION

The questions below are in sequence: you will hear the answer to question 1, then question 2, then question 3, etc. If you miss an answer, do not worry about it; simply move on to the next question.

1. According to Judith Levine, our definition of "a need"—and how we differentiate a need from a desire—is constantly shifting. In her opinion, what influences how we define what is essential?

   _____

   _____

2. According to Judith Levine, the consumer culture gives us an identity, since "who we are" is a function of what we read, what we wear and the people we spend time with.

    True   ☐ False

3. Which of the following statements is false?
   According to Judith Levine, a frugal lifestyle

   a) encouraged her to spend more time with her partner and her friends.

   b) reduced the number of distractions in her life.

   c) allowed her and her mate to spend more time in the public sphere (e.g., libraries and parks).

   d) was nearly impossible to lead in the United States.

4. Gretel Meyer Odell started up the Brockton neighbourhood listserv,[10] a virtual place where people can "meet" to borrow items from one another. She mentions ten examples of items that people have borrowed over the last year. Name three.

---

10. A listserv is an e-mail system that automatically sends messages to groups of subscribers, allowing people with similar interests to exchange information.

a) _____

b) _____

c) _____

5. Elizabeth May and her team came up with a creative solution to reduce their costs and carbon footprint. What was their "creative" solution?

_____

_____

6. Ms. Levine applauds Ms. May's creative solution, but makes three suggestions as to how to improve it. Name one.

_____

_____

7. While campaigning, Ms. May claims that she met one very nice woman who allowed an entire documentary film crew to sit in the back seat of her car.

☐ True   ☐ False

8. What example of mooching does Ms. Levine give?

_____

_____

9. What is the subject of the segment?

_____

10. What is the main idea of the segment?

_____

A Question of PERSPECTIVE

As the interview continues, the examples of thrift discussed grow more extreme: reusing dental floss, setting up a community toilet, eating opossum and racoon, etc. By the end of the piece, it is clear that it is a joke. However, most listeners will have begun listening to the broadcast assuming it was serious. Some listeners are offended by being fooled; others, amused. In your opinion, why do people react so differently to being fooled? Provide a minimum of three reasons.

DISCUSSION

→ Discuss each of the questions in small groups.

→ Be prepared to share your answers with the rest of the class and to explain them.

1. A **parody** is a satirical imitation of something more serious. Explain how the interview you heard could be considered a parody.

2. Gretel Meyer Odell's listserv is real, as are the examples of borrowing she provided. When given a choice, do you prefer to borrow or buy? Explain your preference.

3. At what point in the interview would you have realized you were listening to an April Fool's Day joke?

VOCABULARY REVIEW

→ Without looking back at the synonyms that you found for the terms in italics on pages 65 and 66, correctly fill in the blanks with the words from the chart below.

→ Pluralize nouns and conjugate verbs as required.

ADJECTIVE	EXPRESSIONS	NOUNS	VERBS
frugal	be in a pinch cut corners pinch pennies the milk of human kindness	bartering glitch	hang out hitchhiking mooch

1. "_____" is a Shakespearean phrase from the play *Macbeth*. In it, Lady Macbeth reveals her fears that her husband is too kind to kill Duncan.

2. _____ is a way to obtain what you need without having to spend any money.

3. — Have you asked Joan about babysitting on Friday night?
   — Yeah, but she's not free.
   — Well, I guess I could call my mom and tell her we're _____ a bit of _____. I'm sure she'd watch the kids for a couple of hours.

4. If you have no money, I guess you'll just have to _____ some from your father.

5. Jack Benny (1894–1974) was an American comedian who was famously _____ : many of his comedy routines centred around his being ridiculously tight with his money.

6. _____ your _____ and watch your savings grow.

7. The plan just might work—once all the _____ have been taken care of.

8. While _____ across the country, they had a couple of scary rides so they decided to return home by train.

9. Why don't we just stay in tonight, eat popcorn and watch a DVD? It's been ages since we've just _____ together.

10. With no salary increase, we'll have to _____ to survive.

ost

A Rhyme

A rhyme is a repetition of similar sound: "*how now brown cow.*"

When used in songs or poetry, a rhyme scheme (pattern) can be identified.

Take, for example, the first stanza of "Smart," the poem by Shel Silverstein found at the start of this unit (p. 50).

> *My dad gave me one dollar bill (A)*
> *'Cause I'm his smartest* **son**, *(B)*
> *And I swapped it for two shiny quarters (C)*
> *'Cause two is more than* **one**! *(B)*

The rhyme scheme ABCB, a simple four-line sonnet, is used. Many alternate schemes are possible: ABAB; AABB; AABBCCDD; etc.

For this writing assignment, you are asked to write a 100- to 125-word rhyming poem about money using any rhyme scheme you wish.

The Process Essay

The process essay explains how to do something: how to drive a car; how to get great marks in English; how to make friends; etc.

For this writing assignment, you are asked to write a 400- to 450-word process essay using one of the following titles:

1. How to Barter
2. How to Be Conspicuously Wasteful
3. How to Compost
4. How to Differentiate Wants from Needs
5. How to Get into Debt

6. How to Get Out of Debt
7. How to Lead a Healthy Life
8. How to Mooch
9. How to Pinch Pennies
10. How to Stick to a Budget

Base your process essay on the academic essay outlined on page 9: you will need an introduction, a development and a conclusion.

Unlike in most academic essays,

→ you are allowed to use the second person singular; for example, "To be conspicuously wasteful, you must ..."

→ you do not need to do any research, so referencing and a "Works Cited" section are probably not required.

The chart below provides a structural overview, detailing elements to consider. Remember always to proofread your work before submitting it.

ESSAY SECTIONS	PARAGRAPHS	STRUCTURAL ELEMENTS
Introduction	1	• Begin with an effective grabber. • Indicate what process you wish to explain. • Indicate why the process is important. • Define key terms. • Write a thesis statement, complete with one main and two or three supporting points; for example, "To be conspicuously wasteful, you must have a great deal of money; you must have a public forum in which to display your waste; and you must have no shame!"
Development	2 3 4 (optional)	• Begin each of the body paragraphs with a transition term. • Within each body paragraph, present steps in chronological (or logical) order, using appropriate transition terms.
Conclusion	5	• Begin the paragraph with the transition term "In summary" followed by a brief recapping of the main and supporting points. • End with an effective clincher.

℗resent

Some Financial Advice

VOCABULARY TIP

Advise is a verb and *advice* is a noun. Be careful to spell each correctly!

In *Hamlet*, William Shakespeare's Polonius **advises** his son to "... neither a borrower nor a lender be." While the adage is familiar to most, few people today actually heed this **advice**. In this small-group exercise, you and three or four of your classmates are asked to analyze case studies about borrowing and lending gone wrong and offer some advice of your own. Be prepared to share your ideas with other groups.

Case Study 1: The Mostly Happy Couple

James and his wife Barbara have been married for five years, and they have saved $50,000 dollars for a down payment on a house. The bank has agreed to lend them as much as $300,000 in mortgage money. James and Barbara have found a house they love, but the selling price is $400,000—and the seller will not lower her price. Barbara's father is well off, but he and James don't get along. James refuses to ask Barbara's father for a loan. Barbara doesn't want to lose the house of her dreams due to James's pride. What should they do?

Case Study 2: Brothers at Odds

Charles has been a caring and devoted son; however, he is always short of cash. His mother Claire is a widow living on a fixed income. Charles is constantly asking to "borrow" money to pay the rent, a "loan" he never repays. His brother Steven, a successful businessman, is worried that their mother is depriving herself of basic necessities to help Charles out. What should Steven do?

Case Study 3: Friends at Any Cost?

Charlene is a student living on student loans. She is good with her money and normally only spends money on the essentials. Every once in a while, Charlene splurges on a meal out with her best friend Grace. Charlene orders an inexpensive main course and drinks water with her meal. Grace orders two or three appetizers, a main course and a small carafe of wine. When the bill comes, Grace always suggests they just "split it down the middle," claiming that things will all "even out" in the end. Charlene has tried to object in the past, but each time Grace has gotten furious. Charlene doesn't have a lot of friends and looks forward to what is otherwise a pleasant evening out. What should Charlene do?

Case Study 4: Poor Party Girl

Paula is everybody's best friend: she's generous with her time and money. Once a month, she throws a party for friends and family and always pays for the food and refreshments. You know Paula is getting into serious debt to pay for these shindigs. You also know she gets terribly insulted if anyone offers to chip in. You're Paula's boyfriend, and you enjoy the parties as much as she does. What should you do?

Case Study 5: The New Neighbours

A young couple with a toddler move into the apartment next door. The parents are both recently unemployed and live on employment benefits. They provide their child with life's necessities, but you suspect the child does not always get enough healthy food to eat. You broach the subject with your neighbours, offering a loan to help them until they're back on their feet. They politely tell you to mind your own business. You are concerned about the child's well-being. What should you do?

Proverbially Speaking

A proverb is a short, well-known statement that gives advice or expresses something that is generally believed to be true. Examples of proverbs seen in this unit include "money can't buy happiness" and "a stitch in time saves nine."

Proverbs about money are numerous. Other examples include:

1. A bird in the hand is worth two in the bush.
2. A fool and his money are soon parted.
3. He who pays the piper calls the tune.
4. It is better to give than to receive.
5. Money talks.
6. Nothing ventured, nothing gained.
7. One man's loss is another man's gain.
8. The best things in life are free.
9. Time is money.
10. When poverty comes in at the door, love flies out of the window.

→ Select any one of the proverbs on page 71 and use it as the thesis of a formal speech. Your speech should last five to seven minutes.

→ In your introduction, be sure to explain the meaning of the proverb in your own words. (For information on structuring and giving a formal speech, see page 17.)

For example:

My objective today is to demonstrate the truth of the proverb, "[insert chosen proverb]," and I will do so in the following three ways: first, I will ...; second, I will ...; and third, I will ...

𝒫articipate

In this section, you will work with another student on a joint writing and speaking project.

Writing a Fable

A **fable** is a traditional short story that teaches a moral lesson, using animals, plants, inanimate objects and/or forces of nature as main characters.

In this project, you and your partner will write a modern-day fable about money and share it with your classmates.

Procedure

1. Research fables on the Internet and analyze the basic structure: fables have non-human characters behaving like humans; there is a conflict to be resolved; a dialogue exists between a protagonist (main character) and an antagonist (character working in opposition to the protagonist)—both of whom are often natural enemies; and a definite moral is revealed at the end of the story (i.e., a lesson is learned through the resolution of the conflict). Focus your research on "Aesop's Fables," "The Jataka Tales" and/or Dr. Seuss.

2. Decide which moral lesson about money you would like your fable to teach; for example, "money can't buy happiness." Research proverbs about money on the Internet, since a proverb can easily be used as a moral. (Or see the activity "Proverbially Speaking" on page 71 for ten proverbs you might wish to consider.)

3. Select two main characters that may or may not be considered natural enemies, and give these characters suitable names.

4. Determine the setting (time and place) of your story.

5. Write down your story. Be sure to give your story a beginning, a middle and a conclusion—and end with a definite moral, such as a proverb. Include lots of dialogue between the two main characters and use descriptive language when writing about the setting and characters.

6. Proofread and correct your work.

7. Tell your story to your classmates; ask them whether they agree or disagree with the moral you selected.

ⓟursue

Related Works

The following works may be of interest for continued study.

TYPES OF WORKS	TITLES

Animated Short	*John Law and the Mississippi Bubble*. Dir. Richard Condie. National Film Board of Canada, 1978.
	    • Available online at:
	    http://www.nfb.ca/film/john_law_and_the_mississippi_bubble
	    (9 minutes and 20 seconds)
	    • An entertaining history lesson about a financial bubble—and subsequent financial crash—involving the exchange of paper money for gold in France more than 200 years ago; some interesting parallels to modern get-rich-quick schemes—and the resulting modern financial disasters

Documentary	*Maxed Out: Hard Times, Easy Credit and the Era of Predatory Lenders*. Dir. James Scurlock. Magnolia Pictures, 2006. • Film about abusive practices in the credit-card industry

Fiction	Kinsella, Sophie. *Shopaholic*. 2000–2007. Print.
	    • Series of popular novels about a woman whose spending is often out of control
	
	Steinbeck, John. *The Grapes of Wrath*. New York: Viking, 1939. Print.
	    • Set in the Great Depression

Movie	*Cinderella Man*. Dir. Ron Howard. Miramax, 2005.
	    • Actor Russell Crowe takes on the role of Jim Braddock, a washed-up boxer who makes an amazing comeback to pull himself and his family out of poverty
	
	The Pursuit of Happyness. Dir. Gabriele Muccino. Columbia, 2006.
	    • Actor Will Smith plays Chris Gardner, a salesman who falls on hard times; based on a real-life story

Non-Fiction	Atwood, Margaret. *Payback: Debt and the Shadow Side of Wealth*. Toronto: Anansi, 2008. Print.
	    • Exploration of the concept of debt
	
	Levine, Judith. *Not Buying It: My Year without Shopping*. New York: Free Press, 2006. Print.
	    • Book by author interviewed in the Listening activity (see page 65)
	
	Roseman, Ellen. *Money 101: Every Canadian's Guide to Personal Finance*. Etobicoke: Wiley, 2002. Print.
	    • Book by consumer reporter interviewed in the Watching activity (see page 56)

Short Story	Leacock, Stephen. "How to Borrow Money." *Short Circuits*. Toronto: Macmillan, 1928. Print. • Entertaining short story with an enduring moral

My eLab 🖉 Visit My eLab for additional reading, listening and vocabulary practice.

Too Young, Too Old, Too Bad

A staircase in the
Messberghof building in
Hamburg, Germany

review

WORD CULTURE

The expression *time flies*
means "time moves quickly."
The expression has its origins
in antiquity as demonstrated
by the Roman proverb *tempus
fugit*, which translates as
"time flees." Today, the
expression is sometimes
completed with "when you're
having fun!"

We all have one.

An age, that is.

Some of us are young, some of us are old, and some of us fall somewhere
in between.

The young wish they were older, the old wish they were younger and the
middle-aged wish they had time to wish!

Whether **time** "stands still" or "**flies**" depends on how old you are; it depends
on your perspective.

People of all ages, young and not so young alike, experience discrimination
because they are "too young" or "too old." They experience ageism.

Ageism and aging are the topics of this unit, and they are "timely" ones
in developed countries with aging populations that, somewhat ironically, tend
to appreciate the young and depreciate the old.

Too young, too old—too bad!

 **repare**

In this section, two warm-up exercises are proposed: the first deals with aging, the focus of Reading 4.1 and of the Watching activity; the second, with ageism, the focus of Reading 4.2 and of the Listening activity.

WARM UP 4.1 What Do You Know about Aging?

Aging is simply the process of getting old. For most the process is gradual, occurring over a long lifetime. For others, the process is comparatively rapid.[1] How much do you know about aging? Take the following quiz to find out.

1. The average life expectancy of a Canadian woman is _____ years; the average life expectancy of a Canadian man is _____ years.

   a) eighty-five / eighty-one

   b) eighty-one / eighty-five

   c) eighty-eight / eighty-four

   d) eighty-four / eighty-eight

2. On average, men in their seventies are _____ centimetres shorter than when they were in their twenties.

   a) one-and-a half

   b) two

   c) two-and-a half

   d) three

3. On average, women in their seventies are _____ centimetres shorter than when they were in their twenties.

   a) two

   b) three

   c) four

   d) five

4. The human brain stops growing in the

   a) teens.

   b) early twenties.

   c) early thirties.

   d) early forties.

5. In general, at approximately what age is muscle strength at its peak?

   a) Eighteen

   b) Twenty-one

   c) Twenty-five

   d) Thirty-five

6. Eyesight begins to weaken in your

   a) twenties.

   b) thirties.

   c) forties.

   d) fifties.

7. Men and women start to "shrink" in their

   a) twenties.

   b) thirties.

   c) forties.

   d) fifties.

1. In the Post section you will be given an opportunity to learn about progeria, a rare genetic condition in which symptoms characteristic of aging occur in childhood.

8. Women's brains shrink less than men's brains.

□ True □ False

9. Brain shrinkage affects cognitive abilities such as memory, attention and speed of processing information.

□ True □ False

10. In 1921, approximately 5 percent of Canadians were aged sixty-five or older. In 2056, Statistics Canada projects that approximately _____ percent of the population will be aged sixty-five or older.

a) 10   **c)** 20

b) 15   **d)** 25

Sources:
- "Aging: A Canadian Snapshot." *Rage against the Darkness*. CBC Documentaries, Sept. 2004. Web. 5 Jan. 2010.
- CBC News Online. "Strength, Brain Power and Shrinking through the Ages." *CBC News*. 5 Aug. 2006. Web. 5 Jan. 2010.
- Morales, Steve. "A Greying Population: What Does It Mean for Canada?" *CBC News*. 28 Feb. 2007. Web. 5 Jan. 2010.

 **WARM UP 4.2** **Is It Ageist?**

Ageism is discrimination based on age. Typically, ageism has referred to actions that treat the old unfairly; however, ageism also refers to actions that treat the young and middle-aged unfairly.

→ For each of the actions below, decide whether the action is fair or unfair (i.e., ageist).

→ Be prepared to discuss your answers with the rest of the class.

ACTIONS	FAIR	UNFAIR
1. Charging young and middle-aged adults more than seniors for the same services (bus passes, movie tickets, etc.)		
2. Charging young and middle-aged adults more than children for the same services (bus passes, movie tickets, etc.)		
3. Not allowing those under the age of eighteen to drink alcohol		
4. Not giving those under the age of eighteen the right to vote		
5. Not hiring someone because he or she is too old		
6. Not providing costly medical care because a patient is too old to benefit from the treatment for very long		
7. Requiring employees to retire at sixty-five		
8. Requiring parental permission to marry if sixteen or seventeen years of age		
9. Requiring those over the age of seventy to pass a yearly driving test		
10. Setting stricter rules on obtaining and retaining drivers' licenses for those under the age of twenty-five		

© PEARSON LONGMAN • REPRODUCTION PROHIBITED

GRAMMAR TIP

The **past unreal conditional** is composed of an *if clause* in the past perfect and a *result clause* in the conditional perfect: *If I **had known** then what I know now, I **would have done** things differently.* The past unreal conditional is used to talk about unreal past situations. For more information on conditionals, see page 212.

Ponder

Erma Bombeck was a popular American humorist who authored more than 4000 newspaper columns and many bestselling books from the mid-'60s before her death in 1996.

If I Had My Life to Live Over

By Erma Bombeck

Someone asked me the other day if I had my life to live over, would I change anything.

My answer was no, but then I
⁵ thought about it and changed my mind.

If I had my life to live over, I would have talked less and listened more.

Instead of wishing away nine
¹⁰ months of pregnancy and complaining about the shadow over my feet, I would have cherished every minute of it and realized that the wonderment growing inside me was
¹⁵ to be my only chance in life to assist God in a miracle.

I would never have insisted the car windows be rolled up on a summer day because my hair had just
²⁰ been teased and sprayed.

I would have invited friends over to dinner even if the carpet was stained and the sofa faded.

I would have eaten popcorn in
²⁵ the "good" living room and worried less about the dirt when you lit the fireplace.

I would have taken the time to listen to my grandfather ramble about
³⁰ his youth.

I would have burnt the pink candle that was sculptured like a rose before it melted in storage.

I would have sat cross-legged on
³⁵ the lawn with my children and never worried about grass stains.

I would have cried and laughed less while watching television … and more while watching real life.

⁴⁰ I would have shared more of the responsibility carried by my husband.

I would have eaten less cottage cheese and more ice cream.

⁴⁵ I would have gone to bed when I was sick instead of pretending the Earth would go into a holding pattern if I weren't there for a day.

I would never have bought *any-*
⁵⁰ *thing* just because it was practical / wouldn't show soil / guaranteed to last a lifetime.

When my child kissed me impetuously, I would never have said,
⁵⁵ "Later. Now, go get washed up for dinner."

There would have been more I love yous … more I'm sorrys … more I'm listenings … but mostly,
⁶⁰ given another shot at life, I would seize every minute of it … look at it and really see it … try it on … live it … exhaust it … and never give that minute back until there
⁶⁵ was nothing left of it.

(378 words)

Source: Bombeck, Erma. "If I Had My Life to Live Over." *Eat Less Cottage Cheese and More Ice Cream*. Kansas City: Andrews McMeel, 2003. Print.

VOCABULARY AND COMPREHENSION

You may wish to work with a partner as you answer the questions below.

1. Which words from the poem have the following meanings?

    a) Discoloured: _____

    b) Talk aimlessly: _____

    c) State in which no progress is made: _____

    d) Impulsively: _____

    e) Given another chance at life: _____

    f) Take advantage of every moment: _____

2. From whose perspective is the poem written?

    _____

3. What does the author mean when she writes, "... I would have eaten less cottage cheese and more ice cream ..."?

    _____

4. In lines 49 and 50, why does the author write "anything" in *italics*?

    _____

5. What is the author's biggest regret?

    _____

DISCUSSION

→ Discuss each of the questions below in small groups.

→ Be prepared to share your answers with the rest of the class and to explain them.

1. Many believe that wisdom comes with age; "If I Had My Life to Live Over" seems to support this belief as Ms. Bombeck alludes to several "life lessons" when listing her regrets. In your opinion, what are the three most important lessons she learned over time? Justify your choice.

2. Name an important life lesson not mentioned in the text that you have learned over time. How did you learn this lesson?

3. Many people, especially older people, find the piece inspiring. Did you? Why or why not?

READING 4.1 Relics of a Former Life

Gail Kerbel is a Canadian actress and writer whose article "Relics of a Former Life" appeared in *The Globe and Mail* on April 7, 2009.

BEFORE READING

→ Scan the article, circling the vocabulary terms listed on page 79.

→ Define these terms according to the context in which each is used.

VOCABULARY TIP

Sashay is a variant of "chassé," a term used in dance to describe a sliding movement

1. sibling (n.): _____

2. cram (v.): _____

3. digs (n.): _____

4. hoist (v.): _____

5. feeble (adj.): _____

6. rally (v.): _____

7. stench (n.): _____

8. linger (v.): _____

9. bounty (n.): _____

10. **sashay** (v.): _____

Examine the reading strategies suggested in "Appendix B: Effective Reading and Active Listening." Then read the questions on page 81 *before* reading the article itself.

Relics of a Former Life

By Gail Kerbel

When my father moved from his rambling house to a three-room apartment, my siblings and I were enlisted to help.

Since we didn't know what to do with all the stuff from our childhood home, we crammed everything into his new digs. The silver and crystal that was brought out for company, the entire *Encyclopedia Britannica*, 1965 edition, the dusty boxes of report cards extolling our virtues as friendly, co-operative children, the massive dining room table with its twelve gold flocked chairs—we transferred all of it.

"Have I told you how much I love this place?" my father would ask.

"You have, Dad."

"I come home from work, make a coffee and relax in the Florida room. I just love it."

The Florida room was a narrow, enclosed porch overlooking a parking lot. I don't know what it had to do with Florida. "That's great, Dad."

My father was telling me he had no intention of leaving his apartment and moving to a nursing home.

Sorry, Dad.

We put it off as long as we could, longer than we should have. But when his arms were too weak to hoist himself from his chair, when his legs were too feeble to carry his weight, we moved him to a home. We thought that if we brought some items from the apartment—a pink velvet loveseat, a blue ottoman—maybe that would cheer him up, maybe he would rally. As if upholstery had magical restorative powers. He was there for five days, and then he died.

Once again, we had to pack up the stuff. My two brothers, my sister and I held a family meeting to figure out how to close the apartment.

We sat in his living room with our coats on, four adult orphans wishing we were anywhere but there. It would have been more comfortable if we could have taken our coats off, but all the windows were open to let in fresh air. In the weeks before we had to move him, our father sealed up his apartment, sat in a chair and smoked, and a bitter stench still lingered in the place.

We sorted through the items quickly because no one wanted much. We all had our own stuff, and our father had suggested the furniture might be worth an interesting sum. We spent the rest of the afternoon shivering and discussing what we would do with the proceeds from a sale. I was considering a trip to Andalusia.[2]

I arrived one morning to prepare for a meeting with a woman from a high-end consignment store. I displayed the crystal and silver on the dining room table, lit one of my father's stale cigarettes, sat on the pink loveseat and calculated what we'd make from this bounty. I figured we'd clear about $40,000.

But I miscalculated. It turned out the woman wanted … nothing. Apparently, the furniture that I thought was so exquisite, that I used to sashay around pretending to be Scarlett O'Hara receiving gentlemen callers, was faux French Provincial from Eaton's. The market was flooded with the stuff and nobody wanted it.

Adios Andalusia.

I took a green garbage bag into my father's office, opened it wide and tossed in some old bookends. Then I sat at the desk, fired up another cigarette, opened the top drawer and nearly choked on my sadness. There was his handwriting on squares of white notepaper: reminders of doctor's appointments, shopping lists, little conversations with himself in script so familiar I could hear his voice.

I closed the drawer and opened another. It contained a number of plaques honouring my mother's charitable work. One of them had her photo mounted between two acrylic plates. I already had the picture, but how do you throw out an item with your mother's face on it? You don't.

I had been there for an hour, and all that I'd managed to throw out were the bookends and a chipped mug. My brother came by to pick up some documents and spied the mug in the garbage.

"You're throwing that out?" he asked.

"It's broken," I said.

"But that's the mug that held the pencils on the shelf by the phone."

I pulled it from the bag.

It was becoming clear that we were never going to have the place cleaned out by the time the lease expired. There was only one thing to do: renew the lease.

Just because my father couldn't stay in his beloved apartment didn't mean everything else had to go. I could keep the apartment and pay the rent on all the relics of a former life. And when my husband and I died, our sons could inherit the lease and stuff in the boxes of hockey trophies and Mother's Day cards and the old pine table around which we've spent so many happy hours. And then their children, if they were creative enough to make space, could cram in the mementos from their childhoods, and nobody would ever have to let go of anything again. Then I remembered the building was going to be turned into a condo.

It's been a year since the furniture was trucked off to a flea market and the garbage collectors carted away the rest. Yet still when I think of the chipped mug, the acrylic plaque, the pink velvet loveseat, I want it all back.

(897 words)

Source: Kerbel, Gail. "Relics of a Former Life." *Globe and Mail* 7 Apr. 2009. Web. 5 Jan. 2010.

2. A region in southern Spain.

VOCABULARY AND COMPREHENSION

You may have to use external sources (dictionary, website, etc.) to find some of the answers to the questions below.

1. How many times did the author and her brothers and sister move their father's possessions? Indicate from which place and to which place the items were moved each time.

   _____

   _____

   _____

   _____

   _____

2. Why did the author and her siblings have difficulty fitting their father's things into his apartment?

   _____

   _____

3. The author and her brothers and sister maintained their father's apartment even after he had moved to a nursing home.

   ☐ True   ☐ False

4. How long did the author's father live in a nursing home?

   _____

5. Why did the author and her siblings wear their coats while closing up their father's apartment?

   _____

   _____

6. Circle the letter of the correct answer(s). More than one answer is possible. Which of the following statements is(are) false?

   a) The author and her siblings fought over their father's possessions.

   b) The father thought his furniture was valuable.

   c) The father's furniture sold for $40,000.

   d) The author's father spoke to her while she was closing up his apartment.

7. In the second-last paragraph (lines 108–123), the author is writing facetiously.

   ☐ True   ☐ False

8. What is the subject of the article?

   _____

9. What is the author's opinion on the subject?

   _____

A Question of PERSPECTIVE

If you were elderly and enfeebled, would you expect to be cared for by your adult children in one of their homes?

DISCUSSION

→ Discuss each of the questions in small groups.

→ Be prepared to share your answers with the rest of the class and to explain them.

1. In your own words, what is a relic? Have you kept any relics from your childhood? If so, why? If not, why not?

2. What is the one object you would never want to be without? Why is it so important to you?

3. In your opinion, why did the father seal up his apartment and smoke in the weeks before he was moved to a nursing home?

 WATCHING Send in the Robots

Due to an aging workforce and a low birth rate, Japan will soon be facing a labour shortage. One potential solution to the shortage is the production of working robots. On January 31, 2009, CBC's *The National* aired journalist Saša Petricic's report on this very inventive idea. Guests include Professor Hiroshi Kobayashi and Saya, a robotic receptionist; Takanori Shibata and Paro, a robotic baby seal; Tutomi Turada, a hospital orderly; Toshiharu Mukai and RI-MAN, a robotic health-care worker; Shinya Ono, a Japanese member of parliament; Takao Kobayashi, a researcher; ASIMO, a robotic superstar; a robotic security guard made by ALSOK; and Timutsu Titaku, an elderly Japanese man.

BEFORE WATCHING

The terms listed at the top of page 83 are used in the video clip.

→ Working alone or with a partner, write the letter of the correct term beside each definition. The first one has been done for you as an example.

Examine the listening strategies suggested in "Appendix B: Effective Reading and Active Listening." Then read the comprehension questions on pages 83 and 84 *before* watching the clip.

DEFINITIONS		TERMS
1. Making you feel nervous or a little afraid	d	a) From abroad (exp.)
2. An unkind or disrespectful smile		b) Attendant (n.)
3. Fear of foreigners		c) The bulk (n.)
4. Person whose job is to look after or care for someone else		d) Creepy (adj.)
5. Make something (or someone) else seem less important		e) Overflow (v.)
6. From a foreign country		f) Overshadow (v.)
7. Be filled beyond capacity		g) Reluctant (adj.)
8. Unwilling, hesitant		h) Slowdown (n.)
9. The greater part		i) Sneer (n.)
10. Decline		j) Xenophobia (n.)

COMPREHENSION

The questions below are in sequence: you will hear the answer to question 1, then question 2, then question 3, etc. If you miss an answer, do not worry about it; simply move on to the next question.

1. Fill in the blanks. "The work is delicate and deliberate and, frankly, just a little bit _____ ! Robotic muscle made of gears and glue, heads not quite comfortable in their own skins. Smiles and _____ not yet quite right. Still under construction, this is the face of the new Japan." (Saša Petricic)

2. According to Professor Hiroshi Kobayashi (as expressed by Saša Petricic), what does Japan "desperately need"?

   _____

3. Japan's projected labour shortage is almost as important as the global economic crisis occurring at the time of the report.

   ☐ True   ☐ False

4. Fill in the blanks with the correct numbers. "Japan's problem is not unique. Just about every developed country is having fewer babies and more aging baby boomers. But nowhere are the numbers as dramatic as they are right here. _____ percent of the population is over the age of _____ right now; Canada won't hit that for at least _____ decades. In Japan by the middle of the century, _____ percent or more of its people will be senior citizens. That's something Canada, the United States and most European countries will likely never see." (Saša Petricic)

5. List two implications of an aging population mentioned in the report.

a) _____

b) _____

_____

6. According to orderly Tutomi Turada (through an interpreter), what effect did the arrival of Paro have on the seniors living in the seniors' home?

_____

7. How long did inventor Takanori Shibata spend developing Paro?

_____

8. Circle the letter of the correct answer(s). More than one answer is possible. RI-MAN can

a) talk   **c)** see

b) hear   **d)** feel

9. According to Toshiharu Mukai (as expressed by Saša Petricic), what is the biggest challenge with RI-MAN robots? The biggest problem?

_____

10. Japanese children learn to trust and rely on technology to resolve problems.

☐ True   ☐ False

11. Fill in the blanks. "Still, some say this reliance on technology is necessary precisely because the country is so uncomfortable with workers _____ _____ . Researcher Takao Kobayashi says for some Japanese, it's nothing short of _____ ." (Saša Petricic)

12. What percentage of Japan's population is made up of immigrants?

_____

13. What are bento boxes?

_____

14. Fill in the blanks. "We have always known Japan was going to have a large population of the aged. Though big corporations have become so successful in pursuing profit in the global economy, the _____ of the ordinary people in Japan are suffering." (Timutsu Titaku, through an interpreter)

15. Japanese youth have a negative opinion of robotics.

☐ True   ☐ False

A Question of PERSPECTIVE

Would your opinion on robotics be different if you had been raised in Japan? (If you were actually raised in Japan, would your opinion on robotics be different if you had been raised in North America?) Explain your response.

DISCUSSION

→ Discuss each of the questions in small groups.

→ Be prepared to share your answers with the rest of the class and to explain them

1. At the start of the video, why did Saša Petricic describe the robots being manufactured as "creepy"? Do you share his point of view?

2. What do you think about Paro, the robotic seal, being used as a therapeutic aid in seniors' homes? How do you feel about this?

3. Do you think North American youth share their Japanese counterparts' viewpoint on robotics? Why or why not?

VOCABULARY REVIEW

→ Without looking back at the terms and definitions provided on page 83, correctly fill in the blanks with seven of the words from the chart below.

→ Correctly use each of the remaining three words in sentences of your own creation.

→ Pluralize nouns and conjugate verbs as required.

ADJECTIVES	EXPRESSION	NOUNS	VERBS
creepy	from abroad	attendant	overflow
reluctant		bulk	overshadow
		slowdown	
		sneer	
		xenophobia	

Don't you think it would be somewhat (1) _____ having a robot "living" in your home? Most people I know would be (2) _____ to share their abode with a machine. The (3) _____ of their concern probably has to do with the issue of trust: can you rely on a robot to do what you tell it to do—and not do you in? Robotics is likely to become a "hot" issue in the coming years as the population ages and more and more people are in need of (4) _____ from home or (5) _____ .

In countries where (6) _____ is widespread, aging inhabitants will likely opt for automated companions—unless there's yet another economic (7) _____ and robots prove too expensive to buy.

Sentence 1: _____

_____

Sentence 2: _____

_____

Sentence 3: _____

_____

READING 4.2

"Too Old" or "Too Young"; Stop Judging by Age

Brett Anningson is a freelance journalist who writes on social issues. His article "'Too Old' or 'Too Young'; Stop Judging by Age" appeared in New Brunswick's *Times & Transcript* on May 26, 2008.

BEFORE READING

→ Scan the article, circling the vocabulary terms listed below.

→ Define each term according to the context in which each is used.

1. blessing (n.): _____

2. curse (n.): _____

3. wisdom (n.): _____

4. old-fashioned (adj.): _____

5. trivial (adj.): _____

6. verge on (v.): _____

7. knee-jerk (adj.): _____

8. blind spot (n.): _____

9. lump together (v.): _____

Examine the reading strategies suggested in "Appendix B: Effective Reading and Active Listening." Then read the questions on pages 88 and 89 *before* reading the article itself.

"Too Old" or "Too Young"; Stop Judging by Age

By Brett Anningson

Aging: blessing or curse?

Now there is a question that starts all sorts of discussions; because whether we like it or not, we are all in the same boat.
5 We age, our bodies break down, our minds skip a beat, the world changes around us ... and, unfortunately, I think our attitude makes it worse.

Consider how it works against the young:
10 he is too young to be a lawyer; she is too young to be a doctor, that job would be done **better** by someone with more experience. Have you ever said anything like that? You must have at least heard
15 someone say it.

GRAMMAR TIP

Better is the comparative form of *good* when functioning as an adjective and of *well* when functioning as an adverb. For more information on comparative adjectives and adverbs, see page 230.

We have a preconceived notion that with age comes wisdom—and although it may be right that some types of wisdom come with the passing of years, such as
20 patience, all wisdom is not time dependent. But society is focused on the idea that the most capable person has been doing the job for some time.

But not a lot of time: there comes a
25 moment, all too soon, when you are too old; old-fashioned, too slow, out of touch, antiquated. That same doctor and lawyer are working from an old-fashioned way of doing things—we do not value the wisdom
30 of the aged either.

I figure, if you are a man, and I suppose it is slightly different for a woman, but for a man I figure forty-seven is the only age where you are perfect.

35 This applies to wisdom, capability, sports, and of course, beauty. There is an optimum age and once you have surpassed it, there is no going back.

I remember the day I became too old
40 to be a US Marine—it was always one of those childhood dreams like firefighter and Disney World Jungle Cruise ride attendant ... but there comes a time when it is impossible to go back to childhood
45 dreams. And I suppose that is the beginning of wisdom.

But what I want to argue against is that this all too often becomes the beginning of a long list of things that we are told we are
50 too old for.

Think of the President of the United States. That is a job it seems you have to be older in order to have it; and in fact, a lot of people serve in elected office of all
55 sorts that are beyond the age of normal retirement. We trust them with such trivial things as grain storage and nuclear missile codes; and yet in the day-to-day world we think that those who are older, and I am
60 even talking just a little older than us, are verging on useless.

I could counter this on many fronts. Halle Berry is 42 for example, and Demi Moore is 46. Sean Connery is 78 and still a
65 sex symbol. I am pressed for time so I am not going to try and look up all the names of celebrities and work back on their ages, but you get my drift. We have this knee-jerk default reaction that says that
70 younger is better when it comes to beauty and celebrity—but even then, if we stop and think about it, we are wrong.

So why the blind spot when it comes to age? We cannot make claims about people

[75] and their abilities based on race, or sex, or religion, but it is still perfectly acceptable to say that someone is too old or too young.

Officially, it is called "ageism," which [80] is defined as stereotyping and prejudice against individuals or groups because of their age. The term was coined in 1969 by US gerontologist Robert Neil Butler to describe discrimination against seniors [85] and patterned on sexism and racism.[3]

Butler defined ageism as a combination of three connected elements. These were: prejudicial attitudes toward older people, old age and the aging process; discrimina-[90]tory practices against older people; and institutional practices and policies that perpetuate stereotypes about older people.[4]

This is a real problem; a study by [95] Joanna Lahey, economics professor at Texas A&M University, for example, found that firms are more than 40 percent more likely to interview a younger job applicant than an older job applicant.[5]

[100] As people became more and more aware of the inherent problems, the terms were broadened to include other ages;

and it is also true that there is economic and employment inequity for the younger [105] set—kids under eighteen are hired for less than minimum wage; in fact, it is allowed by law in the United States. And there are other restrictions as well—such as hours allowed to work.

[110] Now, there is clearly a difference between older and younger folks—and experience plays into it sometimes. But really, I know a lot of sixty-year-olds who have never matured and a lot of fifteen-[115]year-olds I would trust with my life. I am merely trying to say that we should not lump groups together based on one characteristic and say it is absolutely true for the whole; especially something as [120] arbitrary as age.

My hope is always that we will be able to see beyond the stereotype to the individual.

I know that is not always easy, but it is [125] necessary.

My three-year-old teaches me a lot of things, so did my seventy-year-old grandfather; and almost everyone I have ever met in between.

(908 words)

Source: Anningson, Brett. "'Too Old' or 'Too Young'; Stop Judging by Age." *Times & Transcript* [Moncton] 26 May 2008. Web. 6 Jan. 2010.

VOCABULARY AND COMPREHENSION

You may have to use external sources (dictionary, website, etc.) and reread the article above to find the answers to the questions below.

1. Paraphrase the following sentence from the second paragraph: "We age, our bodies break down, our minds skip a beat, the world changes around us ... and unfortunately, I think our attitude makes it worse."

_____

_____

_____

_____

3. Kramarae, C., and D. Spender. *Routledge Encyclopedia of Women: Global Women's Issues and Knowledge.* New York: Routledge, 2000. 29. Print.
4. Wilkinson, J., and K. Ferraro. "Thirty Years of Ageism Research." *Ageism: Stereotyping and Prejudice against Older Persons.* Ed. Nelson T. Cambridge: MIT, 2002. Print.
5. Lahey, J. "Do Older Workers Face Discrimination?" *An Issue in Brief — Center for Retirement Research at Boston College* 33 (2005):3. Web. 18 Jan. 2010.

2. Which of the following statements is(are) false? More than one answer is possible.

   According to the author:

   a) Society is prejudiced against young professionals, assuming they are too inexperienced to be good at their work.

   b) As we get older, our patience probably increases.

   c) The older one gets, the wiser and more respected one becomes in one's profession.

   d) A man is at his best in his forties.

3. In the tenth paragraph (lines 51–61), the author uses the adjective *trivial* sarcastically to underscore the irony of a certain situation. What is the situation, and how is it ironic? (See question 4 on page 51 for a working definition of "ironic situation.")

   _____

   _____

4. What idiom in the eleventh paragraph (lines 62–72) means "you understand"?

   _____

5. According to the author, society accepts stereotyping and prejudice based on age, while it condemns the same when based on race, sex or religious affiliation.

   ☐ True   ☐ False

6. In the text, **ageism** is defined as, "… stereotyping and prejudice against individuals or groups because of their age." (Lines 80–82) Working from this definition, what is

   a) racism? _____

   _____

   b) sexism? _____

   _____

7. Which of the following statements is(are) true? More than one answer is possible.

   The author believes that

   a) the young and the old differ from one another.

   b) many teenagers are more trustworthy than many seniors.

   c) we should not hold ageist attitudes.

   d) changing ageist attitudes is really quite simple.

8. What is the subject of the article?

   _____

9. What is the author's opinion on the subject?

   _____

   _____

A Question of PERSPECTIVE

If you were twice your current age, how would you feel about being treated by a doctor in his late twenties, fresh out of medical school?

DISCUSSION

→ Discuss each of the questions in small groups.

→ Be prepared to share your answers with the rest of the class and to explain them.

1. How does being wise differ from being smart?

2. Is younger "better" when it comes to beauty? Explain.

3. In the text, the author provides many examples of ageism: assuming young professionals are too inexperienced to be good at their work; believing those who are older are "almost useless"; companies preferring to interview younger rather than older job candidates; and paying minors less than adults. List five other examples of ageism or ageist practices in North American society.

LISTENING Designing for Seniors

Nora Young hosts CBC's *Spark*, a radio program about technology and culture. You are about to hear an excerpt of her interview with Glen Hougan, assistant professor in product design at the Nova Scotia College of Art & Design (NSCAD) in Halifax. The interview, entitled "Glen Hougan on Designing for Seniors," first aired on February 17, 2009.

BEFORE LISTENING

The terms listed on page 91 are used in the audio clip.

→ Working alone or with a partner, write the letter of the correct term beside each definition. The first one has been done for you as an example.

Examine the listening strategies suggested in "Appendix B: Effective Reading and Active Listening." Then read the listening comprehension questions on pages 91 to 93 *before* listening to the clip.

DEFINITIONS		TERMS
1. Understand somebody's feelings	d	a) Bulky (adj.)
2. Tolerate something		b) Coveralls (n.)
3. Sticks put under your arms to help you walk when you have injured a leg		c) Crutches (n.)
4. Put things together to compare or contrast (formal)		d) Empathize (v.)
5. Protective piece of clothing worn over other clothing		e) Funding (n.)
6. Part of body that can bend (knee, elbow, etc.)		f) Go mainstream (exp.)
7. Move from being used or owned by a small segment of a population to being used or owned by the population as a whole		g) Joint (n.)
		h) Juxtapose (v.)
		i) Lack (n.)
8. Financing		j) Put up with something (v.)
9. Insufficient amount		
10. Big and awkward		

COMPREHENSION

The questions below are in sequence: you will hear the answer to question 1, then question 2, then question 3, etc. If you miss an answer, do not worry about it; simply move on to the next question.

1. Why did Professor Hougan have his students design an "aging suit"?

   _____

   _____

2. Fill in the blanks. "So I had them look at designing an aging suit that would physically simulate ... some of the _____ of mobility and flexibility issues that people have as they get older." (Glen Hougan)

3. Which of the following statements is(are) true? More than one response is possible.
   The aging suit

   a) restricts movement.

   b) includes special glasses.

   c) limits hearing.

4. Which of the following statements is(are) false? More than one answer is possible.

    a) Professor Hougan believes it is important for today's young design students to look at the issue of ageism in design, especially at a time when a large number of older baby boomers[6]—a large and influential demographic that decides what gets made—are retiring.

    b) The wearing of the aging suit had an enormous effect on the students' designs.

    c) The wearing of the aging suit coupled with interviewing their grandparents affected the students' designs.

    d) The students came to understand how difficult tying shoes is for some seniors.

5. Professor Hougan refers to a "classic" example of ageism in industrial design: "the walker with tennis balls split in half and placed on the bottom of the feet to make the walker slide." (He refers to this as a "product hack.") In your own words, explain how this is an example of ageism in industrial design.

_____

_____

6. Fill in the blank. "The aesthetics and the image actually influence our opinions of them [the elderly]. It's almost like looking at the products, we see the people. If the products are ugly and _____ , then we have that perception of that population." (Glen Hougan)

7. What is universal design?

_____

_____

8. Professor Hougan provides a classic example of universal design: large grip OXO kitchen utensils. For what population was this product designed? Who uses it now?

_____

_____

9. When designing for seniors, Professor Hougan encourages his students to concentrate on good design—designs that would appeal to the larger population as well as the seniors themselves.

    ☐ True   ☐ False

10. According to Professor Hougan, what image do Nordic Walkers[7] project when used by people in their sixties? Canes?

Nordic Walkers: _____

_____

Cane: _____

---

6. Those born between 1946 and 1964.
7. Poles similar to ski poles originally used as an off-season ski training activity.

11. Fill in the blanks. "You know, a friend of mine who is really athletic had a sports accident and initially she was using a cane and then she switched over to using _____ and she said she really noticed a difference in the way people reacted to her and perceived her. Because when she was on _____ it was like, that's a person who has had an injury versus when she had the cane, she felt she was looked at … as though she was feeble." (Nora Young)

12. Professor Hougan suspects baby boomers will resist aging, and that such resistance is a good thing.

☐ True   ☐ False

13. What is the subject of the radio excerpt?

_____

14. What is Professor Hougan's opinion on the subject of the article?

_____

_____

A Question of PERSPECTIVE

The middle-aged often treat the elderly as if they were children, using terms like "dear" when referring to the old—especially older women—and adopting a tone of voice similar to that used with preschool children. If you were a senior citizen, how would you feel about being treated in this way? What would you think of a middle-aged person who treated you this way?

DISCUSSION

→ Discuss each of the questions in small groups.

→ Be prepared to share your answers with the rest of the class and to explain them.

1. Can ageism be eradicated from North American society? Why or why not?

2. Is one generation more ageist than another? Justify your response.

3. Do youth care more about aesthetics than function? Explain.

VOCABULARY REVIEW

→ Without looking back at the terms and definitions provided on page 91, correctly fill in the blanks with the words from the chart below.

→ Pluralize nouns and conjugate verbs as required.

ADJECTIVE	EXPRESSION	NOUNS	VERBS
bulky	go mainstream	coveralls crutches funding joint lack	empathize juxtapose put up with (something)

1. Arthritis causes mild to severe pain in a patient's _____ : treatment options range from lifestyle changes to surgery.

2. Darlene is a popular designer who _____ classic with modern design elements.

3. Due to a _____ of evidence, the accused was acquitted of the crime.

4. Kayla's new laptop has all the latest add-ons, but I find it somewhat _____ at just over four kilograms.

5. Living "green," once a fairly marginalized lifestyle, _____ _____ ; everyday people are consuming less and living increasingly eco-friendly lifestyles.

6. Painters often wear _____ to protect their clothing.

7. Philip is using _____ because he sprained his ankle yesterday.

8. Some people living with autism may find it difficult to _____ with others.

9. Sue and Harold are finally divorcing. It's no surprise, really: I don't know how he _____ her moodiness for all of those years.

10. When the government cut _____ to the arts, artists from across the country demonstrated on Parliament Hill.

𝒫ost

Sentence Completions

→ Choose one of the ideas below.

→ Complete the sentence any way you wish.

→ Write a 100- to 125-word paragraph to support what you have written.

→ Include a word count.

1. My best age was when I was …

2. The best age for a man/woman is …

3. What I like most about my current age is …

4. What pleases me most about getting old is …

5. What worries me most about getting old is …

6. When I am old, I …

7. When I see a newborn child, I …

8. When I see a very old person, I …

9. If I had my life to live over, I …

10. When people tell me I am too young/old to do something, I …

EXAMPLE PARAGRAPH

My best age was when I was six years old. It seems to me that I was comparatively carefree and happy. I remember getting a sled for Christmas that year. The sled probably cost my parents no more than ten dollars. But it was shiny and new—and mine! I couldn't wait to get outside and try it out. The hill in the park close to our home couldn't have been more than twenty feet high … but to me it held all the excitement of climbing Mount Everest! I spent hours that winter walking to the top, sliding down and walking back up again. I've never had so little—and yet been so happy!

(113 words)

The Informative Essay

The informative essay requires that you take on the role of teacher, adopting a thesis on a topic about which your audience may or may not be informed: nutrients that slow the aging process; factors related to increased longevity in North Americans; reasons for differential aging in men and women; etc.

→ Choose a topic from the list below.

→ Write a 400- to 450-word informative essay on one of the following topics. Base your informative essay on the academic essay outlined on page 9.

1. Alzheimer's Disease
2. Andropause
3. Caloric Restriction
4. Mandatory Retirement
5. Menopause

6. Progeria
7. The Minimum Voting Age
8. The Raging Grannies
9. The Red Hat Society
10. The Zimmers

When writing an informative essay, remember to

→ use credible sources, paraphrasing and quoting as appropriate;

→ provide essential information on the topic selected;

→ support points with expert opinion as well as facts and statistics rather than anecdote.

ESSAY SECTIONS	PARAGRAPHS	STRUCTURAL ELEMENTS
Introduction	1	• Begin with an effective grabber. • Indicate why it is important to understand the topic selected. • Define key terms. • Write a thesis statement, complete with main and three supporting points; for example, "Treatments for Alzheimer's can be divided into three categories: pharmaceutical, psychosocial and caregiving."
Development	2 3 4 (optional)	• Begin each of the body paragraphs with a transition term. • Paraphrase or quote experts on the topic. • Provide relevant statistics.
Conclusion	5	• Begin the paragraph with the transition term "In summary," followed by a brief recapping of main and supporting points. • Do not introduce any new information. • End with an effective clincher.

Present

Why Do You Think ...?

→ In small groups, explain why you think the statements below are true.

→ Be prepared to share your answers with the rest of the class.

Why do you think ...

1. it is illegal to sell alcohol or cigarettes to minors?

2. people shrink as they age?

3. society has different expectations for young and old people?

4. the North American population is aging?

5. women live longer than men?

Running a Seminar

A **seminar** is a meeting in which participants exchange information and hold discussions on a specific topic. For this exercise, you are asked to participate in a seminar based on one of the following:

1. Adolescent Rebellion
2. Big Brothers Big Sisters of Canada
3. Foster Grandparent Programs
4. Intergenerational Living
5. Meals on Wheels

6. Mentorship
7. School Breakfast Programs
8. Teen Marriage
9. The Sandwich Generation
10. The Stages of Childhood Development

→ Divide into groups of four or five and select a topic.

→ Each person in the group commits to researching one aspect of the selected topic (a subtopic.) Take the topic "the stages of childhood development" as an example: one member could focus his or her research on infancy, while another, on early childhood.

→ Get teacher approval for each of the subtopics.

→ Each member researches his or her subtopic and prepares a five- to seven-minute formal presentation (see page 17) and a list of five related discussion questions.

→ Each member takes a turn at leading part of the seminar, presenting his or her subtopic and running a five-minute discussion based on the prepared list of questions. When presenting, it would be a good idea for each member to use visual aids (a PowerPoint presentation, posters, handouts, a multimedia presentation, etc.). During the discussion, the leader should direct questions to specific group members to ensure equal participation.

Participate

Taking an Oral History

Taking an oral history is an important way of preserving a piece of the past: an interviewer asks a person about his or her life experiences and records the interview in audio or video format.

In this activity, you and your partner are going to interview an elderly person about events in his or her life and produce a written report (in English) on one segment of the interview.

Procedure

The following outlines what you should do before, during and after the interview.

Before the Interview

1. Select an elderly person you would like to interview—someone you feel has led a particularly interesting life and whom you know well and trust (a grandparent, a close friend or neighbour, etc.). While it is preferable to select an English-speaking person, it is not necessary (or perhaps possible) to do so. Note: If you are interviewing in another language, make sure that both you and your partner speak this language and be aware that you will have to translate the content of part of the interview into English when writing up your report.

2. Prepare a list of topics for discussion for the interviewee: early childhood, adolescence, work history, extraordinary events, retirement, etc. As at least one of you knows the interviewee fairly well, focus on an aspect of his or her life about which you would both like to know more.

3. Contact the potential interviewee, informing the person that you would like to conduct a thirty-minute interview with him or her to complete a class project for your English course. If the person agrees to be interviewed, send him or her the list of prepared interview topics for approval.

4. Once the list of topics has been approved and returned to you, contact the interviewee again: agree upon a date, time and quiet place for the interview. Tell the interviewee that he or she will be asked to sign a permission slip allowing you to share interview content (in both written and audio or audiovisual formats) with your teacher and classmates and that there will be two interviewers present. Make sure the interviewee has contact information (phone numbers, e-mail addresses, etc.) for both of you.

5. Prepare a list of open questions to ask the interviewee based on the approved topics. Open questions are those that require more than a "yes" or a "no" as a response. For example, "Tell us about your time in the army." Yes/no (or closed) questions are allowed; however, use them sparingly!

6. Set up and test the audio or video recording equipment. Make sure the equipment is functioning properly.

7. When the interviewee arrives, have him or her sign the permission slip. (Your teacher will provide you with a blank permission slip.) Chat a while to put everyone at ease.

During the Interview

8. Begin with an open question; for example, "What is your happiest moment?" Refer to your list of questions appropriately: do not just read one question after the other. Formulate new questions based on the interviewee's responses.

9. Make sure both of you have a chance to ask questions: conduct the interview in a conversational manner but do not interrupt the interviewee. If something is unclear, wait for a natural pause in the conversation and ask for clarification. Maintain appropriate eye contact throughout.

10. Listen to the interviewee's answers and do not argue—even if you disagree strongly with something he or she has said. The interview is about the interviewee's thoughts and feelings, not yours!

11. Be aware of the time: do not let the interview last longer than thirty minutes. (If the interviewee seems fatigued, end the interview.)

12. Turn off the recording equipment.

After the Interview

13. Chat a while, responding to any questions the interviewee might have about the project.

14. If necessary, ensure the interviewee's safe return home.

15. Contact the interviewee within a few days after the interview, thanking him or her for participating.

16. Select a seven- to ten-minute segment of the interview that you feel is of particular interest. Write up a 400-word report on the segment. Use past tenses when referring directly to interview content; for example, She said, *"If we'd known each other better, I'm not sure we would have gotten married!"* Your report should include the following elements:

   a) An introduction in which you identify the interviewee and interviewers as well as the time, place and duration of the interview

   b) A brief overview of the topics discussed during the interview

   c) A detailed account of the segment selected for your report and why you chose the segment

   d) A direct quote of special interest. (If the quote is in another language, write the quote in the language spoken and provide an English paraphrase—and not a direct translation—immediately thereafter.)

   e) An appreciation of oral histories in general and your interview in particular. (Are oral histories relevant? Did you enjoy the interview process? Did you learn anything? What are your thoughts and feelings about participating in such a project?)

   f) An appendix containing your prepared list of questions (See Step 5 on page 98.)

17. Submit both the recording and the report to your teacher for evaluation. Your teacher may ask you to present your recording and/or your report to the rest of the class.

ursue

Related Works

The following works may be of interest for continued study.

TYPES OF WORKS	TITLES
Animated Short	*Mabel's Saga/Le voyage de Mabelle*. Dir. JoDee Samuelson. National Film Board of Canada, 2004. • Available online at http://onfnfb.gc.ca/eng/collection/film/?id=51514 (14 minutes and 25 seconds) • A celebration of menopause
Child Fiction	Munsch, Robert N. *Love You Forever*. Scarborough: Firefly Books, 1986. Print. • Story about enduring love of parents for their children
Documentary	*Complaints of a Dutiful Daughter*. Dir. Deborah Hoffmann. Women Make Movies, 1994. • A daughter documents her mother's experience with Alzheimer's *Young@Heart*. Dir. Stephen Walker. Fox Searchlight, 2007. • Story of seniors' chorus that performs classic rock and pop music
Fiction	Laurence, Margaret. *The Stone Angel*. Toronto: McClelland & Stewart, 1964. Print. • Reminiscences of an elderly woman
Movie	*The Company of Strangers (Strangers in Good Company)*. Dir. Cynthia Scott. National Film Board of Canada, 1990. • Available online at http://www.nfb.ca/film/company_of_strangers • Eight older women on a tour who become stranded when their bus breaks down
Non-Fiction	Alford, Henry. *How to Live: A Search for Wisdom from Old People (While They Are Still on This Earth)*. New York: Twelve, 2009. Print. • Author interviews seniors about their lives and insights
Online Video Clips	The Zimmers. Web. 7 Jan. 2010. <http://www.thezimmersonline.com/Videos.html>. • The world's oldest band members perform their music
Poetry	Sarton, May. *Coming into Eighty*. New York: Norton, 1994. Print. • Poems written by a woman in "the land of old age"
Short Story	Fitzgerald, F. Scott. *The Curious Case of Benjamin Button*. 1922. New York: Scribner, 2007. Print. • Short story about a newborn who begins life as an old man and gets younger as he "ages"

My eLab ✐ Visit My eLab for additional reading, listening and vocabulary practice.

5

Mind Matters

Part of the Gateway buildings in Minsk, Belarus, reflected in the city's central railway station

*P*review

VOCABULARY TIP

The terms *disease* (or *illness*) and *disorder* are often used interchangeably and refer to "abnormal" conditions that impair functioning; however, the term *disorder* is less stigmatizing than *disease*. Advocates for those living with mental disorders often reject both terms, preferring the term *differences* instead.

Sadly, some prejudices continue to exist. A case in point is the prejudice associated with **disorders** and **diseases** of the mind. Many people with autism, bipolar disorder, depression and schizophrenia experience prejudicial treatment for being different.

In North America, discrimination based on age, race and gender have been vehemently and collectively denounced for decades; however, discrimination based on differences of the mind has not been condemned to the same extent, and that is a shame—because minds matter!

In this unit, you will read and hear about accomplished people living with different minds, minds that have contributed, do contribute, and will continue to contribute to society in spite of the prejudice associated with differences of the mind.

℗repare

In this section, two warm-up exercises are proposed: the first deals with autism, the focus of Reading 5.1 and the Watching activity; the second, with mental illness, the focus of Reading 5.2 and the Listening activity.

How Much Do You Know about Autism?

Autism is a developmental disorder and the focus of the first part of this unit. How much do you know about autism? Take the following quiz to find out.

1. Circle the letter of the correct answer.

   Autism is characterized by

   a) impaired social interaction.

   b) impaired communication.

   c) restrictive and repetitive behaviour and interests.

   d) All of the above.

2. Asperger syndrome is a form of autism.

   ☒ True   ☐ False

3. The signs of autism manifest themselves

   a) before the age of three.

   b) between the ages of three and five.

   c) between the ages of five and seven.

   d) between the ages of seven and nine.

4. Approximately _____ people in 1000 have some form of autism.

   a) two   **b)** four   **c)** six   **d)** eight

5. Approximately four times as many _____ as _____ have been diagnosed with some form of autism.

   a) males / females   **b)** females / males

6. The causes of autism are unclear, but it probably has a strong genetic basis.

   ☐ True   ☒ False

7. The autism rights movement considers autism a "difference" and not a "disorder." Similar to other human rights movements, autism has its own "pride day." Autism Pride Day falls on _____ each year.

   a) January 1   **b)** May 30   **c)** June 18   **d)** December 25

8. Most autistic people are also savants.

   ☐ True   ☒ False

9. Which of the following is(are) signs of autism?

   a) No babbling by twelve months of age.

   b) No gesturing by twelve months.

   c) No single words by sixteen months.

   d) All of the above.

10. There is no known "cure" for autism.

   ☒ True   ☐ False

WARM UP 5.2

Stamping Out the Stigma Associated with Mental Illness

The website Stamp Out Stigma provides a list of famous people who lived (or are living) with mental illness. As the name of the website suggests, mental illness remains a highly stigmatized disorder, a stigma that can (and should) be eliminated. One way to eliminate the stigma is to list well-known and hugely talented individuals who experienced (or have experienced) mental illness at some point in their lives.

→ Working alone or with a partner, match the names of famous people with brief descriptions of their lives.

a) Ernest Hemingway	f) Vincent Van Gogh	k) Virginia Woolf
b) Isaac Newton	g) Sylvia Plath	l) Abraham Lincoln
c) Leo Tolstoy	h) Vaslav Nijinsky	m) Tennessee Williams
d) John Forbes Nash Jr.	i) Patty Duke	n) Lionel Aldridge
e) Ludwig van Beethoven	j) Eugene O'Neill	o) Charles Dickens

DESCRIPTIONS	
1. Academy Award-winning actress living with bipolar disorder	
2. American football player who helped the Green Bay Packers win Super Bowls I and II; he suffered from schizophrenia.	
3. American novelist and winner of the 1953 Pulitzer Prize for *The Old Man and the Sea* and the 1954 Nobel Prize in Literature; he experienced suicidal depression.	
4. American playwright and winner of the Pulitzer Prize in Drama for *A Streetcar Named Desire* (1948) and *Cat on a Hot Tin Roof* (1955); he suffered from clinical depression.	
5. American playwright, author of *Long Day's Journey into Night*, who suffered from clinical depression	

DESCRIPTIONS	
6. American writer of *The Bell Jar* whose battle with depression sadly ended in suicide	*g*
7. British novelist, author of *Orlando*, who experienced mood swings characteristic of bipolar disorder	
8. Dutch artist who struggled with mental illness throughout his life	
9. English mathematician and scientist suspected of suffering from bipolar disorder	
10. English novelist, author of *A Tale of Two Cities* and *Great Expectations*; he is purported to have suffered from clinical depression.	*O*
11. German composer and pianist believed to have suffered from bipolar disorder	
12. Mathematician and winner of the 1994 Nobel Prize in Economics. His struggle with schizophrenia was portrayed by Russell Crowe in the movie *A Beautiful Mind*.	
13. Russian ballet dancer and choreographer of Polish descent, diagnosed with schizophrenia	
14. Russian novelist, author of *War and Peace*, who suffered from clinical depression	
15. Sixteenth president of the United States, who suffered from severe clinical depression	*L*

Ernest Hemingway

Source: "Famous People with Mental Illness." Stamp Out Stigma, 2005. Web. 19 August 2009.

*P*onder

Lennard J. Davis is a professor of English and teaches about disability and human development at the University of Illinois at Chicago. The passage you are about to read is from the introductory chapter of his book, *Obsession: A History*.

Obsessive Me

By Lennard J. Davis

When I was around six or seven, I began to have thoughts about death and dying that I couldn't push out of my mind. I realized that I was mortal and would die. I'd lie in bed and panic, sweat, and thrash around wrestling with the inevitability of my personal demise. To get those thoughts out of my mind, I developed certain rituals. I would try to envision in my mind's eye a black kitten that I had actually earlier brought home and was allowed to keep only until nightfall. That mental image comforted me, as did the vision of a white and clearly wrapped loaf of Silvercup bread, whose advertising campaign had no doubt made me feel the comfort of food and the safety of home. But mostly, I would lie in bed at night and look out my window at the apartment building next to mine. I decided that I had to count every

CULTURAL NOTE

Zeno of Elea (fifth century BC) was a Greek philosopher who supposedly proposed the so-called "racetrack paradox," in which the runner never reaches the finish line, because no matter how close he comes to the end of the track, he must first travel halfway there.

single window that was illuminated, and once the thought occurred to me, I began to do it compulsively. Since the building was substantial, the count took a fair amount of time. After I had arrived at a total number of illuminated windows, I would begin to doubt whether I had counted correctly. I would then recount. Then it would occur to me that someone might have turned their lights on or off. So another recount was necessary. I did this for hours until I was exhausted.

In the morning my mother worried about the dark circles under my eyes. I assured her everything was fine, since it would be pointless to explain what I had been doing and thinking. On the way to school, I might hit my shoe against a curb by mistake, so of course I had to scuff the other shoe to keep things symmetrical. When I arrived at the traffic light, I had a formula I had to say to myself—"I defy justice. Light change!"—over and over again until the light changed. [...] When I ate elbow macaroni, I would slide each elbow on the tine of a fork, so that the utensil contained four straightened tubes of pasta, and then I would swallow each one whole. Continuing on the culinary front, I divided my food into absolute and irrevocable sections that must never mix or touch one another. Also, in eating mashed potatoes or any mouldable foods, I would create a circle, divide it into four quadrants, eat one quadrant, and then completely remake the food into a slightly smaller circle. And then I would repeat the whole process, as the circle got asymptotically smaller and smaller. In illustrating **Zeno's paradox** three dimensionally with my food, I was always satisfied, and endlessly caught in my web of complex rituals.

While I was doing that, my father and brother were compulsively washing their hands and surviving through their own developed rituals. Every night my father checked and rechecked the locks on the doors, the faucets, and gas jets while closing and rechecking all the kitchen cabinets, accompanied all the while by repetitive throat clearings and nasal sniffles. My brother lathered himself up so much that he eventually developed a skin rash. My mother was strangely untouched by all these machinations. In the 1950s and in an immigrant, working-class, and under-educated family, we didn't have a name for these kinds of activities. We didn't know we were engaged in obsessional and compulsive activities. We were just doing what came naturally to us in our time and place.

(588 Words)

Source: Davis, Lennard J. *Obsession: A History*. Chicago: University of Chicago Press, 2008. Print.

VOCABULARY AND COMPREHENSION

You may wish to work with a partner as you answer the questions below.

1. What noun in line 7 means "death"?

   demise

2. How did the author stop focusing on death and dying?

   by counting how many windows were lit up

3. What two reasons does the author give for recounting the illuminated windows in the apartment building next to his?

   a) *maybe someone shut/opened a light*

   b) *maybe he counted wrong*

4. Why did the author hide his obsessive counting from his mother?

   he thought it would be pointless

5. Which of the following statements is(are) true? More than one answer is possible.

   As a school-aged child, the author

   (a) was obsessed with symmetry.

   (b) thought he could make things happen by *willing* them to happen.

   (c) had complex eating rituals.

   d) was obsessed with Greek philosophy.

6. In addition to compulsive handwashing, what other compulsions did the author's father exhibit?

7. All members of the author's family exhibited obsessive compulsive behaviours.

   ☐ True   ☒ False

8. As a child, how did the author and members of his family perceive their obsessive compulsive behaviours?

   like it was normal, It was all they knew

DISCUSSION

→ Discuss each of the questions in small groups.

→ Be prepared to share your answers with the rest of the class and to explain them.

1. In your opinion, are OCD-like behaviours common or uncommon? Justify your answer.

2. Should those with OCD reveal their disorder to friends and colleagues or conceal it? Justify your point of view.

3. A disorder is a mental or physical condition that prevents proper functioning. In your opinion, did the author's OCD prevent him from functioning properly? Explain.

READING 5.1 Exploring Inner Space

Jim Withers is a copy editor and former reporter whose article "Exploring Inner Space" features Daniel Tammet, an autistic savant. Mr. Withers and Mr. Tammet both experience synesthesia, a mysterious condition in which one type of stimulation evokes the sensation of another; for example, Mr. Withers and Mr. Tammet both see numbers as having specific colours. Mr. Withers's article appeared in Montreal's *The Gazette* in June of 2009.

BEFORE READING

→ Scan the article, circling the vocabulary terms listed below.

→ Define these terms according to the context in which each is used.

1. mind-boggling (adj.): _____

2. surefire (adj.): _____

3. feat (n.): _____

4. insight (n.): _____

5. enthralling (adj.): _____

6. hodgepodge (n.): _____

7. breathtakingly (adv.): _____

8. boundless (adj.): _____

9. clumsy (adj.): _____

10. pivotal (adj.): _____

Examine the reading strategies suggested in "Appendix B: Effective Reading and Active Listening." Then read the questions on pages 111 and 112 *before* reading the article itself.

Exploring Inner Space

By Jim Withers

He knows a dozen languages and can perform astronomical calculations in his head. He learned to speak Icelandic in only a week and he once recited from memory the first 22,514 decimal places of pi.

But Daniel Tammet insists he's no superhuman. In fact, the autistic savant, linguist and author says we all possess amazing brains, capable of more than we can imagine. It's the leitmotif[1] of his latest book, *Embracing the Wide Sky: A Tour across the Horizons of the Mind.*

Tammet has a prodigious memory and sense of detail, along with mind-boggling mathematical and linguistic abilities.

As a party trick, reciting pi for more than five hours would be a surefire way to clear a room, but done as a charity fundraiser five years ago, it catapulted the now thirty-year-old Englishman to international fame. Tammet's pi recitation and inhaling-Icelandic-in-a-week feat were featured in an award-winning British documentary film, *The Boy with the Incredible Brain.* Also known as *Brainman*, the film showed Tammet beating the house at blackjack in Las Vegas and meeting Kim Peek, the real-life inspiration behind the 1988 Oscar-winning movie *Rain Man*, starring Dustin Hoffman.

Brainman helped land Tammet appearances on such television programs as the *Late Show* with David Letterman, the *Today Show* and CBC's *The Hour.*

Slight of build, with a blondish brush cut, shy smile and wire-rim glasses framing penetrating blue eyes, Tammet explains to TV hosts in his soft-spoken, unhurried manner the downside of being an autistic savant: the lack of social instincts, the underdeveloped sense of empathy and abstract thought, the inability to remember faces and the daily minutiae (trivia, gossip, etc). He's taught himself to overcome his weaknesses and do what comes naturally to others, like looking people in the eye when speaking to them.

No Tammet TV appearance is complete without a freak-show trick or two, like quickly being able to conjure up what thirty-seven to the fourth power is, or, once given the date, being able to say on what day of the week the host was born. But he gives the impression he's more interested in dispelling misconceptions about autistic people and savants—that the former are uncreative and the latter are like computers, for example.

"Every autistic person is different," Tammet says.

His is a relatively mild form, Asperger syndrome, so he is highly functioning.

Unlike most of the millions of people with autism, and the estimated fifty or fewer other savants on the planet, Tammet is able to articulate what it's like to have such an unusual perspective.

While not all savants are autistic, their skill is commonly accompanied by developmental disorders.

Tammet has been studied by some of the world's leading neuroscientists, hoping to decode autism's secrets and, more generally, gain insight into what makes the human brain tick.

"I've intrigued scientists," Tammet says of the tests he's undergone over the years, adding that he's proud of any contribution he can make to bridging the worlds of autism and non-autism, savantism and non-savantism.

---

1. Dominant or recurring theme.

"My relationship with scientists has changed," he says. "Now, they consider me more of a peer than a guinea pig, and I'm part of the scientific discussion."

Indeed, he is, through public speaking and writing.

If you're keeping score, with *Embracing the Wide Sky*, Tammet is **batting a thousand** when it comes to cracking the *New York Times* bestseller list.

His first book, the 2006 autobiography *Born on a Blue Day*, has sold more than half a million copies. It tells how he suffered a series of severe epileptic seizures when he was four, something he believes changed the circuitry in his brain, causing him to see pictures in his mind and recognize patterns in numbers. It's a condition known as synesthesia, a mingling of the senses and cross-activation in different regions of the brain, a subject Tammet explores in *Embracing the Wide Sky*.

Tammet visualizes numbers not simply as symbols representing different quantities, but as shapes, colours and textures with individual personalities.

His favourite is four, which is shy and quiet like him; five is like a clap of thunder or a wave slapping against a rock; six is a small black hole while nine is large, blue and threatening. Numbers can resemble such wildly different things as oatmeal and waterfalls. Tammet remembers that his pi recitation felt like taking a ride through especially enthralling terrain.

Tammet explains that he is able to perform his astonishing mathematical calculations "intuitively," by manipulating the colourful numerical patterns and shapes in his mind, the way most people instinctively do with words—mentally arranging a hodgepodge of thoughts into meaning and coherent, grammatical sentences.

Citing work by researchers such as neurologist V. S. Ramachandran—who has been studying synesthesia for two decades — Tammet says that such "cross talk" in the brain can spawn great creativity, from puns and metaphors to art and music.

"Hyperconnected brains are the very opposite of coolly calculating machines, operating not from any step-by-step mental rule book, but instead as a kind of beautiful, swirling chaos that draws on information from all over the brain to arrive at results that are truly, breathtakingly creative," he writes.

Everyone has synesthesia to some degree, Tammet says, offering such common terms as "loud shirt" and "feeling blue" to demonstrate its prevalence.

His passion for numbers and languages and the unique, fascinating patterns he finds in each is boundless, like his curiosity.

As Tammet puts it: "When someone asks me, 'Do you speak Breton or Inuktitut?' I say, 'Not yet.'"

Given that he has learned a dozen languages—including Welsh and Esperanto (invented in the nineteenth century) and created one of his own, Mänti—it would be hard to dispute Tammet's contention that he relies on intuitive techniques. In fact, he runs online language courses in French and Spanish using those methods.

Everyone is born with intuitive numerical and linguistic abilities, he says, adding that the human brain—including those of non-savants—is a flexible, plastic thing capable of amazing cognitive skills, changing as we age.

There was little indication that his isolated, self-absorbed childhood and

adolescence in working-class London would lead to anything like the life Tammet now enjoys. Taunted, teased, but mostly ignored, he spent long stretches of time
170 alone, in his bedroom or studying tree leaves at school recess, with an obsessive need for order and routine, taking refuge in repetitive behaviour and numbers.

"I had no idea why I was so different,"
175 he recalls.

He wanted to fit in, to have real friends, but he didn't know how. It helped that he was part of a large, loving family and that his eight younger siblings were non-
180 judgmental role models.

But he is somewhat at a loss as to how he was able to emerge from his insular, "small pleasures" world.

"It was a clumsy process, but I persisted."

185 A pivotal point occurred at age nineteen, when Tammet volunteered for a job teaching English in Lithuania.

"I had read that travel can help people find themselves."

190 And it did. It was while in that Baltic land that he became more open to the world, and to awakening feelings.

The Lithuanians Tammet met were friendly, curious and willing to look be-
195 yond differences. It didn't hurt that he learned their language. The Lithuanians were flattered.

"I came back confident," Tammet says. "I vanquished the prison of autism. I'm a
200 combatant, not a prisoner, but you never completely lose your autism."

He also overcame the added trepidation many young people must deal with when they inform their parents that they are gay
205 —coming out in another sense. Happily

for Tammet, his parents were accepting of their son's sexual orientation.

[…]

Tammet met his current partner,
210 French photographer Jérôme Tabet, in New York after a couple of years of online correspondence. (Internet communication is a boon to autistic people because they don't have to initiate a conversation, or
215 know when to smile, as you do in face-to-face meetings, Tammet explains.)

[…]

Now at home with his partner in France, Tammet is writing his next book.
220 This one will tackle religion and faith.

He became a Christian in his early twenties despite the fact that his upbringing was non-religious.

"It was a decision based on reflection
225 and life experience," he says. "I made a leap of faith, a great fundamental leap."

Religious belief comes down to human subjective experience, such as "falling in love or one's sense of self," Tammet says.
230 "All those things go out the window if there is no faith. And every faith is unique."

Living outside Avignon, once the home of popes, Tammet says he feels less foreign, in a way, than he does in England.
235 He is often recognized by locals, especially after the magazine *Paris Match* did a feature story about him recently.

Long gone are the days when he just wanted to be like everyone else.

240 "I try to be true to myself and come to peace with the world. I want to have a life I feel proud of, with unique things to offer," he says.

"I think that's true of everyone."

(1518 words)

Source: Withers, Jim. "Exploring Inner Space." *Gazette* [Montreal] 7 June 2009. Web. 15 Jan. 2010.

VOCABULARY AND COMPREHENSION

You may have to use external sources (dictionary, website, etc.) to find some of the answers to the questions below.

1. Which of the following statements is(are) false? More than one answer is possible.

   Daniel Tammet

   a) lauds the human brain—a brain capable of more than we think.

   b) achieved worldwide fame due to astonishing mathematical abilities.

   c) is an imposing man.

   d) has acquired the social skills innate to most people.

2. What two misconceptions about autistic savants does Daniel Tammet wish to correct?

   a) _____

   b) _____

3. Which of the following statements is(are) true? More than one answer is possible.

   a) Asperger syndrome is a mild form of autism.

   c) Few people are savants.

   d) All savants have autism.

   b) Few people have autism.

4. Paraphrase the following: "Tammet has been studied by some of the world's leading neuroscientists, hoping to … gain insight into what makes the human brain tick." (Lines 72–76)

   _____

   _____

5. With time, how have Tammet's relationships with neuroscientists changed?

   _____

   _____

6. To what does Tammet attribute his synesthesia?

   _____

7. According to neurologist V. S. Ramachandran, synesthesia can engender creativity.

   ☐ True   ☐ False

8. Paraphrase the following: "Hyperconnected brains are the very opposite of coolly calculating machines, operating not from any step-by-step mental rule book, but instead as a kind of beautiful, swirling chaos that draws on information from all over the brain to arrive at results that are truly, breathtakingly creative."

   _____

   _____

9. Which of the following statements is(are) false? More than one answer is possible.

Tammet

a) was accepted by his classmates.

b) was accepted by his brothers and sisters.

c) doesn't fully understand how he emerged from the isolation of his childhood.

d) credits travel with helping him to open himself to others.

e) considers himself "cured" of autism.

f) is gay.

g) comes from a religious family.

10. In lines 225 and 226, the author quotes Tammet as saying he "made a leap of faith" when becoming a Christian. What does the expression *leap of faith* mean?

_____

11. Which of the following mottos best expresses Tammet's viewpoint on life?

a) Strive for normalcy.

b) Conform to society's expectations.

c) Be true to yourself and proud of who and what you are.

d) Fundamentally, we're all the same.

A Question of PERSPECTIVE

If you had a child with autism, would you accept or reject your child's "developmental difference?" Explain.

DISCUSSION

→ Discuss each of the questions in small groups.

→ Be prepared to share your answers with the rest of the class and to explain them.

1. Explain the significance of the title of the article.

2. Tammet argues that everyone has synesthesia to some degree and offers a "loud shirt" and "feeling blue" as examples of expressions that demonstrate its prevalence. What do these expressions mean? Can you think of any other expressions that demonstrate synesthesia? Have you ever experienced synesthesia?

3. Does travel help people find themselves? Justify your response.

DVD ← **WATCHING** Positively Autistic

On October 27, 2008, CBC's *The National* ran a documentary entitled "Positively Autistic." In the documentary, three people with autism and one person who is living with a person who has autism are interviewed: Amanda Baggs, a young woman with autism; Michelle Dawson, a university researcher with autism; Ari Ne'eman, founding president of the Autistic Self Advocacy Network; and Estée Klar-Wolfond, whose son Adam is autistic. (Ms. Klar-Wolfond wrote The Joy of Autism blog and is the founder and executive director of the Autism Acceptance Project.) The documentary begins with a brief overview of autism and is divided into four distinct parts: People, Ability and Disability, Neurodiversity,[2] and Acceptance. The documentary was produced by Lani Selick and edited by Bob Schroeder.

CULTURAL NOTE

Jonathan Lerman is an American artist with autism whose work has been exhibited in art galleries. Vernon Smith won the 2002 Nobel Prize in Economics. Mr. Smith has Asperger syndrome. Both men are referred to in the documentary.

Jonathan Lerman

---

2. Neurodiversity is the belief that atypical neurological development is a normal human difference to be recognized, accepted and respected.

BEFORE WATCHING

The following quotes were taken directly from the segment:

1. "One way to look at autism, and it's a very common way ... is ... you start with a typical *baseline* and you say, 'This is how people should be.'" (Michelle Dawson)

2. "... autism is not some appendage that attaches itself to people. It is a part of who we are. It is a part of our existences, and it is not something that necessarily *precludes* a high quality of life." (Ari Ne'eman)

3. "He [Adam] never fit the images of what people said he had to be like as an autistic person ... He's very affectionate. He's very *outgoing*. He is intelligent. He's curious. He's able to learn without a particular methodology." (Estée Klar-Wolfond)

4. "If an autistic child does not turn their head to orient toward a sound, it's assumed that that child is *unaware*. It's assumed that if a child is not ... you know ... often if a child does not speak, that they have no understanding of language, that they can't possibly be intelligent, and so on." (Michelle Dawson)

5. "Adam reads books, and he jumps up and down, and then he used to run around and then come back and jump up ... We put it on the edge of his bed ... and jump up and down and you think, 'Well what can he be reading from that?' You know, a *bookworm* has to be sitting in place and sitting still and looking at this. But he was! He was reading dictionaries. He was reading encyclopedias. He's been reading all of his life."

6. "I process and analyze information in a different way from the other researchers I work with. I suppose my main role is reading and writing papers and looking at a lot of ***data***." (Michelle Dawson)

7. "The normalization to me is a negative. If I were to extinguish Adam's hand flapping or jumping up and down to make that behaviour look more appropriate, that's taking away a movement that he needs to feel his body in space—the way he learns and perceives his world. So if I take that away, I'm almost *impairing* him more." (Estée Klar-Wolfond)

8. "This past December, New York University Child Study Center put forward a[n] advertising campaign that offended *countless* people throughout the disability community. It consisted of a series of phony ransom notes, each claiming to be from a particular disability that had supposedly kidnapped a child ... Thanks to our efforts, these ads were removed." (Ari Ne'eman)

9. "The presentation of autism is sort of a tragedy, like losing a child, like a death in the family ... All these things that have been said ... and you know, all these other things: describing autistic children as rotting on the vine, autistic people as a *blight* on society, as, you know, not human unless we've had one particular intervention starting early in life ..." (Michelle Dawson)

10. "The problem is ... [that] right now, the research and policy agenda around autism is not *geared* toward those things [helping people with autism to communicate, hold a job, live in the community, marry and have children], it is geared toward trying to make us indistinguishable from our peers—to try and force us to be normal for normal's sake." (Ari Ne'eman)

GRAMMAR TIP

Some nouns of Greek or Latin origin form their plurals according to the rules of those languages; for example, *data* is the plural of the Latin noun *datum*. For more information on irregular plural forms, see page 220.

→ Copy the terms that are in *italics* on page 114 into the left column of the table below.

→ Write a synonym for each term in the right column. The first one has been done for you as an example. You may wish to use a thesaurus.

ITALICIZED TERMS	SYNONYMS
1. *baseline*	reference point
2. precludes	
3. outgoing	
4. unaware	
5. bookworm	
6. data	
7. impairing	
8. countless	
9. blight	
10. geared	

Examine the listening strategies suggested in "Appendix B: Effective Reading and Active Listening." Then read the comprehension questions below *before* watching the clip.

COMPREHENSION

The questions below are in sequence: you will hear the answer to question 1, then question 2, then question 3, etc. If you miss an answer, do not worry about it; simply move on to the next question.

1. What is the focus of most therapies for autism?

   _____

2. Michelle Dawson claims that there is an "optimal way to be human."

   ☐ True   ☒ False

3. From Ari Ne'eman's point of view, who *must* be involved when setting policy about autism?
   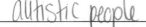
   autistic people

4. Estée Klar-Wolfond considered her son's autism to be a tragedy.

   ☐ True   ☒ False

5. What does Michelle say she has trouble doing?

   _____

6. When talking about her self-injurious behaviour, Michelle claims that this behaviour is used to scare the public about people like her.

☒ True ☐ False

7. Michelle works on a research team. She mentions that she "looks at things differently" from her fellow researchers and affirms that on the team, two different kinds of minds are at work. For Michelle, is it positive or negative to have two minds working together?

It is positive because they are complimentary

8. What does Michelle say she has been called? Why is it hard for Michelle to talk about her experience?

animal, it is too recent

9. Estée Klar-Wolfond maintains that she was once "ambushed" on radio and asked two accusatory questions. What two questions was she asked?

a) how could you not want to cure your son?

b) what kind of parent are you?

10. In Estée Klar-Wolfond's view, what constitutes "the best parenting"?

love your kids for who they are and not expect them to change.

A Question of PERSPECTIVE

If you had a child with autism, would you want your child to learn how to modify behaviours such as hand flapping or jumping up and down in order to appear "normal?" Explain.

DISCUSSION

→ Discuss each of the questions in small groups.

→ Be prepared to share your answers with the rest of the class and to explain them.

1. Early in the video clip, Michelle Dawson states, "Differences can be profound, without necessarily being disorders. You know, it's only in autism where we assume that if people are very different, then they must be sick." In your opinion, is autism a difference or a disorder? Justify your response.

2. About halfway through the documentary, Amanda states, "Nobody is truly independent." Do you agree or disagree with her statement? She goes on to ask, "Why is it that I am not considered to live independently because I can't cook for myself, but other people are considered to live independently if they can't fix their computers?" How would you respond to her question?

3. Paraphrase and comment upon the following statement: "We should view neurology through the same civil rights lens that we view race, religion, sexual orientation and other forms of what's termed 'legitimate human difference.' And basically from that perspective, instead of trying to find a way of making autistic people 'normal' or making people with other forms of neurological difference 'normal,' what we should be doing is addressing the true problems and barriers that exist in our lives." (Ari Ne'eman)

VOCABULARY REVIEW

→ Without looking back at the synonyms that you found for the words in italics on page 115, correctly fill in the blanks with the words from the chart below.

→ Pluralize nouns and conjugate verbs as required.

ADJECTIVES	NOUNS	VERBS
countless	baseline	impair
outgoing	blight	preclude
unaware	bookworm	gear (toward)
	data	

1. Excessive drinking _____ judgement.

2. — Have you received sufficient _____ to complete the report?
   — Yes, I have all the information I require.

3. Jake slipped into the back of the class while his teacher, Ms. Millman, wasn't looking; she was _____ he'd been absent.

4. My brother is a real _____ : he has read a book a day since he was a child.

5. Racism is a _____ on society, a belief that is incompatible with the values of social justice.

6. Studying full-time _____ working full-time: if you try to do both, you'll soon burn out!

7. Sue has an _____ personality: she has a lot of friends and is the life of every party!

8. The president _____ his speech toward very young children: he spoke simply and succinctly.

9. They spent _____ hours working on the project: every waking hour was devoted to completing the task.

10. To lose 10 percent of my body weight, I must first establish a _____: I have to know what I weigh now in order to know how many pounds I need to lose to attain my goal.

Awakening in a Twilight Zone Not to Be Feared

Davidicus Wong is a family physician living in British Columbia. His article appeared in *The Vancouver Courier* on May 15, 2009.

BEFORE READING

→ Scan the article, circling the vocabulary terms listed below.

→ Define these terms according to the context in which each is used.

1. lineup (n.): _____

2. rerun (n.): _____

3. dogfight (n.): _____

4. distress (v.): _____

5. disrupt (v.): _____

6. strike (v.): _____

7. chatty (adj.): _____

8. chore (n.): _____

9. quirk (n.): _____

10. fizzle (v.): _____

> Examine the reading strategies suggested in "Appendix B: Effective Reading and Active Listening." Then read the questions on pages 120 and 121 *before* reading the article itself.

Awakening in a Twilight Zone Not to Be Feared

By Davidicus Wong

On our last trip to Disneyland, I took my boys to the Twilight Zone[3] Tower of Terror. Set in a ritzy hotel from the 1930s, the ride begins with an introduction by the late Rod Serling, who explains how an ordinary hotel check-in and elevator ride can take us to the Twilight Zone. The out-of-control elevator is not for guests with osteoporosis,[4] gastroesophageal reflux,[5] herniated discs[6] or a fear of elevators.

What I like best about amusement park lineups is the opportunity to talk with my teenaged sons. They're used to me turning a conversation about the here and now into a discussion about deeper life lessons.

---

3. *The Twilight Zone* was a popular American TV series created and hosted by Rod Serling. The series focused on the paranormal or futuristic and ran from 1959 to 1964.
4. Disorder in which bones become increasingly brittle due to a lack of calcium and other minerals.
5. Disease characterized by stomach acids moving back up into the esophagus.
6. Discs between the backbones that have protruded to put pressure on the spinal nerves, causing pain.

Waiting to get into the Tower of Terror, I told them that at their age, episodes of *The Twilight Zone* were my favourite afternoon reruns. Characters would awaken to strange new worlds. The shows fuelled my imagination, suspended my growing adolescent disbelief and informed me of the human condition.

In one episode, a man in mid-life crisis drives to his hometown, finds himself back in time and meets himself as a child. In another, a Second World War fighter pilot abandons his partner in a dogfight by flying into a strange cloud. He emerges in the 1960s, tries to convince a doctor he's not delusional and finally decides to fly back into the cloud for a second chance at heroism.

Many of my patients have crossed over into the Twilight Zone. Every few years, one patient will present with delusions, often paranoid, sometimes provoked by illicit drug use but sometimes arising *de novo*.[7] Patients vary in their insight. Some will recognize that their beliefs are illogical and a manifestation of mental illness. Others are so firmly fixated on their false beliefs that they distress their friends and families.

I sometimes wonder what I would do if a patient presented a really good story about time travel with convincing evidence that he was from the past or future. It hasn't happened yet.

In the absence of drugs and psychiatric disease, each of us can enter the Twilight Zone several times throughout our lives. Each week, I see patients distressed by unexpected, sometimes catastrophic circumstance. Last week, a patient with no risk factors other than age (he's a non-smoker with normal cholesterol, blood pressure and blood sugar) had a stroke.[8] Another has metastatic cancer[9] in spite of a healthy lifestyle. Sometimes complications disrupt the happiness of pregnancy and childbirth.

Taking care of ourselves, not smoking, eating fresh vegetables, driving carefully and exercising can greatly reduce our risks, but none of us can be risk-free. Medical misfortune can still strike the nicest people who do everything right.

All we can do is to learn what we can about what happened, talk about how we feel with our loved ones and health professionals, and discover how we can make the most of what we have in this new and different life. A couple who survived a stillbirth[10] with their first pregnancy now have four healthy and happy children. They are achieving their potential as great parents.

Circumstances beyond our control can plunge us into the Twilight Zone. Many have lost their jobs due to the economic downturn and corporate downsizing. Others have found their job descriptions expand. One positive side effect of stock devaluation is that many doctors who were planning to retire early have decided to keep on working.

When we lose a close friend, parent or other loved one, we enter an altered state. We ride an emotional roller coaster and struggle with existential confusion. Somehow, we must accept the help of friends, family and professionals to survive our losses, make sense of what has happened, find peace in a new world, and discover meaning in our everyday lives.

In the living of life, we find ourselves in unexpected places. All of a sudden,

.............➤

7. Latin, meaning "again" or "anew."
8. A blocked or broken blood vessel in the brain.
9. Cancer that has spread to other parts of the body.
10. Giving birth to a dead baby.

school's a **drag**, we hate our jobs or we
100 aren't getting along at home. We discover
that our adorable, chatty children who
once thought the world of us have morphed
into teens who think we're totally uncool;
we have entered the age of mutual embar-
105 rassment. Work and school are not what
we expected them to be; what once was
interesting and fun has become a stressful
chore. The funny quirks that once endeared
us now drive us nuts when the fire of
110 romance has fizzled and the pilot light of
daily tolerance just went out.

At various times, we can awaken to
greying or thinning hair, new wrinkles and
extra pounds. All of a sudden, we are a
115 decade older.

Obviously, these changes didn't happen
overnight. You weren't bitten by a radioac-
tive spider yesterday, becoming Spider-
Man this morning. We, and everything else

120 in our lives, are always changing. Nothing
is exactly as it was a year, a day or a
moment ago. The beach may look as it did
yesterday, but the water is in constant
motion. Each wave is unique and shifts
125 the sand into a new pattern.

We can cross the sand of the beach,
leaving footprints soon to be washed away.
We can surf the waves, adapt to what the
ocean gives us, and still ride our own path.

130 Life is always changing. What we
mistake for permanence is only shifting
sand. We sometimes get so busy we don't
notice the subtle changes that take us
adrift from where we really want to be.
135 By watching the waves, keeping our landmarks in sight, and correcting our course,
we can find our way.

Adapting to change, maintaining our important relationships and living our lives
140 more deliberately can reduce our risk for
entering the Twilight Zone, but of course,
we are never risk-free.

Sometimes to awaken in the Twilight
Zone can open new and positive possibili-
145 ties. Suspend your disbelief.

(959 words)

Source: Wong, Davidicus. "Awakening in a Twilight Zone Not to Be Feared." *Vancouver Courier* 15 May 2009. Web. 12 Jan. 2010.

VOCABULARY AND COMPREHENSION

You may have to use external sources (dictionary, website, etc.) to find some of the answers to the questions below.

1. What is a twilight zone?

    _____

2. The Twilight Zone provided the author with mindless entertainment.
    ☐ True   ☐ False

3. Initially, the author uses the Twilight Zone as a metaphor to describe the al-
    tered state in which those who experience the trauma of mental illness find
    themselves. As the article progresses, this metaphor is expanded to include
    altered states brought on by other types of traumatic events. What (three)
    types of traumatic events does the author mention?

a) _____

b) _____

_____

c) _____

4. In line 109, the author uses the informal expression *to drive someone nuts.* From the context in which it is used, what does this expression mean?

_____

5. What metaphor does the author use to illustrate the fact that our lives are in constant change even though we may perceive them as unchanging?

_____

_____

6. Paraphrase the following sentence: "We sometimes get so busy we don't notice the subtle changes that take us adrift from where we really want to be. By watching the waves, keeping our landmarks in sight, and correcting our course, we can find our way."

_____

_____

_____

7. According to the author, what three things can we do to reduce the risk of entering the Twilight Zone?

a) _____

b) _____

c) _____

8. According to the author, entering the Twilight Zone is a negative experience.

☐ True   ☐ False

9. What is the subject of the article?

_____

10. What is the author's opinion on the subject?

_____

_____

A Question of PERSPECTIVE

Everyone experiences some degree of emotional pain from ordinary events, such as not getting admitted to a university program or breaking up with a girlfriend/boyfriend to extraordinary events such as experiencing a natural disaster firsthand or being hit by a car. If you could remove all pain from human existence, would you? Would a pain-free world be a better world? Would *your* world be a better world? Explain.

DISCUSSION

→ Discuss each of the questions in small groups.

→ Be prepared to share your answers with the rest of the class and to explain them.

1. The author writes that some circumstances are beyond our control. Other than the examples mentioned in the article, what circumstances are beyond our control? Provide a minimum of ten examples.

2. What is the best way to deal with traumatic events?

3. Why are some people able "to make the most" of any situation while others are not?

CD

LISTENING Mental Health Stand-up

Hallie Cotnam hosts the CBC radio program *Ottawa Morning*. On May 8, 2009, Ms. Cotnam interviewed Sonja Cronkhite about an upcoming stand-up comedy show given by people living with mental illness. Ms. Cronkhite is the program coordinator of Psychiatric Survivors of Ottawa (PSO) and a comic in recovery from mental health challenges. Before the interview begins, two clips are heard: in the first, we hear Mary Hill practising her stand-up act; in the second, we hear David Granirer, Vancouver counsellor and founder of Stand Up for Mental Health, explaining the benefits of stand-up for people facing mental health challenges. Also heard during the show is a short stand-up segment by Emily Olding, **a.k.a.** Emily Oh.

GRAMMAR TIP

The term *a.k.a.* is an abbreviation of "also known as." Abbreviations that can be pronounced as words are referred to as "acronyms": *AIDS* is an acronym for "Acquired Immune Deficiency Syndrome." For more information on abbreviations and acronyms, see pages 238 and 239.

BEFORE LISTENING

The following quotes were taken directly from the segment:

1. "I am overweight because of my *meds*. Maybe I shouldn't be taking them with chocolate chip cookies." (Mary Hill)

2. "Like many of the people in that room she [Mary Hill] was struggling, she's been struggling with mental illness for years, but now, she and others are using their challenges as a *muse* for their comedy." (Hallie Cotnam)

3. "… and it [the shame associated with mental illness] turns into this black *toxic waste* in our soul." (David Granirer)

4. "… there are seventeen new comics that have sort of *stepped up* … to become comics." (Hallie Cotnam)

David Granirer

5. —"Well there are seventeen comics total. There are ten who are new, and seven of us who are ..." (Sonja Cronkhite)

—"Alumni ..." (Hallie Cotnam)

—"*Seasoned*!" (Sonja Cronkhite)

6. "We handed out little *flyers* saying, 'if you're interested in learning more on becoming a comic ... fill this out ....'" (Sonja Cronkhite)

7. "So they were hearing ... the Alumni comics, and we *were* really *striking a chord with* them ...." (Sonja Cronkhite)

8. "You bring up very strong emotions from people with stuff that's your most shameful and your ugliest pieces. And ... and suddenly realizing, 'Hey all that *yucky* stuff, that's good; that's material.'" (Sonja Cronkhite)

9. —"And then you start going through your day-to-day life, and every person you run into, who's an obstacle to you in the mental health system, and you're like, 'Oh buddy, you're in my next act.' And it really ..." (Sonja Cronkhite)

—"*Payback*!" (Hallie Cotnam)

—"It's payback, but it changes your ability to deal with all the obstacles in your life because you're realizing that this may be painful now, but oh this has got to pay off in the next show. This is so great!" (Sonja Cronkhite)

10. "... this kind of comedy and the strength that people draw from it help to reduce the stigma and mental illness ... do you *concur* with that and how does that work? How does that happen? How does that reduce the stigma?" (Hallie Cotnam)

→ Copy the terms that are in *italics* above into the left column of the table below.

→ Write a synonym for each term in the right column. You may wish to use a thesaurus. The first one has been done for you as an example.

VOCABULARY TIP

Meds and *yucky* are examples of slang. English vocabulary ranges from the very informal to the very formal. It is important to use the appropriate level when speaking or writing. As a rule, the spoken form tends to be more informal than the written. The obvious exception to this rule is formal speeches, such as those proposed in the Present section in each unit of this textbook.

ITALICIZED TERMS	SYNONYMS
1. *meds*	medications
2.	
3.	
4.	
5.	
6.	
7.	
8.	
9.	
10.	

COMPREHENSION

The questions are in sequence: you will hear the answer to question 1, then question 2, then question 3, etc. If you miss an answer, do not worry about it; simply move on to the next question.

1. According to host Hallie Cotnam, what does the program "Stand-up for Mental Health" help people do? It helps people with mental illness

   a) become comics.

   b) build confidence.

   c) fight stigma in their communities.

2. According to David Granirer, people facing mental health challenges benefit from performing stand-up because they lose the feeling of shame associated with a diagnosis of mental illness.

   ☐ True   ☐ False

3. What does Sonja Cronkhite say she felt while listening to Mary Hill's comedy?

   _____

4. At a comedy show in 2006, ten audience members filled out a flyer indicating they wanted to learn more about becoming comics. Why did they have to wait until 2009 [the year the interview was recorded] for the chance to perform?

   _____

   _____

5. Which of the following statements is(are) true? More than one answer is possible.

   According to Sonja Cronkhite,

   a) the ten new comics in the upcoming show wanted to participate because they had felt an emotional connection with the performers at the 2006 show.

   b) making people laugh is very powerful.

   c) people facing mental health challenges are used to making the people in their lives cry—it's good to be able to use the same bad stuff that makes some people cry to make other people laugh.

   d) her comedy is inspired by obstacles faced in daily life, making the obstacles easier to deal with.

   e) painful experiences from the distant past and present can both easily and readily be turned into comedy.

6. What awful situation was comic Emily Oh able to make into a funny (and rather poignant) situation?

   _____

   _____

7. Emily Oh chose not to use the awful situation referred to in the previous question in her act. According to Sonja Cronkhite, what types of experiences do not work as comedy?

8. In Sonja Cronkhite's opinion, how does watching stand-up comedy performed by people living with mental health challenges help reduce the stigma associated with mental illness?

A Question of PERSPECTIVE

How comfortable would you be attending a stand-up comedy show about mental illness? Would knowing the comedians make you more comfortable or less comfortable?

DISCUSSION

→ Discuss each of the questions in small groups.

→ Be prepared to share your answers with the rest of the class and to explain them.

1. Black humour is a type of comedy in which taboo topics are treated in a humorous manner, while retaining their seriousness. Mental illness is a taboo topic. Is treating mental illness in a humorous way helpful or harmful? Justify your response.

2. At the start of the clip, comedian Mary Hill uses black humour, joking: "My family is dysfunctional and not at all supportive of what I do. Maybe I shouldn't keep trying to burn their house down… [and] … I have a younger brother who also suffers with a mental disorder; he won't eat anything I make because he thinks it is poison. My question is, 'How does he know?'" Do you find these two examples of black humour funny or disquieting? Explain.

3. Why do you think Emily Oh chose not to include the awful situation referred to in question 6 (p. 124) in her act?

VOCABULARY REVIEW

→ Without looking back at the synonyms that you found for the words in italics on page 123, correctly fill in the blanks with the words from the lists below.

→ Pluralize nouns and conjugate verbs as required.

ADJECTIVES	EXPRESSIONS	NOUNS	VERBS
seasoned	strike a chord with (someone)	flyer	concur
yucky	toxic waste	meds	step up
		muse	
		payback	

1. For stand-up comics living with mental health challenges, their illness is also their _____.

2. In my opinion, laughter is indeed the best medicine. Do you _____?

3. Many household cleaners should be treated as _____ and kept well out of the reach of children.

4. Most grocery stores publish weekly _____ containing coupons.

5. President Obama's 2008 campaign slogan, "yes we can" _____ _____ many American voters.

6. To paraphrase a well-known proverb, "_____ is a meal best served cold!"

7. When faced with cutbacks in education, the teachers at my son's school _____ to help: they organized a charity auction and raised $10,000 for new library books.

8. When taking _____, it's important to follow the doctor's instructions: some pills need to be taken with food and others, on an empty stomach.

9. You can easily spot the difference between a _____ player and a rookie.

10. You know what my three-year-old daughter's favourite word is? _____! She uses it to describe anything she doesn't like.

Laugh at Yourself!

We all do "crazy" things from time to time, and we all find ourselves in ludicrous circumstances (often beyond our control) every once in a while. Think back over your life and choose a funny moment that involved you and about which you can laugh today. Write approximately 100 to 150 words.

The Definition Essay

The definition essay requires that you explain the meaning of a term.

→ Write a 400- to 450-word definition essay on one of the abstract topics from the list below. (Note: You may need to refine your topic prior to defining; for example, refine the term *illness* as "mental illness" and define *mental illness* as opposed to *illness*.)

→ Base your definition essay on the five-paragraph academic essay outlined on page 9.

1. Acceptance
2. Change
3. Compulsion
4. Conformity

5. Difference
6. Health
7. Humour

8. Illness
9. Normalcy
10. Obsession

When writing a definition essay, remember to

→ tell readers what term is being defined.

→ refer to a dictionary, without copying the definition.

→ define the term in your own words.

→ proofread your work before submitting it.

The chart below provides a structural overview, detailing elements to consider.

ESSAY SECTIONS	PARAGRAPHS	STRUCTURAL ELEMENTS
Introduction	1	• Begin with an effective grabber. • Your thesis statement is a personalized definition of the term consisting of three (supporting) points; for example, "Normalcy means aspiring to mediocrity at home, school and in society at large."
Development	2 3 4 (optional)	• Begin each of the paragraphs of the development with a transition term. • Paraphrase or quote experts on the topic. • Provide relevant statistics. • Illustrate with anecdotes.
Conclusion	5	• Begin the final paragraph with the transition term "In summary," followed by a brief recapping of main and supporting points. • Do not introduce any new information. • End with an effective clincher.

resent

Taboo Topics

→ In small groups, discuss the following:

In the not-so-distant past, mental disorders and diseases were taboo topics: they were not discussed in public—or (in some cases) even in private! In modern North American society, are any topics taboo? Should any topics be taboo? What factors influence whether or not a topic is taboo?

Accomplished People

In Warm Up 5.2 on page 103, you participated in a matching exercise that underscored the accomplishments of famous people who lived (or who are living) with mental disorders or diseases. In this exercise, you are asked to give an oral presentation on the life of one of these accomplished people.

→ Select one of the people listed in Warm Up 5.2.

→ Research his or her life, focusing on significant events in childhood, adolescence and/or adulthood; his or her experience with mental illness; and his or her greatest professional accomplishments.

→ Speak for five to seven minutes.

→ Respect the structure of a formal presentation. (See page 17.)

The chart below provides a suggested presentation outline.

PRESENTATION PARTS	CONTENTS
Introduction	• Begin with a short, inspiring anecdote based on the person's life. • End with a preview statement along the lines of, "In this presentation, I will talk about [name of famous person]; first, I will present a chronological overview of his or her life; then I will talk about his or her experience with mental illness; and finally, I will discuss his or her greatest accomplishments."
Development	• Present chronological overview. • Talk about his or her experience with mental illness. • Discuss greatest achievements.
Conclusion	• Recap main points. • Use a clincher in which you refer back to the anecdote used in the introduction.

℗articipate

In this section, you will work with another student on a joint writing and speaking project.

Blogging to Stamp Out Social Stigma

This activity was inspired by the website Stamp Out Stigma,[11] which was designed to help stamp out the stigma associated with mental disorders and diseases.

The term *social stigma* means "something that harms a person's reputation." Examples of social stigmas include, but are not limited to, criminality, drug addiction, mental or physical illness, nationality, physical disability and religion.

In this exercise, you and your partner are asked to write weblogs (blogs), the purpose of each is to stamp out a social stigma.

Procedure

1. Working alone, type "free blog hosting sites" into a search engine such as Google or Yahoo!

2. From the list generated by the search engine, select a user-friendly site that guides you through the blog creation process, choosing a "catchy" title and an attractive template. Immediately after creating your blog, go to "settings" to restrict blog access and ensure that you have adequately protected your identity. (You may wish to use a pseudonym or post anonymously.)

3. Post an introductory article in which you clearly explain the purpose of your blog. Your article should be approximately 100 to 150 words long. Edit your article until you are satisfied with content and form (i.e., correct grammar and spelling).

4. Contact your partner for his or her e-mail address in order to grant him or her access to your blog. Ask your partner to reply to your introductory article. (Verify in "settings" that you have allowed readers to post responses!) Your partner may reply to the content of your article and/or comment on the correctness of your grammar and spelling. Your partner should post a reply of 100 to 150 words.

5. Continue working together over the coming weeks, posting 100- to 150-word articles and replies on each other's blog sites. Be creative: in your articles and replies, include links to pertinent websites, video and audio clips, Word documents, pictures, etc.

6. Your teacher will set a due date for your blogs. Once the due date has been reached, your teacher will provide you with his or her e-mail address so that you and your partner can grant access to your blogs. Your teacher will evaluate your blogs, giving you and your partner a shared grade. Your teacher will then make an appointment with you and your partner to talk about the blog-writing process. Prepare for the discussion by anticipating the types of questions your teacher might ask. The oral part of this project may or may not be evaluated.

11. The source cited for Warm Up 5.2 on page 103 of this unit.

**ursue**

Related Works

The following works may be of interest for continued study.

TYPES OF WORKS	TITLES
Documentary	*Autism: The Musical*. Dir. Tricia Regan. Bunim-Murray Productions, 2007. • Profiles five children with autism as they write and rehearse a stage production *Cracking Up*. Dir. Tara Shortt. HDTV Vancouver Productions, 2007. • Documentary about David Granirer's Stand Up for Mental Health program, which was discussed in the Listening activity (p. 122)
Fiction	Haddon, Mark. *The Curious Incident of the Dog in the Night-Time*. London: Jonathan Cape, 2003. Print. • Story told from the standpoint of a fifteen-year-old autistic boy
Movie	*A Beautiful Mind*. Dir. Ron Howard. Universal, 2001. • Film based on the life of John Forbes Nash Jr., a Nobel laureate in Economics living with schizophrenia *As Good As It Gets*. Dir. James L. Brooks. TriStar, 1997. • Academy Award-winning film about an obsessive-compulsive man and his relationships with a single mother and his gay neighbour *Brainman/The Boy with the Incredible Brain*. Dir. Martin Weitz. Discovery, 2005. • Documentary about Daniel Tammet, the man living with Asperger syndrome who is described in Reading 5.1 (p. 108) *Rain Man*. Dir. Barry Levinson. United Artists, 1988. • Story of two brothers on a road trip, one of whom is an autistic savant
Non-Fiction	Davis, Lennard J. *Obsession: A History*. Chicago: University of Chicago Press, 2008. • An excerpt from this book can be found in the Ponder section of this unit (p. 105). Granirer, David. *The Happy Neurotic: How Fear and Angst Can Lead to Happiness and Success*. Toronto: Warwick, 2007. • Book by the counsellor pictured on page 122 and heard in the Listening section of this unit Tammet, Daniel. *Embracing the Wide Sky: A Tour across the Horizons of the Mind*. New York: Free Press, 2009. • By the author profiled in Reading 5.1 (p. 108)

My eLab ✎ Visit My eLab for additional reading, listening and vocabulary practice.

All or Nothing

Happy silhouette
standing at the
end of a bridge

P review

Betting all or nothing is a risky bet indeed: you put everything on the line and could come out a big winner or a big loser. There is no in-between.

This unit is about risk: risks all of us take on a daily basis, extreme risks that only some of us have the stomach to take (hang-gliding, bungee jumping and backcountry skiing to name but a few), risks that end up advancing society, risks that put ourselves and others in danger, risks to escape the daily grind and risks to venture into places few have dared visit.

In this unit, you will read and hear about such risks and will be asked to share your thoughts and feelings about all kinds of risky behaviours. If you are ready to take a risk, turn the page!

repare

In this section, two warm-up exercises are proposed: the first deals with risk-taking and risk-takers, the focus of Reading 6.1 and the Listening activity; the second deals with particularly dangerous and potentially self-injurious risks, the focus of Reading 6.2 and the Watching activity.

WARM UP 6.1

Cautious or Cowardly? Courageous or Crazy?

Later in this unit, you will read and hear about the actions listed in the chart below. In Part A, indicate with a checkmark whether the actions listed are cautious or cowardly. In Part B, indicate whether the actions listed are courageous or crazy. Be prepared to share your answers.

PART A	ACTIONS	CAUTIOUS	COWARDLY
1.	Avoiding air travel		
2.	Respecting prohibitions on skiing off-trail		
3.	Only travelling to "safe" destinations		
4.	Never travelling alone		
5.	Refusing to hang-glide		

PART B	ACTIONS	COURAGEOUS	CRAZY
6.	Wearing your underwear in public		
7.	Ice fishing in spring		
8.	Volunteering for search and rescue missions		
9.	Flying to the moon		
10.	Building and flying your own airplane		

WARM UP 6.2 How Dangerous Is It?

Later in this unit, you will be examining risks that many qualify as dangerous.

→ In the space provided, indicate the level of risk that you associate with each action in the list on page 133.

→ Be prepared to share your answers.

1. Driving skidoos on a lake in early winter and late spring   ———
2. Drag racing   ———
3. Crossing the US-Canadian border without going through customs   ———
4. Bungee jumping   ———
5. Volunteering to fight in a war   ———
6. Helicopter skiing   ———
7. Driving 140 kilometres an hour   ———
8. Skydiving   ———
9. Binge drinking   ———
10. Eating junk food   ———

ⓟonder

David Sedaris is an American humorist, bestselling author and radio commentator who lives in France. Mr. Sedaris has published several collections of short stories and essays. The story you are about to read was taken from his book *When You Are Engulfed in Flames*, published in 2008.

In the Waiting Room

By David Sedaris

Six months after moving to Paris, I gave up on French school and decided to take the easy way out. All I ever said was "Could you repeat that?" And for what? I rarely
⁵ understood things the second time around, and when I did it was usually something banal, the speaker was wondering how I felt about toast, or telling me that the store would close in twenty minutes. All that
¹⁰ work for something that didn't really matter, and so I began saying "*D'accord*," which translates to "I am in agreement," and means basically, "OK." The word was a key to a magic door, and every time I said
¹⁵ it I felt the thrill of possibility.

"*D'accord*," I told the concierge, and the next thing I knew I was sewing the eye onto a stuffed animal belonging to her granddaughter. "*D'accord*," I said to the
²⁰ dentist, and she sent me to a periodontist, who took some X-rays and called me into his conference room for a little talk. "*D'accord*," I said, and a week later I returned to his office, where he sliced my
²⁵ gums from top to bottom and scraped great deposits of plaque from the roots of my teeth. If I'd had any idea that this was going to happen, I'd never have said "*D'accord*" to my French publisher, who'd
³⁰ scheduled me the following evening for

a television appearance. It was a weekly cultural program, and very popular. I followed the pop star Robbie Williams, and as the producer settled me into my chair I ran my tongue over my stitches. It was like having a mouthful of spiders—spooky, but it gave me something to talk about on TV, and for that I was grateful.

I said "*D'accord*" to a waiter and received a pig's nose standing erect on a bed of tender greens. I said it to a woman in a department store and walked away drenched in cologne. Every day was an adventure.

When I got a kidney stone, I took the Métro to a hospital and said "*D'accord*," to a cheerful redheaded nurse, who led me to a private room and hooked me up to a Demerol drip. That was undoubtedly the best that *d'accord* got me, and it was followed by the worst. After the stone had passed, I spoke to a doctor, who filled out an appointment card and told me to return

GRAMMAR TIP

Most regular verbs ending in a "consonant-vowel-consonant" structure require that you double the last consonant before adding *-ed*: occur → occurred. For more *-ed* spelling tips, see pages 191 and 194.

the following Monday, when we would do whatever it was I'd just agreed to. "*D'accord*," I said, and then I supersized it with "*génial*," which means "great!"

On the day of my appointment, I returned to the hospital, where I signed the register and was led by a slightly less cheerful nurse to a large dressing room. "Strip to your underwear," she told me, and I said, "*D'accord*." As the woman turned to leave, she said something else, and, looking back, I really should have asked her to repeat it, to draw a picture if that's what it took, because once you take your pants off, *d'accord* isn't really OK anymore.

There were three doors in the dressing room, and after removing my clothes I put my ear against each one, trying to determine which was the safest for someone in my condition. The first was loud, with lots of ringing telephones, so that was out. The second didn't sound much different, and so I chose the third and entered a brightly painted waiting room set with plastic chairs and a glass-topped coffee table stacked high with magazines. A potted plant stood in the corner, and beside it was a second door, which was open and led into a hallway.

I took a seat and had been there for a minute or so when a couple came in and filled two of the unoccupied chairs. The first thing I noticed was that they were fully dressed, and nicely, too—no sneakers or sweat suits for them. The woman wore a nubby[1] gray skirt that fell to her knees and matched the fabric of her husband's sport coat. Their black hair, which was obviously dyed, formed another match, but looked better on her than it did on him—less vain, I supposed.

"*Bonjour*," I said, and it **occurred** to me that possibly the nurse had mentioned something about a robe, perhaps the one that had been hanging in the dressing room. I wanted more than anything to go back and get it, but if I did the couple would see my mistake. They'd think I was stupid, so to prove them wrong I decided to remain where I was and pretend that everything was normal. *La la la.*

It's funny the things that run through your mind when you're sitting in your underpants in front of a pair of strangers. Suicide comes up, but just as you embrace it as a viable option you remember that you don't have the proper tools: no belt to wrap around your neck, no pen to drive through your nose or ear and up into your brain. I thought briefly of swallowing my

---

1. Textured.

watch, but there was no guarantee I'd choke on it. It's embarrassing, but, given the way I normally eat, it would probably go down fairly easily, strap and all. A clock might be a challenge, but a Timex the size of a fifty-cent piece—no problem.

The man with the dyed black hair pulled a pair of glasses from his jacket pocket, and as he unfolded them I recalled a summer evening in my parents' backyard. This was ages ago, a dinner for my sister Gretchen's tenth birthday. My father grilled steaks. My mother set the picnic table with insect-repelling candles, and just as we started to eat she caught me chewing a hunk of beef the size of a coin purse. Gorging always set her off, but on this occasion, it bothered her more than usual.

"I hope you choke to death," she said.

I was twelve years old, and paused, thinking, *Did I hear her correctly?*

"That's right, piggy, suffocate."

In that moment, I hoped I *would* choke to death. The knot of beef would lodge itself in my throat, and for the rest of her life my mother would feel haunted and responsible. Every time she passed a steak house or browsed the meat counter of a grocery store, she would think of me and reflect upon what she had said, the words "hope" and "death" in the same sentence. But, of course, I hadn't choked. Instead, I had lived and grown to adult-hood, so that I could sit in this waiting room dressed in nothing but my under-pants. *La la la.*

It was around this time that two more people entered. The woman looked to be in her mid-fifties, and accompanied an elderly man who was, if anything, over-dressed: a suit, a sweater, a scarf, and an overcoat, which he removed with great difficulty, every button a challenge. *Give it to me,* I thought. *Over here.* But he was deaf to my telepathy and handed his coat to the woman, who folded it over the back of her chair. Our eyes met for a moment—hers widening as they moved from my face to my chest—and then she picked a magazine of her own, and as she turned the pages I allowed myself to relax a little. She was just a woman reading a copy of *Paris Match*, and I was just the person sitting across from her. True, I had no clothes on, but maybe she wouldn't dwell on that, maybe none of these people would. The old man, the couple with their matching hair: "How was the hospital?" their friends might ask, and they'd answer, "Fine," or "Oh, you know, the same."

"Did you see anything messed up?"

"No, not that I can think of."

It sometimes helps to remind myself that not everyone is like me. Not everyone writes things down in a notebook and then transcribes them into a diary. Fewer still will take that diary, clean it up a bit, and read it in front of an audience:

"March 14. Paris. Went with Dad to the hospital, where we sat across from a man in his underpants. They were briefs, not boxers, a little on the grey side, the elastic slack from too many washings. I later said to Father, 'Other people have to use those chairs, too, you know,' and he agreed that it was unsanitary.

"Odd little guy, creepy. Hair on his shoulders. Big idiot smile plastered on his face, just sitting there, mumbling to himself."

How conceited I am to think I might be remembered, especially in a busy hospital where human misery is a matter of course. If any of these people did keep a diary, their day's entry would likely have to do with a diagnosis, some piece of news either inconvenient, or life-altering: the liver's not a match, the cancer has spread to the spinal column. Compared with that, a man in his underpants is no more re-markable than a dust-covered plant, or the magazine subscription card lying on the floor beside the table. Then, too, good news or bad, these people would eventually leave the hospital and return to the street, where any number of things might [210] wipe me from their memory.

Perhaps on their way home they'll see a dog with a wooden leg, which I saw myself one afternoon. It was a German shepherd, and his prosthesis looked as though it had [215] been fashioned from a billy club. The network of straps holding the thing in place was a real eye-opener, but stranger still was the noise it made against the floor of the subway car, a dull thud that managed [220] to sound both plaintive and forceful at the same time. Then there was the dog's owner, who looked at the homemade leg and then at me, with an expression reading, "Not bad, huh?"

[225] Or maybe they'll run into something comparatively small yet no less astonishing. I was walking to the bus stop one morning and came upon a well-dressed woman lying on the sidewalk in front of an [230] office-supply store. A small crowd had formed, and just as I joined it a fire truck pulled up. In America, if someone dropped to the ground, you'd call an ambulance, but in France it's the firemen who do most [235] of the rescuing. There were four of them, and, after checking to see that the woman was okay, one of them returned to the truck and opened the door. I thought he was looking for an aluminum blanket, the [240] type they use for people in shock, but instead he pulled out a goblet. Anywhere else it would have been a cup, made of

paper or plastic, but this was glass and had a stem. I guess they carry it around in [245] the front seat, next to the axes or whatever.

The fireman filled the goblet with bottled water, and then he handed it to the woman, who was sitting up now and running her hand over her hair, the way one might [250] when waking from a nap. It was the lead story in my diary that night, but no matter how hard I fiddled with it I felt that something was missing. Had I mentioned that it was autumn? Did the leaves on the [255] sidewalk contribute to my sense of utter delight, or was it just the goblet and the dignity it bespoke: "Yes, you may be on the ground; yes, this drink may be your last—but let's do it right, shall we?"

[260] Everyone has his own standards, but in my opinion a sight like that is at least fifty times better than what I was providing. A goblet will keep you going for years, while a man in his underpants is good for [265] maybe two days, a week at most. Unless, of course, you are the man in his underpants, in which case it will probably stay with you for the rest of your life—not floating on the exact edge of your [270] consciousness, not handy like a phone number, but still within easy reach, like a mouthful of steak, or a dog with a wooden leg. How often you'll think of the cold plastic chair, and of the nurse's face as [275] she passes the room and discovers you with your hands between your knees. Such surprise, such amusement, as she proposes some new adventure, then stands there, waiting for your "*d'accord.*"

(2090 words)

Source: Sedaris, David. *When You Are Engulfed in Flames.* New York: Little, Brown, 2008. Print.

VOCABULARY AND COMPREHENSION

You may wish to work with a partner as you answer the questions below.

1. Why did saying "*d'accord*" to every question "thrill" the author?

_____

_____

2. The author blindly replied "*D'accord*" to nine different people. Indicate what happened to the author each time by completing the chart below.
The first one has been done for you as an example.

WHEN THE AUTHOR SAID "*D'ACCORD*" TO THE	HE
a) concierge,	had to sew the eye onto a stuffed animal.
b) dentist,	
c) periodontist,	
d) French publisher,	
e) waiter,	
f) woman in the department store,	
g) red-headed nurse,	
h) doctor,	
i) "slightly less cheerful" nurse,	

3. A **simile** is a figure of speech in which two dissimilar things are compared, often in a phrase introduced by *like* or *as*. Copy out the simile used by the author in the second paragraph (lines 35–36).

_____

4. Why did the author not go back to the dressing room and put on a robe?

_____

_____

_____

5. The author seriously considered taking his own life while sitting in his underwear in a room with two dressed strangers.

☐ True　☐ False

6. A **gerund** is a noun made of the *-ing* form of the verb: *Her **singing** is beautiful.* What gerund in the tenth paragraph (line 129) means "eating greedily"?

_____

7. Why did the author write that he wanted to "choke to death" when he was twelve years old?

_____

_____

8. Why does the author think he is being conceited when he fears that those with him in the waiting room will remember his lack of clothing in the years to come?

_____

_____

_____

9. The author conjectures that outside the hospital setting, those with him in the waiting room are likely to witness any number of events more memorable than seeing a man in his underwear waiting for medical treatment. What two events, based on his own experience, does the author mention?

a) _____

b) _____

_____

10. According to the author, why will he remember sitting nearly naked in a waiting room with other people long after the other people have forgotten the event?

_____

DISCUSSION

→ Discuss each of the questions in small groups.

→ Be prepared to share your answers with the rest of the class and to explain them.

1. The author expresses a certain frustration about not understanding everything he hears in French, which is not his first language. To combat his frustration, he "gives up" and pretends that he understands what is said to him, when in reality, he does not. Have you ever done this or been tempted to do this when learning a new language? Explain.

2. If you **go with the flow**, you accept what comes your way and do not try to change anything: it is the opposite of *going it alone*. In the essay, the author goes with the flow when he agrees to whatever is asked of him. What are the advantages of going with the flow? Of going it alone?

3. The essay was intended to be funny. Did you find the essay funny? Why or why not? What factors may have influenced your appreciation of the essay?

Sarah Regan is a writer living in Toronto. Her essay "Sometimes You Have to Just Jump" was published in *The Globe and Mail* on Thursday, June 28, 2007.

BEFORE READING

→ Scan the article, circling the vocabulary terms listed below.

→ Define these terms according to the context in which each is used.

1. jam-packed (adj.): _____

2. glossy (adj.): _____

3. dog-eared (adj.): _____

_____

4. peered (v.): _____

5. helmets (n.): _____

6. fling (v.): _____

7. hardships (n.): _____

8. swift (adj.): _____

9. carefree (adj.): _____

10. milestone (n.): _____

Examine the reading strategies suggested in "Appendix B: Effective Reading and Active Listening." Then read the questions on pages 141 and 142 *before* reading the article itself.

Sometimes You Have to Just Jump

By Sarah Regan

I carefully scanned my to-do list one last time before jumping into one of the waiting taxis.

Day 1 of our vacation in Rio de Janeiro was jam-packed with museum exhibitions, tourist attractions and a guided tour of the city. My father and I had come to Brazil to celebrate my graduation from university.

I thought I had planned everything to ensure we got the most out of our seven-day vacation.

Turns out I had scheduled everything except fun.

"Hey, why don't we try hang-gliding," my father said, holding up a dusty brochure he found on the back seat of the cab.

The glossy brochure showed a young man sailing through the air attached to what looked like an enormous kite, Copacabana Beach in the background.

The man's open-mouth expression was enough to entice my adventure-seeking father and terrify his overly cautious daughter.

"Uh ... I don't think that's on our list of things to do," I said, nervously tapping the dog-eared copy of *Lonely Planet* on my lap.

"Oh, come on, sweets," he said. "We're
30 here to have fun. Forget that list of yours
and let's live a little."

An hour later I reluctantly watched my
middle-aged father jump off Pedra Bonita
Mountain, plunging 520 metres to the
35 ground.

I took two unsteady steps toward the
edge of the cliff and cautiously peered
over. I saw an ant-size version of my father

WORD CULTURE

Pep is an abbreviation of "pepper." In a figurative sense, *pepper* means "energy."
A *pep talk*, an expression first used in the twentieth century, is a talk designed
to energize. The expression is often used in a sports context: *After a short pep talk,
the team went on to win the championship.*

land softly on the sandy beach below.
40 Even from the top of a mountain, his white
Canadian body was hard to miss on a
beach sprinkled with bronzed Brazilians.
He waved excitedly at me, encouraging me
to follow.

45 Behind me, a pack of jumpers, consisting mostly of young males in their twenties, tightened the straps on their helmets
and harnesses, as taught in the tandem
training course.

50 *What makes seemingly intelligent people
want to fling themselves off a mountain?*

I asked myself. Even more puzzling, what
would inspire my fifty-four-year-old father
to participate in such a daring sport and
55 take his eldest daughter along for the ride?

I sighed and fastened my last safety
buckle. I reflected on how hard I worked
during these past few years in university.

I thought about the hardships I endured
60 to get to where I am today: bad apartments,
bad roommates, badly paying part-time jobs.

I remembered the many sleepless nights
I lay in bed at 3:00 a.m. wondering if I had
answered that exam question to the best
65 of my ability. Or if my professor had received the research paper I sent via e-mail.

Four years of meticulous planning had
led me to the top of this mountain. Was I
really prepared to jeopardize my future in
70 the name of one swift celebratory act?

I didn't think so.

My instructor, who sensed my fear,
leaned over and whispered in my ear,
"Sometimes you have to stop thinking and
75 just jump."

By this point my father could see my
hesitation. He stood helplessly on the
beach below, probably wishing he was
beside me so he could offer his trademark
80 you-can-do-this **pep talk**.

But this was a challenge I had to face on
my own.

He had saved up for a year to take me
on this trip. A proud father who worked
85 fourteen-hour days as a bus driver just to
afford to take his daughter on a vacation
she would never forget. I envied his work-
hard, play-hard mentality and wanted to
own it myself.

90 Years of studying had taught me the
importance of work, but I had forgotten
how to play.

I took one last look at him waiting for
me below and backed away from the cliff.
95 "I can't do this, I can't do this," I repeated
aloud.

Then a thought occurred to me: I am my father's daughter after all. Maybe I had a touch of his carefree spirit hidden inside me.

100 I took five large steps backward, gripped the handlebar tightly against my chest and shut my eyes. I ran as fast as I could toward the ledge and jumped.

Ten minutes later I was back on the 105 ground, yet something in me had changed.

Years later I look back on this moment as a milestone. I still make lists and probably always will. I'm just a list kind of person. But that day on the mountain

110 taught me that life can't be neatly organized into a column prioritized by coloured highlighters.

The best moments in life are scary and disorganized.

115 I am now about to graduate from university with my second degree, but this time around I'm prepared to let go. I now know that when life's to-do list is long and everyday tasks become predictable, all 120 I have to do is jump.

I know I'll land with two feet on the ground.

(796 words)

Source: Regan, Sarah. "Sometimes You Have to Just Jump." *Globe and Mail* 28 June 2007. Web. 8 Feb. 2010.

VOCABULARY AND COMPREHENSION

You may have to use external sources (dictionary, website, etc.) to find some of the answers to the questions below.

1. **Antonyms** are words with opposite meanings. In the seventh paragraph (lines 23-24), what two antonymous adjectives does the author use to describe her father and herself?

   Father: _____

   Author: _____

2. The author describes her copy of *Lonely Planet*, a travel guide, as "dog-eared." What does this descriptive term suggest?

   _____

   _____

3. The author reflects upon the difficulties she went through and the worries she had during the four years it took her to get a university degree. List the difficulties and the worries in the chart below.

DIFFICULTIES	WORRIES

4. Why do you think the father wanted his daughter to jump off the cliff?

_____

5. How does the author finally find the courage to jump off the cliff?

_____

_____

6. Rewrite the sentence word-for-word in which the author expresses her opinion on life.

_____

7. What personal experience (obviously) influenced the author's perspective?

_____

A Question of PERSPECTIVE

Do you live a *careful* or a *carefree* life? Do you think you will live your life in the same way twenty years from now? Why or why not?

DISCUSSION

→ Discuss each of the questions in small groups.

→ Be prepared to share your answers with the rest of the class and to explain them.

1. The author's father suggested hang-gliding. While the author was preparing to jump off the cliff, she describes those waiting behind her as "mostly young males in their twenties." Are men really drawn to extreme sports more than women? If so, why would this be? Is gender alone in influencing perspective on this issue? Could there be other influences?

2. In the thirteenth paragraph (lines 50–51), the author asks the following question: "What makes seemingly intelligent people want to fling themselves off a mountain?" Respond to her question; offer at least three different reasons.

3. Do you agree or disagree with the hang-gliding instructor's advice? "Sometimes you have to stop thinking and just jump." Explain.

CD ◄ **LISTENING** Risk-Takers: Boon or Burden?

The Point was a popular CBC radio program hosted by Aamer Haleem. On the program, informed guests discussed and debated topics of general interest. On January 7, 2009, Mr. Haleem's guests included Canadian Senator Larry Campbell[2] and Mike Bradley, mayor of Sarnia, Ontario. At the start of the excerpt you are about to hear, skier James Hillier explains how he received

2. Senator Campbell is a former mayor of Vancouver who served as BC's Chief Coroner from 1996 to 2000. The Canadian television series *Da Vinci's Inquest* was based on his life.

a lifetime ban from Grouse Mountain, a ski resort north of Vancouver. The subjects of the day's show were government involvement in people's personal lives and bipartisan politics. The subject of the excerpt? The title of the clip says it all!

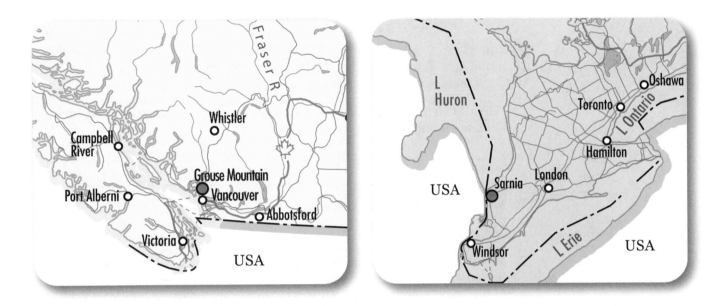

BEFORE LISTENING

The terms in the first column were taken from the audio clip.

→ Match each term with the correct synonym. The first one has been done for you as an example.

TERMS	
1. Aegis (n.)	c
2. Beyond (prep.)	
3. Daredevil (n.)	
4. Disturbing (adj.)	
5. Off the beaten track (exp.)	
6. Out of bounds (exp.)	
7. Prone (adj.)	
8. Self-indulgent (adj.)	
9. Sing a different tune (exp.)	
10. Vicarious (adj.)	

SYNONYMS

a) Thrill-seeker or adventurer

b) Second-hand

c) Protection or support

d) Outside of prescribed limits

e) Out of the way (not on the main road)

f) Narcissistic

g) Inclined

h) Farther on than

i) Distressing

j) Change one's ways, attitudes or behaviour

COMPREHENSION

The questions below are in sequence: you will hear the answer to question 1, then question 2, then question 3, etc. If you miss an answer, do not worry about it; simply move on to the next question.

1. Why did Mr. Hillier and his three companions receive a lifetime ban from Grouse Mountain?

    _____

    _____

2. Mr. Hillier needed to be rescued.

    ☐ True   ☐ False

3. Mayor Mike Bradley and Senator Larry Campbell express many opinions on risk-taking and risk-takers. Seven of their opinions are summarized in the chart below. Indicate the sequence in which these opinions are expressed by writing a number from 1 to 7 in the space provided. The first one has been done for you as an example.

OPINIONS EXPRESSED	SEQUENCE
a) Extreme risk-takers needing rescue should pay for the cost of the rescue and face criminal charges. (Mike Bradley)	
b) Ice fishermen needing rescue in the spring by the Coast Guard should pay for the cost of the rescue, because the danger of spring ice fishing is recurrent and therefore foreseeable. (Mike Bradley)	
c) Life is all about taking risk, but this risk must be calculated. (Mike Bradley)	
d) Risk-takers are irresponsible, as they potentially put others [first-care responders] at risk. (Mike Bradley)	
e) Risk-takers needing rescue should pay for the cost of the rescue and face criminal charges. (Larry Campbell)	
f) Risk-takers over-romanticize themselves. (Mike Bradley)	1
g) Risk-takers put volunteer rescuers at risk as a result of their [the risk-takers'] stupidity and quest for personal glory. (Larry Campbell)	

4. About halfway through the clip, host Aamer Haleem tries to open up the discussion and move beyond the example of James Hillier. Mr. Haleem mentions the Wright brothers,[3] claiming they are examples of risk-takers that society actually rewarded. How do Mr. Campbell (who responds first) and Mr. Bradley respond to this claim?

_____

_____

_____

_____

5. Fill in the blanks. "I think every once in a while you should scare yourself. So when I travel, I tend to get _____ ... _____ ... Nothing has ever happened to me, but it could happen to me ... I'm not going ... outside the boundaries which are laid down. I'm simply wandering around a city ... I do know that there's a bit of a sizzle there!" (Larry Campbell)

6. Fill in the blank. "I think most of us get our risk-taking through others, whether it be watching sports teams ... or this _____ thing ... just what other people do ... but people don't want to be out there doing it themselves." (Mike Bradley)

7. Fill in the blank. "We take risks every day in our lives. We make decisions. The risks may not be life-threatening, but they could be career-threatening. They could be embarrassing, which in some cases is probably worse than life-threatening. And so I think we need to look _____ just the risk-taking as something that's physically dangerous." (Larry Campbell)

8. What example does Mr. Campbell give to support his contention that people who lead quiet lives take risks all the time?

_____

_____

A Question of PERSPECTIVE

If you were a doctor or nurse, how would you feel about treating someone whose injury resulted from participating in an extreme sport? Would you be as sympathetic to that person's plight as you would to someone whose injury was "no fault of his or her own"?

3. Inventors and builders of the world's first successful airplane.

DISCUSSION

→ Discuss each of the questions in small groups.

→ Be prepared to share your answers with the rest of the class and to explain them.

1. Getting out of bed in the morning is a risk: you could fall on the floor. List five risks most people take every day of their lives.

2. Make a list of five famous risk-takers. Explain why each is a risk-taker.

3. Who is more likely to take a risk: a man or a woman? Justify your response.

VOCABULARY REVIEW

Use each of the terms from the first column on page 143 (in the Before Listening section) in a sentence of your own creation, maintaining the meaning of the word as used in the audio clip. Write your sentences on a separate sheet of paper and submit your work to your teacher for verification.

READING 6.2

Self-Indulgent Risks Reflect Larger Issues

....

Brett Anningson is a writer living in Moncton, New Brunswick. He writes a social analysis column for the *Times & Transcript*. His article "Self-Indulgent Risks Reflect Larger Issues" was published on January 19, 2009.

BEFORE READING

→ Scan the article, circling the vocabulary terms listed below.

→ Define these terms according to the context in which each is used.

1. livelihood (n.): _____

2. layoffs (n.): _____

3. bear with (v.): _____

4. buoy (n.): _____

5. plunged (v.): _____

6. lunacy (n.): _____

7. blissfully unaware (col.): _____

8. hedonistic (adj.): _____

9. civic duty (col.): _____

10. portent (n.): _____

VOCABULARY TIP

Words which are often used together are called **collocations (cols.)**: *blissfully unaware* and *civic duty* are examples as are *record numbers* and *round of layoffs*.

> Examine the reading strategies suggested in "Appendix B: Effective Reading and Active Listening." Then read the questions on pages 148 and 149 *before* reading the article itself.

Self-Indulgent Risks Reflect Larger Issues

By Brett Anningson

The travel industry is not noticing any real decline due to the recession. They are offering deals to try and make you take a trip; so they might be losing a bit of money, but they are actually seeing record numbers of vacationers. Carnival Cruise Lines had its largest volume of bookings ever last week.

At first this seems a little strange since there are so many people on the verge of losing their livelihood, their home, or just their way of life. Every day we hear about another round of layoffs. Still we choose to spend thousands of dollars on a one-off disposable item like a trip to Disney World.

I think this has to do with the same reason people buy snowmobiles.

Bear with me, and I will bring this back around. When I lived in the Eastern Townships of Quebec, I lived on the side of Lake Champlain. Everyone, and I mean everyone, drove their Ski-Doos onto the ice as soon as possible and as late as possible. They had drag races, and crossed indiscriminately into the United States. Now, at the same time every single one of them had a buoy tied to the back of the sled [the Ski-Doo]; because every single one of them lost that thing every year when it plunged through the thin ice.

They were also big into ice fishing and parked their big Buicks and Crown Victorias[4] on the ice until May, but that is another level of lunacy.

My brother went to Florida a few years back and jumped off a crane attached to a bungee cord.

This might all seem stream of consciousness but I have a theory that most of what we do nowadays is actually done for escape. The curious thing about that is that the riskier our regular lives, the more pain and hardship we face, the larger the risks we take in our playtime as well.

So think about the world. Iraq and Afghanistan, oil prices and mortgage defaults, more than a thousand killed in Gaza. And what do we do? Go helicopter skiing and snowmobiling in the backcountry of British Columbia where avalanches are a real possibility. We go out on the ice when it is not safe. We drive too fast on highways when it is snowing. We take risks.

It is foolish if you think about it. The more we feel under the gun, the more stressed we are, the more likely we are to do things that will actually get us hurt. All the while, the actual pressure of the situation has made our ability to "talk ourselves down" almost non-existent.

The younger we are, the more we seem to be okay with this. I remember driving to Ottawa at 140 kilometres per hour during the ice storm in Quebec. It just never occurred to me that I might actually get in an accident. I see it all the time here, young people driving by me way too fast for the conditions; blissfully unaware of what is going to happen to them.

But it is not just young people. This phenomenon applies to everyone. The list of risky behaviours is unbelievably long; and it ranges from recreational risks like skydiving and scuba diving right through to the risks we take with alcohol, with sexuality, and even with deep fried foods.

Now, far be it from me to say that this is terrible.

I myself engage in escapism, as tame as

---

4. Full-size car made by Ford.

reading and watching movies, playing World of Warcraft,[5] right up to some real risky behaviours. I know that what I have written is true—when I am stressed I am more likely to overindulge in everything. I also realize I have to learn to cope better.

From all historical accounts it would seem that at the end of the Roman Empire, during the dying days of one of the most powerful, stable, and innovative societies ever, everything went wrong in exactly this way.

People began to overindulge, it became very individualistic, very hedonistic, and the choices people made only made things worse. Instead of a sense of civic duty, everyone turned to a sense of self-fulfillment. I can't even write about the things that went on in ancient Rome's twilight without getting into trouble. You could, however, read some of the other articles in this paper and get a pretty good sense.

Things are not so different here in the decline of the Western Empire.

My real fear is that the risk-taking, self-indulgent attitude that is pervading our society is a real portent of what is on the horizon. This seems to be the end of our society as we know it, and we are, to steal a quote, fiddling as Rome burns.

I am not entirely sure what to turn our energy to; there are prophets and gurus aplenty, like David Suzuki and Eckhart Tolle,[6] who are trying to offer suggestions. I guess I am simply trying to sound the alarm.

Perhaps if we are aware of some of the motivations that go behind our actions we might be better able to fight against the impulse toward self-destruction. At least, that is what my hopeful side keeps arguing. We can start small, by trying to limit our escapism and focus on engagement.

The more we try to be part of the solution, the less impact the problem might have on our lives.

(795 words)

Source: Anningson, Brett. "Self-Indulgent Risks Reflect Larger Issues." *Times & Transcript* [Moncton] 19 Jan. 2009. Web. 8 Feb. 2010.

VOCABULARY AND COMPREHENSION

You may have to reread the article and use external sources (dictionary, website, etc.) to find some of the answers to the questions below.

1. The author asserts that spending money on a vacation when money is tight, driving Ski-Doos on thin ice, and bungee jumping are all motivated by escapism.

   ☐ True   ☐ False

2. Paraphrase the following: "... the more pain and hardship we face, the larger the risks we take in our playtime as well."

   _____

   _____

   _____

5. Multiplayer online role-playing game.
6. David Suzuki is a Canadian science broadcaster and environmental activist; Eckhart Tolle is a German-Canadian spiritual teacher, motivational speaker and writer.

3. What idiomatic expression in the ninth paragraph (line 56) means "feel tremendous pressure"?

_____

4. According to the author, the older we are, the more likely we are to engage in dangerous activities.

☐ True   ☐ False

5. When is the author more likely to overindulge in escapist behaviours?

_____

6. To what does the author attribute the end of the Roman Empire?

_____

7. What idiomatic expression in the seventeenth paragraph (line 110) means "to do something trivial and irresponsible in the middle of an emergency"?

_____

8. What is the subject of the article?

   a) Recreational risks

   b) The impulse toward self-destruction

   c) The end of the Roman Empire

   d) Risks taken by young people

9. What is the author's opinion on the subject?

_____

_____

A Question of PERSPECTIVE

If you lost almost everything you had, would you be more or less willing to risk what little you had left? Justify your response.

DISCUSSION

→ Discuss each of the questions in small groups.

→ Be prepared to share your answers with the rest of the class and to explain them.

1. How do you behave when you are under a lot of stress?

2. Do you agree with the author's contention that, "... the more pain and hardship we face, the larger the risks we take in our playtime as well"? Justify your response.

3. Is age a factor in a person's willingness to engage in risky behaviour? Explain.

WATCHING · Binge Drinking

In October 2008, the CBC ran a series entitled "High Spirits" that took a look at Canadians and their alcohol consumption. The clip you are about to view, entitled "Binge Drinking," first aired on *The National* on October 21. In the clip, reporter Joan Leishman follows three nineteen-year-old university students, Michelle Cooper, Simone Sheen and Brianna Shields, out for a night on the town. The report explores the risks associated with binge drinking as well as those associated with mixing alcohol and caffeine-laced drinks such as Red Bull. Guests include Kathleen Parks and Kathleen (Kate) Miller from the Research Institute on Addictions of the University at Buffalo (SUNY) and Paul Peterson, bartender at a Toronto nightclub.

BEFORE WATCHING

The terms in the first column below were taken from the video clip.

→ Match each term with the correct synonym. The first one has been done for you as an example.

TERMS		SYNONYMS
1. Astonishing (adj.)	h	**a)** Shock
2. Bombed (adj.)		**b)** Danger signal
3. Head start (n.)		**c)** Advantage
4. Hit (somebody) like a ton of bricks (exp.)		**d)** Gradually decrease
5. Jolt (n.)		**e)** Maintain the same rhythm or speed
6. Keep up the pace (exp.)		**f)** Probability
7. Odds (n.)		**g)** Have a surprisingly hard impact on (somebody)
8. Stumble (v.)		**h)** Very surprising
9. Taper off (v.)		**i)** Very drunk (slang)
10. Warning bell (col.)		**j)** Walk unsteadily

Examine the reading strategies suggested in "Appendix B: Effective Reading and Active Listening." Then read the questions on pages 151 and 152 *before* watching the video clip.

COMPREHENSION

The questions below are in sequence: you will hear the answer to question 1, then question 2, then question 3, etc. If you miss an answer, do not worry about it; simply move on to the next question.

1. Fill in the blank. "And as a bartender at Strangelove, Paul Peterson has seen a lot of young women _____ his club." (Joan Leishman)

2. Fill in the blanks. "They're already coming in with some alcohol in them, and then when they come here, they go for that binge 'cause they want to catch up. They want to feel that effect of the alcohol. You know, they're having three, four, five shots within the course of an hour, hour and a half, and then when it's hitting them, it _____ them _____ _____ ."(Paul Peterson)

3. According to Health Canada, what percentage of young women binge drink? What percentage of young men binge drink?

   Women: _____

   Men: _____

4. For young women, how is binge drinking defined?

   _____

5. What was the main finding of the research study conducted by Kathleen Parks?

   _____

   _____

6. Fill in the blank. "If somebody's in a situation that could potentially be dangerous or threatening, they [women who binge drink] are not going to notice the cues that ... set off that little _____ , 'Uh-oh, I might be in trouble,' as early." (Kathleen Parks)

7. Which of the following statements is(are) true? More than one answer is possible. Kate Miller states that mixing caffeinated drinks with alcohol

   a) creates wide-awake drunks who don't realize they're drunk.

   b) leads to an increased risk of vehicle accidents, alcohol poisoning and sexual victimization.

   c) impairs your judgment without your realizing it is impaired.

   d) should be criminalized.

8. Fill in the blank. "We found that on days when women were binge drinking, their _____ of experiencing sexual victimization were nineteen times higher than on days when they didn't drink at all ... It is extraordinary." (Kathleen Parks)

9. The nineteen-year-old university friends featured in the clip believe they are not at risk because they look out for themselves. One of the women mentions four ways they look out for one another. The first two have been listed for you. List the remaining two.

a) They make sure they see each other frequently. _____

b) They tell each other if they leave the club. _____

c) _____

d) _____

10. Fill in the blank. "Usually if you go out with a group of like ten girls, there's always that one girl that's like kind of sober … It's not like ten girls go out and they're all completely _____ and they can't take care of themselves."

11. According to research, what happens to binge drinking after the age of twenty-five?

_____

12. In the chart below, indicate with a checkmark whether each person (or group of people) looks upon binge drinking favourably or unfavourably. If you're unsure, check "unsure."

PEOPLE	FAVOURABLE OPINION OF BINGE DRINKING	UNFAVOURABLE OPINION OF BINGE DRINKING	UNSURE
Joan Leishman			
Kate Miller			
Kathleen Parks			
Brianna Shields Michelle Cooper Simone Sheen			
Paul Peterson			

A Question of PERSPECTIVE

If you were a middle-aged reporter, would you be for or against binge drinking? Explain.

DISCUSSION

→ Discuss each of the questions in small groups.

→ Be prepared to share your answers with the rest of the class and to explain them.

1. Why do young people binge drink more than middle-aged or old people?

2. Why are increasing numbers of young women binge drinking?

3. What do you think about mixing caffeinated drinks with alcohol?

VOCABULARY REVIEW

Choose three terms from the first column on page 150 (in the Before Watching section). Use these terms correctly in a paragraph of your own creation. The paragraph may be on any subject you wish. Reminder: A paragraph must have a controlling idea that is accompanied by supporting details (see page 7). Write your paragraph on a separate sheet of paper and submit your work to your teacher for verification.

𝒫ost

Daringly Different

Write about a time when you dared to be different. Wearing outrageously different clothing? Having an unusual haircut? Eating foods uncommon to most North Americans? Etc. Write approximately 100 to 150 words.

The Personal Essay

The essays in this unit, "In the Waiting Room," "Sometimes You Have to Just Jump" and "Self-Indulgent Risks Reflect Larger Issues," may all be qualified as personal essays. A personal essay expresses something learned about life from a personal experience you have had. Unlike more formal academic essays, you are "allowed" to use the first person singular; in fact, it is an absolute *must*!

For this essay, you are asked to write something you have learned from

1. a funny moment in your life.
2. a memorable moment in your life.
3. a risky moment in your life.
4. a time you got off the beaten track.
5. a time you had to go it alone.
6. a time you had to go with the flow.
7. a time you had to just jump.
8. a time you overindulged.
9. a time you ignored a warning bell.
10. an adventurous moment.

→ Base your essay on the academic essay outlined on page 9: you will need an introduction, a development and a conclusion.

→ Write approximately 400 to 450 words.

When writing your personal essay, remember to

→ choose a real event from your life, not someone else's;

→ provide lots of details when relating your personal experience;

→ clearly state the lesson learned;

→ proofread your work prior to submission.

The chart below provides a structural overview, detailing elements to consider.

ESSAY SECTIONS	PARAGRAPHS	STRUCTURAL ELEMENTS
Introduction	1	• Use your personal experience as the grabber. • Use the lesson learned as the thesis of your essay; for example, "From this experience, I learned the importance of *sober* second thought."
Development	2 3 4 (optional)	• Use transition terms for each of the paragraphs in the development. • Refer back to the personal experience as you are explaining the lesson learned.
Conclusion	5	• Begin with a transition term, a brief recapping of the lesson learned and the main points made in the development. • End with a connection to the grabber (your personal experience).

ⓟresent

Escapist Activities

Escapism is the avoidance of reality through activities that help you forget about your problems for a short period of time. For many, reading books is an escapist activity. In small groups, create a list of ten escapist activities. Then rank the activities from 1 to 10, where 1 is the most popular escapist activity in the list and 10 is the least. When possible, make specific escapist recommendations for each of the ten activities: a really absorbing book, an engrossing film, etc. Compare your group's list to others in the class.

The Adventurers

What do the following people have in common: Amelia Earhart, Cabeza de Vaca, Charles Lindbergh, Christopher Columbus, Sir Henry Morton Stanley, Meriwether Lewis, William Clark, Marco Polo, Mary Kingsley, Sir Edmund Hillary and Steve Fossett? From the title of this activity, you can probably guess that they were all adventurers.

What does it take to be an adventurer?

→ Prepare a five- to seven-minute presentation in response to this question.

→ You may wish to read up on the adventurers listed at the start of this activity.

→ In your presentation, be sure to respect the structure of a formal speech (see page 17).

℗articipate

In this section, you will work with another student on a joint writing and speaking project.

The Adventures of Language Learning

Learning another language is an adventure for many, taking learners out of their "cultural and linguistic comfort zone" and confronting them with a new cultural and linguistic reality. If you are reading this sentence, it is likely that you are learning English as a second language, a language you are well on the way to mastering. To have gotten this far, you and your classmates have likely been learning English for a good many years, both inside and outside of the classroom. In this activity, you and your partner are going to interview others in your class to discover in depth what their adventure in learning English has been like, both the high points and the low! Once the interviews have been completed, you will give an oral report on your findings to your teacher.

Procedure

1. Working with your partner, create a list of twenty questions related to learning English. When creating your list, remember to use the Five W's (and one H): *who, what, where, when, why* and *how*!

2. Pair up with another team and interview one of the members. You and your partner should take turns asking questions. In addition to the questions on your list, ask questions based on responses given. For example:

   Question from List: *When did you start learning English?*
   Response: *When I was a toddler.*
   Question based on response: *Really? That's pretty young. Does your family speak English at home?*

   Jot down the responses. Assure the person interviewed that his or her identity will not be revealed to your teacher when giving the oral report. Note: One of you should now respond to the interview questions prepared by the other team so that they can prepare their oral report.

3. Prepare an outline for your oral report using the template provided on page 19. The thesis of your presentation is your team's opinion as to whether the person interviewed has enjoyed his or her adventure in second language learning. Referring to your notes, find evidence to support your opinion; use quotes whenever possible.

4. Give a joint oral presentation to your teacher, being sure to protect the interviewee's identity. One partner gives the introduction and first piece of evidence; the other, the second (and third) piece(s) of evidence and the conclusion. Each of you should speak for five to seven minutes. Provide your teacher with a copy of your question list and outline before the presentation.

ⓟ ursue

Related Works

The following works may be of interest for continued study.

TYPES OF WORKS	TITLES
Documentary	*Being Caribou*, Dir. Leanne Allison and Diana Wilson. National Film Board of Canada, 2004. • Available online at http://www.nfb.ca/film/being_caribou/ (72 minutes and 19 seconds) • Documentary of an expedition carried out by a husband and wife as they follow a herd of caribou across the Arctic tundra
Fiction	Lewis, C. S. *The Chronicles of Narnia*. 1950–1956. Print. • Series of seven fantasy novels Rowling, J. K. *Harry Potter*. 1997–2007. Print. • Series of seven fantasy novels
Movie	*National Treasure*. Dir. Jon Turteltaub. Buena Vista, 2004. • First in a series of films featuring fictional treasure-seeking Ben Gates *Raiders of the Lost Ark*. Dir. Steven Spielberg. Paramount, 1981. • First in a series of films featuring fictional adventurer Indiana Jones
Non-Fiction	Fox, Michael J. *Always Looking Up: The Adventures of an Incurable Optimist*. New York: Hyperion, 2009. Print. • The well-known actor shares his personal philosophy on life
Short Story	Faulkner, William. "The Bear." *Go Down, Moses and Other Stories*. New York: Random House, 1942. Print. • A boy, a grizzly, an adventure! Hemingway, Ernest. "The Short Happy Life of Francis Macomber." 1936. Print. • A man on safari in a fight for his life London, Jack. "To Build a Fire." 1908. Print. • A man and his dog face the elements in brutally cold weather Proulx, Annie. *Close Range: Wyoming Stories*. New York: Scribner, 1999. Print. • Collection of short stories including "Brokeback Mountain" and "The Mud Below"

My eLab ✎ Visit My eLab for additional reading, listening and vocabulary practice.

One Last Look

View of an archway
with a clear vanishing point
in Aranjuez, Spain

Preview

We end this textbook the way we began, by talking about pants!

In Unit 1, you read a short story by a Hasidic mother who cherishes a pair of red pants scorned by her daughter.

In this unit, you will read a personal essay by a Portuguese-Canadian daughter who embraces a pair of gabardine[1] pants spurned by her mother.

In both cases, the pants are perceived in opposite ways.

In both cases, the opposing perceptions are valid.

In both cases, the pants represent something much greater than the objects themselves.

The subject of this, your final unit, is oh-so-Canadian.

The subject of this, your final unit, is culture: yours, theirs and ours.

---

1. Sturdy, tightly woven fabric.

(P)repare

An **A-OK** is a hand gesture made by joining the thumb and the forefinger in a circle and holding the other fingers in the air. In North America, the gesture is a friendly one, meaning "okay"; however, in other parts of the world, the gesture has quite different meanings.

WORD CULTURE

The adjective *A-OK* means "satisfactory." It is a twentieth-century term derived from the expression "all (systems) OK."

→ Working alone or with a partner, indicate with a checkmark in the left or right column whether each of the statements is true or false.

TRUE	STATEMENTS	FALSE
	1. In Spain, the gesture is an offensive one, meaning "you are nothing."	
	2. In Finland, the gesture means "zero mornings left today" and is used by conscripts in the Finnish Defence Forces to indicate their last day of service in the forces.	
	3. In many European countries, the gesture—when the thumb and the forefinger surround the nose—means "drunk."	
	4. In Japan, the gesture can mean "hello."	
	5. In India, the gesture means "incredible."	
	6. In Bulgaria, the gesture means "time for breakfast."	
	7. In Bulgaria, the gesture—when made with the palm facing toward the gesturer—means "time for lunch."	
	8. In Macedonia, the gesture is a nationalistic symbol of unity.	
	9. For users of American Sign Language (ASL) throughout the world, the gesture can mean the letter B.	
	10. In Brazil, the gesture can be used to mean "okay"—or something quite vulgar!	

Source: "A-ok." *Wikipedia*. Wikimedia Foundation, n.d. Web. 1 Jul. 2009.

Ponder

Isabel Vincent is a Canadian journalist who has written for national newspapers. Her article, "Finding a Nationality That Fits" was first published in *The Globe and Mail* on December 3, 1990.

Finding a Nationality That Fits

By Isabel Vincent

We started to become Canadian the day my mother got her first pair of pants.

They were grey-green gabardine with a high waist, and came wrapped in tissue paper in an Eaton's box. My mother reluc-
5 tantly modelled them for my brother and me, all the while declaring that she couldn't imagine ever feeling comfortable with the stretchy cloth hugging her hips.
10 Portuguese women didn't wear pants, only the *canadianas* dared wear anything so revealing. But in the same breath she'd rationalize that she spent too much money not to wear them, and besides they'd
15 probably be warm in winter.

Houses in the Kensington
Market area in Toronto

That was in 1975, a few years after my family had made the big break and moved from the poor immigrant enclave of Kensington Market[2] to the more upscale
20 neighbourhood of North York,[3] where pockets of European immigrants were just beginning to emerge. We were pioneers in a way. My father had been among the first wave of Portuguese immigrants to Canada
25 in the early '50s, working a bleak stretch of railroad near Port Arthur—now Thunder Bay, Ontario—to earn enough money for my mother's passage across the Atlantic. My mother arrived seasick in Halifax in 1955,
30 and took a slow train to Toronto, where she joined my father in a roach-infested flat on Nassau Avenue in the market.

My mother still speaks of those early *sacrificios*: living in a cold climate with
35 cockroaches and mutely shopping for groceries, pointing out items to a local shopkeeper because she couldn't speak English. Her language skills were so tenuous that she once interpreted a
40 greeting from an Orthodox Jew who lived in the neighbourhood as an offer to buy my brother.

In those days, Toronto police used to disperse small crowds of Portuguese men
45 who lingered too long outside cafes. Despite a burgeoning group of immigrants, there were few Portuguese speakers, even in the market.

2. Multicultural neighbourhood in downtown Toronto, Ontario.
3. Central part of the northern half of Toronto.

But by 1975, the market became a Saturday-morning diversion for us, a place to shop for salted cod and fresh vegetables. To the hearty Portuguese immigrants who still worked in the factories and construction yards, and rented windowless basements in the market, we were on our way up. After all, there were very few Portuguese families north of Eglinton Avenue. Although we lived in a mostly Jewish and Italian neighbourhood, we were finally becoming Canadian. Or so I thought.

I learned English in my first year of school. Multiculturalism was just beginning and hyphenated Canadians were beginning to flourish. I played with Italian-Canadians, Lithuanian-Canadians and Chinese-Canadians, but at that time nobody —especially suburban seven-year-olds— seemed able to pronounce "Portuguese-Canadians," so I told people I was Greek; it was easier to say. My brother went even further, changing his name to something faintly Anglo-Saxon, so his teachers and classmates wouldn't get tongue-tied around those sloshy Portuguese vowels and embarrass him. It seemed a very practical idea at the time, and I reluctantly followed suit.

But we still had problems, and didn't seem to belong. We never quite fit into the emerging Portuguese community, growing up around the parish of St. Mary's Church and the Toronto branch of the popular Benfica soccer club on Queen Street West. We were strangely aloof with our compatriots, most of whom had immigrated from the Azores, and whose guttural form of Portuguese we had difficulty understanding. My brother and I balked at heritage-language classes and remained passive spectators at the annual religious processions.

But if we had trouble dealing with our peers in downtown Toronto, in North York we were not much better off. My mother and aunts spoke disparagingly of the *canadianas*, Canadian women who (they were sure) knew nothing about how to keep a clean house or cook a decent meal. My mother taught me how to cook and sew, and she and my aunts teased my brother, saying someday he'd marry a *canadiana* and would end up doing all his own housework.

For all her predictions, my mother was delighted to find out that she had been wrong. My brother, a physician, did marry a Canadian, but he doesn't do much of the housework. These days, my mother's biggest problem is pronouncing the name of her new grandson, Mathew Loughlin Maclean Vincent.

As I grew older I developed nostalgia for my Lusitanian[4] past, and tried desperately to reintegrate into the community. But I soon grew to hate the hypocrisy of some of my compatriots, most of whom were immigrants who chose to spend several years working in Canada, only to retire to the Portuguese countryside and build their palatial retreats with the fat pensions they collected from the Canadian government. Like my father, who learned English quickly and severed ties with his homeland, I became a staunch Canadian. I could sing "The Maple Leaf For Ever"[5] before I was ten, and I spent my childhood years in French immersion. I became so good at masking my heritage that a few years ago when I applied for a job at a Toronto newspaper I was turned down because I was perceived as being too Anglo-Saxon.

"If you were ethnic, I'm sure they would have hired you on the spot," the wife of the paper's managing editor told me a year later.

---

4. Lusitania is an ancient Roman province that corresponds roughly to modern-day Portugal.
5. "The Maple Leaf For Ever" is a song written by Alexander Muir in 1867 (the year of Canadian Confederation).

135 But for most of my life being Portuguese seemed to me a liability. And then my mother bought that important first pair of pants. For a while it seemed that my life had changed. I was proud of my mother: 140 she was becoming like all the other mothers in the neighbourhood.

But my excitement was short-lived. A few days later, she decided they just wouldn't do. She carefully wrapped them 145 back up in the tissue paper, placed them in the cardboard Eaton's box, and returned them to the store.

(962 words)

Source: Vincent, Isabel. "Finding a Nationality That Fits." *Globe and Mail* 3 Dec. 1990. Print.

VOCABULARY AND COMPREHENSION

You may wish to work with a partner as you answer the questions below.

1. Why was the author's mother reluctant to wear pants?

_____

2. Which noun in the third paragraph (lines 16–32) means "a distinct group isolated within another, larger group?"

_____

Which adjective means "wealthy?"

_____

3. What is a hyphenated Canadian? Provide an example mentioned in the article.

_____

_____

_____

4. Why did the author and her brother anglicize their names?

_____

_____

5. In the seventh paragraph (lines 61–77), the author uses the expression *to follow suit*. From the context in which it is used, what does this expression mean? Why do you think the author was reluctant to follow suit?

_____

_____

6. As Canadian-born children of immigrant Portuguese parents, the author and her brother felt at home both inside and outside of Canada's Portuguese community.

☐ True   ☐ False

7. List two prejudices held by the author's mother and aunts concerning Canadian women.

a) _____

b) _____

8. An **ironic situation** can be defined as a situation in which reality is the opposite of what it appears to be. Working from this definition, explain how it was ironic that the author was refused a job at a Toronto newspaper.

_____

_____

_____

9. From the author's perspective, what did the mother's purchase of her first pair of pants represent?

_____

10. From the author's mother's perspective, what did the purchase of her first pair of pants represent?

_____

_____

DISCUSSION

→ Discuss each of the questions in small groups.

→ Be prepared to share your answers with the rest of the class and to explain them.

1. Is it possible to lay claim to more than one cultural identity? Explain.

2. What are the benefits of being a hyphenated Canadian? What are the challenges?

3. Why did the author's mother return her first pair of pants to the store?

© PEARSON LONGMAN • REPRODUCTION PROHIBITED

CULTURAL NOTE

One of the most famous *feuds* in North American history is that of the "Black Donnellys," which culminated in the massacre by a mob of vigilantes of five members of the Donnelly family on the night of February 4, 1880 in Biddulph Township, Ontario. Although the story is still not a popular one in the area where it happened, it has been enthusiastically enshrined in Canadian mythology—and has been the subject of songs, plays and numerous books.

READING 7.1 Hallway Culture Clash

Matthew Coutts is a reporter for the *National Post*. His article, "Hallway Culture Clash," appeared in the *Post* on May 22, 2009.

BEFORE READING

→ Scan the article, circling the vocabulary terms listed below.

→ Define these terms according to the context in which each is used.

1. salacious (adj.): _____

2. awkward (adj.): _____

3. **feud** (n.): _____

4. strive (v.): _____

5. standoffish (adj.): _____

6. errands (n.): _____

7. standoff (n.): _____

Examine the reading strategies suggested in "Appendix B: Effective Reading and Active Listening." Then read the questions on pages 164 to 166 *before* reading the article itself.

Hallway Culture Clash

By Matthew Coutts

When the **landlady** of my Toronto apartment building said an outraged neighbour had filed a complaint about me over an apparently inappropriate hallway interaction with his wife, my mind raced through the countless conversations I've had with fellow tenants, none of which seemed a possible source of offence.

VOCABULARY TIP

Landlady and *landlord* are examples of gender-specific job titles. There is much debate as to whether gender-specific job titles are appropriate in today's world, particularly when a gender-neutral job title exists. For another perspective on gender-neutral language, see "Humbled by a Real Fight for Women's Rights" in Unit 2 (p. 35).

It turns out it wasn't a salacious transaction that had caused the complaint, but rather a neighbourly and—to me— entirely forgettable greeting, little more than a brief "good morning" as I passed my neighbours on the way to work.

WORD CULTURE

The expression *walk on eggshells* (or *walk on eggs*) means "proceed very carefully." The expression dates from the late sixteenth century.

Still, it was enough of an affront for the man—once a doctor somewhere in the Middle East, my landlady clarified—to feel I had broken a cultural taboo. The incident started an awkward feud which has involved warnings not to repeat my indis-

cretion and one face-to-face shouting match, which included allusions to my impending death.

I expect the battle will wage on, as we appear to be stuck at an impasse.

His Muslim upbringing has ingrained in him a sense of entitlement to demand I not speak directly to his wife; and my prairie upbringing has ingrained in me a duty to strive for polite cohesion with my neighbours.

My landlady, who has handled the complaint with tittering trepidation, hasn't helped dispel the friction. She has told me to adhere to the demands because the man "could be dangerous," directing me to literally turn my back to the couple as they pass, never make eye contact and never hold the elevator for them, no matter what.

Life among neighbours has become increasingly complicated by multiculturalism, in this case making even the most affable salutation or good Samaritan gesture a practice in **walking on eggshells**. But in trying to adapt to a patchwork of often conflicting cultures, has civility become the casualty of accommodation?

I grew up in Manitoba, where it was an affront to your neighbour not to be cordial. If you didn't greet them by name you could be talked about in hushed voices and risked being labelled "standoffish."

Community amongst neighbours was not something to consider, it was a way of life. Call it prairie law.

Since moving to Toronto, I have lived in condos where asking your neighbour for the proverbial cup of sugar is greeted by skeptical, confused faces and closed doors.

But the majority have been open to the time-passing chats that break down barriers.

My midtown apartment building is home mostly to young professionals and is the definition of nondescript. I frequently hold doors for people carrying packages and say "you're welcome" if they show gratitude. I have run errands for unfamiliar neighbours because I was heading out into the rain anyway and there was no point in us both getting wet. I chat like a fool while waiting in the laundry room.

Of course, denying me the right to greet a woman in our shared hallway fails to measure up to reported conflicts that have caused a culture clash, such as Canada's reaction to a recent Afghan law allowing some husbands to withhold food until their wives agree to sex, or the case of a Toronto-area father and son accused of killing a daughter who refused to wear a hijab[6] at school.

I discussed my situation with the head of a prominent Muslim women's rights organization, who was understandably more concerned with the living conditions of the woman in question. She described the segregation of sexes as one of the worst examples of fundamentalist Islamic misinterpretation and dismissed the idea that my greeting could be construed as an offence.

Keep smiling, keep saying hello, she advised. The successful cohesion of cultures requires concessions from both sides. Offence or not, I have continued to greet those I share a building with, although the couple next door continue living in reclusion.

The alternative to this is to live amongst strangers in an icy standoff, fearful that the slightest attempt at community might be viewed as an affront. The alternative is to abandon prairie law, turn your back and close your eyes. And that sounds terrible.

(681 words)

Source: Coutts, Matthew. "Hallway Culture Clash." *National Post* 22 May 2009. Web. 3 Jul. 2009.

VOCABULARY AND COMPREHENSION

You may have to do some research to find some of the answers to the following questions.

1. **Collocations** are combinations of words that are frequently used together: *culture clash* is an example of a collocation. Identify the collocation used in the first paragraph of the article.

_____

_____

6. Piece of cloth covering the head and neck, worn by some Muslim women.

GRAMMAR TIP

Proper nouns ending in *s* can take *'s* or an apostrophe alone to indicate possession: *Mr. Smithers's apartment* or *Mr. Smithers' apartment*. Both are correct. For more information on possessive nouns, see page 222.

2. From the perspective of Mr. **Coutts's** neighbour, what cultural taboo had been broken?

_____

3. What explanation does Mr. Coutts give for greeting his neighbours?

_____

_____

4. In your own words, how does Mr. Coutts's landlady think he should react?

_____

_____

_____

5. How does Mr. Coutts feel about multiculturalism?

_____

_____

6. Paraphrase the following sentence: "But in trying to adapt to a patchwork of often conflicting cultures, has civility become the casualty of accommodation?"

_____

_____

7. According to Mr. Coutts, what is "prairie law"?

_____

_____

8. Most of Mr. Coutts's other neighbours decline his neighbourly overtures.

☐ True   ☐ False

9. Mr. Coutts equates his culture clash with the Canadian–Afghan culture clash over an Afghan law.

☐ True   ☐ False

10. The head of a prominent Muslim women's rights organization thinks Mr. Coutts should continue greeting his neighbours.

☐ True   ☐ False

11. In your own words, why does Mr. Coutts decide not to stop greeting his neighbours?

_____

_____

12. What is the subject of the article?

a) Neighbourly greetings   **c)** Feuding neighbours

b) Multiculturalism   **d)** An Afghan law

13. What is Mr. Coutts's opinion on the subject of the article?

_____

_____

14. List two factors that may have influenced Mr. Coutts's perspective.

a) _____

b) _____

A Question of PERSPECTIVE

If you were Mr. Coutts's Middle Eastern–Canadian neighbour, how would you feel about Mr. Coutts's continued greetings? What would you do?

DISCUSSION

→ Discuss each of the questions in small groups.

→ Be prepared to share your answers with the rest of the class and to explain them.

1. Do you usually greet your neighbours? Why or why not?

2. What do you think about the advice Mr. Coutts's landlady gave him?

3. What do you think about the advice the head of the prominent Muslim women's rights organization gave Mr. Coutts?

CD ← **LISTENING**

Neighbours: When to Say No to Nice?

When Matthew Coutts's article "Hallway Culture Clash" was first published, it caused quite a stir[7]—so much so that he was interviewed by CBC radio four days after publication. The interview to which you are about to listen, entitled "Neighbours: When to Say No to Nice?" was conducted by Aamer Haleem of *The Point* and broadcast on May 26, 2009.

BEFORE LISTENING

The words in the crossword puzzle on page 167 were taken from the radio excerpt.

→ Read the clues and fill in the corresponding blanks.

---

7. The expression *to cause a stir* means "to make people react."

Across

1. A newspaper article; also a homophone of peace. _____

3. Help something develop; encourage; also the family name of a famous Jodie. _____

6. Not offensive; harmless. _____

8. Move head up and down to greet someone. _____

9. Spend time thinking carefully and seriously about something; also the title of a section in each unit of this book. _____

Down

1. Synonym of "swear words." *a string of* _____

2. Synonym of "people," especially in American English. _____

4. Synonym of "unfriendly"; also describes uncleared sidewalks after a winter snow storm. _____

5. Phrasal verb meaning "to do things to complete a plan." *to* _____ *through on something*

7. Phrasal verb meaning "to meet somebody unexpectedly." *to* _____ *into someone*

Examine the reading strategies suggested in "Appendix B: Effective Reading and Active Listening." Then read the questions on pages 168 and 169 *before* listening to the audio clip.

COMPREHENSION

The questions below are in sequence: you will hear the answer to question 1, then question 2, then question 3, etc. If you miss an answer, do not worry about it; simply move on to the next question.

1. Fill in the blanks. "Now hardly anyone feels the need these days to rush over to their new neighbours with a freshly baked pie, but what do you do when you _____ them in the hallway or at the end of the driveway? Do you say, "Hello," make eye contact, _____ or do you just look away?" (Aamer Haleem)

2. What adjective does Mathew Coutts use to describe the atmosphere in the hallway since the incident with his neighbour?

   _____

3. According to Mr. Coutts, his landlady's advice was "... turn your back and close your eyes when your neighbours come by." He responds to this advice with sarcasm. What is his sarcastic response?

   _____

4. Mr. Coutts is from Brandon, Manitoba. What is the unofficial title of Brandon?

   _____

5. What prevented Mr. Coutts from speaking directly to the couple about the hallway incident?

   _____

6. Fill in the blanks. "... have you _____ that [advice to continue to engage the couple, particularly the woman], or have you decided that this is one relationship you don't need to _____ ?" (Aamer Haleem)

7. Since writing his article, Mr. Coutts has received several e-mails in which people describe similar experiences with people from ethnic backgrounds other than Muslim.

   ☐ True ☐ False

8. Circle the correct answer(s). More than one answer is possible.
   The host, Mr. Haleem, has lived in major cities around the world. From his perspective,
   a) people are people (people are pretty much the same wherever you go).
   b) an apartment building is equivalent to a small town (meaning they have comparable populations).
   c) people living in apartment buildings live in closer proximity than many people living in some suburban areas.
   d) someone's refusal to communicate due to religion or ethnic background should **be taken with a grain of salt**.

WORD CULTURE

The expression *to take something with a grain of salt* means "to not take something too seriously" (as used by Mr. Haleem in the Coutts's interview) or (more frequently) "to take something with a great deal of skepticism." In English, the expression has been around for a long time, being used at least as far back as the seventeenth century.

9. About midway through the interview, Mr. Haleem quotes the following sentence from Mr. Coutts's article: "… life among neighbours has become increasingly complicated by multiculturalism …" Mr. Coutts refers to this sentence as the "chin scratcher," meaning he wrote the sentence to make people think. While not explicitly stated during the interview, do you think that the host, Mr. Haleem, thinks that multiculturalism complicates life?

_____

_____

_____

_____

_____

10. What personal experiences do you think may have influenced Mr. Haleem's opinion?

_____

A Question of PERSPECTIVE

If you are well-travelled, how would your perspective on other cultures be different if you had never travelled at all? If you are not well-travelled, how would your perspective on other cultures be different if you had travelled a great deal? Does travel increase or decrease acceptance of other cultures? Explain.

DISCUSSION

→ Discuss each of the questions in small groups.

→ Be prepared to share your answers with the rest of the class and to explain them.

1. Is the reason provided by Mr. Coutts for not speaking directly to the couple after the hallway incident valid? Should he have tried harder? Justify your response.

2. Who knows their neighbours better? City folks or country folks? Explain.

3. With whom do you sympathize more, Mr. Coutts or Mr. Coutts's neighbour? What factors may be influencing your perspective?

VOCABULARY REVIEW

This two-part exercise is designed to review the vocabulary examined in the audio clip and to introduce two common expressions.

Part A

Without looking back at the clues and solutions provided on page 167, fill in the blanks with terms that are synonymous with the words in *italics*. Pluralize nouns and conjugate verbs as required. The first one has been done for you as an example.

Steve: Guess who I *met unexpectedly* (1) _____bumped into_____ yesterday?

Melissa: I couldn't say.

Steve: Bob! My old roommate Bob!

Melissa: The guy you fought with over that girl ... what was her name again?

Steve: Janice.

Melissa: Yup. The last time I saw you and Bob together, the atmosphere was rather *unfriendly* (2) _____ : the tension was so thick you could cut it with a knife—especially after he let out that *series of offensive words* (3) _____ !

Steve: Yeah, well that's all water under the bridge now.

Melissa: Really, how so?

Steve: Because Bob offered me a job. Can you believe it? He read that *article* (4) _____ I wrote for the local paper about the need to *encourage* (5) _____ relationships with the *people* (6) _____ who are important to us and bury the hatchet when there's been a falling-out with a friend. That last bit really struck a cord with him. He told me he *has been thinking carefully about* (7) _____ what I wrote for a couple of weeks now.

Melissa: So how are you going to *pursue* (8) _____ his offer?

Steve: He gave me his number at the publishing company where he works. I'd been afraid of Bob for the longest time, only to find out he's perfectly *harmless* (9) _____ after all.

Part B

In the conversation above, two well-known expressions are used: *water under the bridge* and *bury the hatchet*. From the contexts in which they are used, can you infer their meanings?

1. Water under the bridge: _____

   _____

   _____

2. Bury the hatchet: _____

Customary Behaviour

A custom is a traditional and widely accepted way of behaving that is specific to a particular group of people (a community). Every group has its customs. In a paragraph of 100 to 150 words, write about a custom particular to your family, peer group, culture or country of birth.

The Compare and Contrast Essay

As the name would suggest, a compare and contrast essay is one in which you find similarities and differences between two different subjects. For this essay, you are asked to compare and contrast a custom associated with a particular behaviour from two different cultures: your culture and another one. Base your essay on the academic essay outlined on page 9: you will need an introduction, a development and a conclusion.

→ Choose a custom associated with one particular stage of life: birth, childhood, adolescence, young adulthood (marriage, starting a family, parenting practices, etc.), retirement, old age or death.

→ Brainstorm all potential similarities and differences between your culture's custom and the other culture's custom. Retain the "best" similarities and differences and organize them into an effective whole. A good compare and contrast essay is often the by-product of a good brainstorming session.

→ Write five paragraphs, for a total of approximately 400 to 450 words. Dedicate one paragraph of the development to your culture's custom; one paragraph of the development to the other culture's custom; and one paragraph of the development to comparing and contrasting both cultures' customs.

→ When comparing and contrasting, use appropriate transition terms: on one hand … on the other hand; while one culture values X, the other values Y; etc.

The chart below provides a structural overview, detailing elements to consider. Remember to proofread your work prior to submission.

ESSAY SECTIONS	PARAGRAPHS	STRUCTURAL ELEMENTS
Introduction	1	• Begin with a grabber that introduces the cultures to be compared and contrasted. • End with a preview statement in which you outline the main points you will present and the order in which these points will be presented; for example, "Marriage ceremonies differ across cultures: the author[8] will begin by examining Canadian customs, continue by examining Chinese customs and conclude by comparing and contrasting both cultures' customs."
Development	2 3 4	• Use transition terms for each of the paragraphs in the development. • Present the customary behaviour of culture A in paragraph two. • Present the customary behaviour of culture B in paragraph three. • Compare and contrast the customary behaviours of cultures A and B in paragraph four.

8. Unless your teacher allows you to use the first person singular, use "the author" to refer to yourself.

ESSAY SECTIONS	PARAGRAPHS	STRUCTURAL ELEMENTS
Conclusion	5	• Begin with a transition term and summarize the similarities and differences between the two cultures. • End with a connection to the grabber (the two cultures you compared and contrasted).

Ⓟresent

Customary Clothing

Clothing, like customs, differs from one group to another. Working in a small group, match each article of clothing (or clothing accessory) with its definition by writing the letter of the definition in the space provided; then discuss the questions that follow.

DEFINITIONS

a) A ceremonial dagger worn by baptized Sikhs

b) A horizontal square board fixed on a skull-cap with a tassel worn by university graduates; also called a graduation cap

c) A soft-sided brimless cap worn by Orthodox Christian and Eastern Catholic clergy

d) Distinctive set of garments worn by a religious order

e) Boots popular with some youth subcultures

f) Garment worn by women in some Islamic traditions to cover the entire body

g) Generic name for "cowboy hat"

h) Historical dress of the Han Chinese people

i) Knee-length garment originating in the Scottish Highlands of the sixteenth century; traditionally worn by males

j) Modern Chinese suit

k) Piece of cloth that covers the head; worn to protect straightened hair; popular in some African-American cultures

l) Soft round cap usually made of wool felt; traditionally worn by French men and women

m) Strip of unstitched cloth wrapped around and draped over the body, worn by some Indian women

n) Thin, slightly rounded skullcap traditionally worn by observant Jewish men; also called a kippah

o) Traditional Chinese dress for men; literally means "long shirt"

p) Traditional Japanese garment worn by women, men and children

q) Traditional one-piece Chinese dress for women

r) A dot of red colour applied in the centre of the forehead close to the eyebrows; traditionally worn by South Asian women and girls

s) Turban (mostly) worn by Sikh men

t) Head covering traditionally worn by Muslim women

ARTICLES	ARTICLES
1. Beret	11. Hijab
2. Bindi	12. Kilt
3. Burka	13. Kimono
4. Changshan	14. Kirpan
5. Cheongsam	15. Mao suit
6. Dastar	16. Mortarboard
7. Doc Martens	17. Sari
8. Do-rag	18. Skufia
9. Habit	19. Stetson
10. Hanfu	20. Yarmulke

1. Which of the above-mentioned articles have you actually worn (and are not wearing at this particular moment)?

2. Is it sexist to reserve some items of clothing only for men, and others only for women? Explain your point of view.

3. Should society be allowed to dictate what articles of clothing (or clothing accessories) can and cannot be worn in public places? Justify your response.

You Can't Wear That!

A dress code is a set of rules specifying what can and cannot be worn by a group of people: a company dress code, a police or military dress code, a school dress code, a formal evening dress code, a religious dress code, etc.

For this oral presentation, you are asked to take a position for or against any dress code (or any part of a dress code) of your choosing. Should companies be allowed to ask employees to remove visible body piercings, such as nose rings or flesh tunnels?[9] Should male office workers be forced to wear suits and ties and female office workers, dresses, high heels and nylons? Should military men be forced to wear khakis? Should students be required to wear uniforms? Should North American brides only wear white and North American mourners, only black? Should priests be required to wear clerical collars and nuns, habits? In brief, should any group be allowed to tell its members what they can and cannot wear?

→ Prepare a five- to seven-minute presentation.

→ Refer to the "Oral Presentation Outline" provided for you on page 19.

© PEARSON LONGMAN • REPRODUCTION PROHIBITED

---

9. Type of body piercing jewellery designed to show off the stretching process, exposing holes created in the skin (typically in the earlobe); also known as a spacer.

Participate

In this section, you will work with another student on a joint writing and speaking project.

Interculturalism

Interculturalism is a philosophy that encourages exchanges between cultural groups within a society. Interculturalism strives to

1. fight discrimination and racism;

2. create opportunities for dialogue between cultures;

3. increase understanding of other cultures;

4. highlight cultural commonalities with a view to creating a common civic culture;

5. promote individual rights.[10]

One requirement of interculturalism is openness: you have to be willing to open yourself to others different from yourself, and this is exactly what you will be asked to do to complete this project.

Procedure

1. Working with a partner, brainstorm a list of cultures with which you are unfamiliar but about which you are curious.

2. Choose one cultural group that you would like to explore.

3. Brainstorm ways in which you could experience your chosen cultural group first-hand: visiting a museum, attending a cultural event, eating at a restaurant that serves the culture's traditional foods, downloading the culture's traditional recipes and making some of the foods, exploring a website about your chosen culture, etc. (While it may be easier for those living in large urban centres to explore other cultures, it is not impossible for those living in rural areas to do so: the latter may have to rely on "virtual exchanges" as opposed to "real exchanges.")

4. Experience the cultural group using the method of your choosing. Whenever possible, exchange with that group; for example, find an opportunity to speak to someone from the community and/or correspond with such a person by e-mail. If a true "exchange" is not possible, a true "experience" will do! It is important to ensure your safety: do not reveal your home address or other private information; meet people you do not know in a public place—and never meet them alone; provide friends or family members with the names and contact information of people with whom you wish to have an exchange; etc.

5. Write an appreciation of your exchange (or your experience). In your appreciation, indicate what you learned about the cultural group and list any commonalities noted between your culture and the cultural group explored.

6. Book an appointment with your teacher to discuss your experience and submit your appreciation. Your teacher may evaluate your discussion and your written appreciation.

---

10. Source: "Interculturalism." *Wikipedia.* Wikimedia Foundation, n.d. Web. 15 Dec. 2009.

Pursue

Related Works

The following works may be of interest for continued study.

TYPES OF WORKS	TITLES
Documentary	*Between: Living in the Hyphen*. Dr. Anne Marie Nakagawa. National Film board, 2005. • Documentary profiling seven Canadians of mixed ancestry. Available online at http://www.nfb.ca/film/between_living_in_the_hyphen/
Fiction	Campbell, Maria. *Half-Breed*. Toronto: Saturday Review Press, 1973. Print. • Autobiographical account of a Métis woman's experiences in Western Canada Choy, Wayson. *The Jade Peony*. Vancouver: Douglas & McIntyre, 1995. Print. • Reminiscences of three children growing up in Vancouver's Chinatown in the 1930s and '40s Kogawa, Joy. *Obasan*. Toronto: Lester & Orpen Dennys, 1981. Print. • Story of the Japanese-Canadian internment during the Second World War Vassanji, M. G. *The Gunny Sack*. London: Heinemann, 1989. Print. • Chronicles the lives of four generations of Asians living in East Africa
Movie	*Double Happiness*. Dir. Mina Shum. Fine Line Features, 1994. • A Chinese-Canadian woman tries to assert her independence from her family. *The Joy Luck Club*. Dir. Wayne Wang. Hollywood Pictures, 1993. • Relationships between Chinese-American women and their Chinese mothers
Non-Fiction	Blohm, Judith, and Terri Lapinsky. *Kids Like Me: Voices of the Immigrant Experience*. Boston: Intercultural Press, 2006. Print. • Twenty-six personal accounts of the immigrant experience Granatstein, J. L., and Norman Hillmer. *The Land Newly Found: Eyewitness Accounts of the Canadian Immigrant Experience*. Toronto: Thomas Allen, 2006. Print. • First-hand accounts of the Canadian immigrant experience
Short Story	Atwood, Margaret. "Dancing Girls." *Dancing Girls and Other Stories*.Toronto: McClelland & Stewart, 1977. Print. • Story of a young woman living in a boarding house with people from various cultural backgrounds

My eLab ✏ Visit My eLab for additional reading, listening and vocabulary practice.

Researching, Referencing and Revising

In this appendix, we will examine the three Rs: researching, referencing and revising.

Researching

For some of the writing assignments in *Perspectives*, you may have to conduct some research; this is particularly true for many of the proposed essay assignments.

With the rise of the Internet, research techniques have changed; before the Internet, students were sent to libraries to consult books, magazines, newspapers, academic journals, etc. Since the Internet, students have gone online to consult books, magazines, newspapers and academic journals—as well as web pages, blogs and wikis.

The advantages of researching on the Internet are obvious:

1. **Research can be conducted more quickly.**
   Research can be conducted at a time and in a place convenient to the researcher.

2. **Research can be conducted more efficiently.**
   Ask your parents and grandparents about using card catalogues to find research materials. Long live the search engine!

3. **The sources consulted are current.**
   By the time some books are published, the content may be out of date.

The disadvantage of Internet research is perhaps less obvious: not everything read or heard online is necessarily true because not everyone writing online is necessarily credible. In pre-Internet days, it was the task of publishers and academics to determine the veracity of information and hence the credibility of the information providers. Today, this task falls more squarely on the shoulders of the researcher.

EVALUATING WEBSITE CREDIBILITY

There are eight basic types of websites:[1]

1. Personal (vanity pages)
2. Promotional (sales)
3. Current events (newspapers, magazines, etc.)

---

1. Landsberger, Joe. "Evaluating Website Content." *Study Guides and Strategies.* Joe Landsberger, n.d. Web. 31 Jul. 2008.

4. Informational (specific subjects)
5. Advocacy (propaganda)
6. Instructional (academics)
7. Registrational (product and course registrations)
8. Entertainment

Some of these types of sites are obviously more credible than others.

Consider the following five guidelines when evaluating the credibility of website content:[2]

QUESTIONS	WHERE TO LOOK FOR ANSWERS
Guideline 1: Authority **a)** Who is responsible for the content? **b)** Is the person qualified? **c)** What are his or her academic credentials?	In the footer[3]
Guideline 2: Currency **d)** Are creation and editing dates indicated? **e)** Is the content up to date?	In the footer, header,[4] dateline or wiki "history" pages
Guideline 3: Coverage **f)** What is the focus (main topic) of the site? **g)** Is there a clear outline? Is the site easy to navigate?	In the footer, header, titles, subtitles and navigation menu
Guideline 4: Objectivity **h)** Is the content of the website biased? (e.g., Is a smokers' rights organization downplaying the dangers of second-hand smoke?)	Main content, hyperlinks, header, footer and URL (.gov, .com, .edu, etc.)
Guideline 5: Accuracy **i)** Is the website content accurate? **j)** Are sources listed? **k)** Are sources varied and verifiable? **l)** Are sources reliable?	Content (spelling, grammar and facts), bibliography, hyperlinks, header, footer and URLs cited (.gov, .com, .edu, etc.)

Refer to the Evaluation Sheet on the next page to help you evaluate website credibility when conducting research. Photocopy and complete one sheet for each website consulted.

---

2. Landsberger, Joe. "Evaluating Website Content." *Study Guides and Strategies*. Joe Landsberger, n.d. Web. 31 July 2008.
3. Information placed at the bottom of a page, separated from the main text.
4. Information placed at the top of a page, separated from the main text.

Evaluation Sheet

IDENTIFICATION		
Your Name		
Name of Website Evaluated		
URL of Website Evaluated		
Type of Website Evaluated Circle one: Personal / Promotional / Current Events / Informational / Advocacy / Instructional / Registrational / Entertainment		

EVALUATION		
QUESTIONS	**ANSWERS**	
a) Who is responsible for the content?		
b) Is the person qualified?	☐ Yes	☐ No
c) What are his/her academic credentials?		
d) Are creation and editing dates indicated?	☐ Yes	☐ No
e) Is the content up to date?	☐ Yes	☐ No
f) What is the focus (main topic) of the site?		
g) Is there a clear outline / Is the site easy to navigate?	☐ Yes	☐ No
h) Is the content of the website biased?	☐ Yes	☐ No
i) Are sources listed?	☐ Yes	☐ No
j) Are sources varied and verifiable?	☐ Yes	☐ No
k) Are sources reliable?	☐ Yes	☐ No
l) Is the website content accurate?	☐ Yes	☐ No

In your opinion, is the content of the website credible? Why or why not?

_____

_____

_____

_____

Referencing

Any research referred to in an essay must be correctly cited.

When you quote (use somebody's exact words), paraphrase (rephrase somebody's words) or refer to another writer's work, you must reference the writer to avoid plagiarism.

There are many different citation styles. The style suggested in this text-book is based on the *MLA Handbook for Writers of Research Papers*, seventh edition.

Basically, a citation has two interrelated parts:

1. Parenthetical reference
2. List of works cited

The parenthetical reference is in the body of the essay and the works-cited list appears at the end of the essay.

PARENTHETICAL REFERENCES

Parenthetical references are essential for quotes and paraphrases. Print sources (newspapers, books) and Internet sources are cited differently.

SOURCES	AUTHOR'S NAME *IS* MENTIONED IN THE REFERENCE	AUTHOR'S NAME *IS NOT* MENTIONED IN THE REFERENCE
Print	Parenthetical references should include the **page number**. *Wayson Choy establishes the setting of* The Jade Peony *in the very first sentence:* "The old man first visited our house when I was five, in 1933" (5).	Parenthetical references should include the **author's last name** and the **page number**. *The setting is established in the very first sentence of* The Jade Peony*:* "The old man first visited our house when I was five, in 1933" (Choy 5).
Internet	No parenthetical reference is required. *Claire Ramplin gives a favourable review of Wayson Choy's memoire* Not Yet, *adding that the memoire* "... has cemented his position as one of his country's most beloved elders."	Parenthetical references should include the **author's last name**. *Wayson Choy's memoire* Not Yet "... has cemented his position as one of his country's most beloved elders" (Ramplin).

Complete references to Choy and Ramplin must appear in the works-cited list. If the author of your quote is cited in somebody else's work, put the abbreviation *qtd. in* (quoted in) before the indirect source you quote. For example: (Smith, qtd. in Jones 25). In this case, a complete reference to Jones should appear in the works-cited list.

Remember: If an organization writes an article, the organization is considered to be the author.

WORKS CITED

On a separate page at the end of your essay, you must list all the sources that you paraphrased or quoted. Follow these guidelines:

- The sources are in alphabetical order by last name (or by organization or title if no author has been identified).
- *Italicize* or <u>underline</u> (if not using a word processor) all titles of complete works (newspapers, books, TV series, etc.).
- Use quotation marks for titles of works contained in another work (articles, book chapters, TV episodes, etc.).
- Capitalize all important words in a title.
- If using an Internet source, indicate the title of the work or website in italics, the name of the publisher or sponsor in regular print, the date of publication (using the form "Day Month Year"),[5] the medium (web) and the date accessed.
- All entries are double-spaced, and the second (and third and fourth) lines of each entry are indented.

The following chart lists common types of sources accompanied by examples.

TYPE OF SOURCES	EXAMPLES
Book with one author	Choy, Wayson. *The Jade Peony*. Vancouver: Douglas & McIntyre, 1995. Print.
Article in a newspaper or magazine	Coutts, Matthew. "Hallway Culture Clash." *National Post* [Toronto] 22 May 2009: A13. Print.
Article on a website	Ramplin, Claire. "Surviving Two Big Heart Attacks Made Wayson Choy a Firm Believer in Luck." *Sunday Times* [Perth]. The Sunday Times, 19 Sept. 2009. Web. 9 Nov. 2009.
Website	Citizenship and Immigration Canada. "Asian Heritage Month." *Multiculturalism*. Citizenship and Immigration Canada, 28 Apr. 2009. Web. 9 Nov. 2009.

Revising

Before submitting your writing for evaluation, you must revise your work. Revising requires that you carefully reread your work, improving your writing (editing) and isolating and correcting any errors you might have made (proofreading).

---

5. Write "n.d." if the publication date is not indicated.

THE PROOFREADING PROCESS

When proofreading your work:

1. Make a list of the types of errors you commonly make on a separate sheet of paper. (It is easier to spot errors when you know what you are looking for!) Update your list on a regular basis as you receive feedback from your instructor.

2. Read your work aloud (if the context permits), circling any parts you have trouble reading (difficulty reading may indicate a mistake) and any words that "look wrong."

3. Read your work again (silently or aloud)—this time from the end to the beginning—circling any words that look misspelled: this strategy is great for identifying spelling mistakes and spotting typos!

4. Reread your paper one final time (silently or aloud), completing the checklist below.

5. Rewrite your paragraph or essay, using reference materials (your common error checklist, dictionaries and a grammar book) to help you correct any mistakes.[6]

Proofreading Checklist

Refer to the checklist below when proofreading your work.

TASKS	✓	TASKS	✓
1. All important words in the title of my essay are capitalized.		9. The simple form of the verb is used after modal auxiliaries.	
2. Each sentence starts with a capital letter and ends with a period, a question mark or an exclamation mark.		10. All conditionals are correctly used.	
		11. Regular and irregular nouns are correctly pluralized.	
3. All verbs are conjugated correctly.		12. All verbs used with non-count nouns are singular.	
4. Pronouns agree with the nouns for which they stand.		13. Comparative and superlative adjective and adverb forms are correctly used.	
5. I have verified my spelling in a dictionary.			
6. I have verified my choice of vocabulary in a dictionary.		14. Adjectives and adverbs are placed in the correct order.	
7. I have verified all punctuation in a grammar book.		15. My writing is double-spaced and my handwriting (if the assignment is not completed on a word processor) is legible.	
8. The number of words used meets the minimum (and maximum) word counts.			

6. Wells, Jaclyn M. et al. "Proofreading Your Writing." *The Purdue OWL.* Purdue U Writing Lab, n.d. Web. 31 Dec. 2008.
Writing@CSU. "Editing and Proofreading Strategies." *Writing Guides.* Colorado State University, n.d. Web. 31 Dec. 2008.

Effective Reading and Active Listening

Effective Reading

The definition of *effective reading* depends in large part on *what* you are reading and on *how deeply* you are asked to delve into the topic at hand.

In this textbook, you are asked to read poems, short stories and novels as well as opinion, news and research articles. What you are reading should influence how you read it!

In addition, readings included in this textbook always come with questions; however, this is not necessarily true for other readings (for example, Internet readings completed for research). In the first case, you know how deeply you need to delve into a given topic from the number and complexity of questions asked. In the second case, you alone must make the decision.

Bearing this in mind, the following general reading strategies are suggested to optimize reading comprehension:

1. **Read at a time and in a place that optimize your ability to concentrate.**
   Are you an early bird or a night owl? Do you need complete silence to read, or do you like a bit of background noise? When possible, choose what works best for you.

2. **Think about why you're reading what you're reading.**
   Thinking about why the reading was assigned (or why you chose to read it) will help you focus on the reading at hand.

3. **Think about what you already know about the reading topic.**
   You usually have some knowledge about a topic before reading. Thinking about prior knowledge puts you into a context conducive to getting the most out of your reading.

4. **Skim first; read second.**
   When reading news, opinion or research articles, skim the title and subtitles, any comprehension questions, the first and last paragraphs, the first sentence of other paragraphs, diagrams, illustrations, references, etc. The idea is to get an overall picture of what you are about to read before you actually read it. Skimming (or surveying) is the first step in SQ3R, an abbreviation for a well-known reading strategy: **S**urvey, **Q**uestion, **R**ead, **R**e-cite (or Recall) and **R**eview.

5. **Read actively.**
   While reading, make charts, draw mind maps (visually connect ideas together) or pictures, highlight, underline or create an outline to maximize comprehension. Circle transition terms. In the absence of questions, make a list of your own questions, the answers to which can be found in the text.

6. **Use a dictionary effectively.**
   Try to understand the meaning of a new word from the context in which it is used. Looking up every new word in a dictionary can be distracting: look up words the meanings of which cannot be inferred from context alone and the meanings of which are essential to understanding.

7. **Reread!**
   If time permits, reread poems, short stories or articles a second (or third) time, taking a short break (if possible) between each rereading. This strategy is particularly important when reading complex texts or texts containing a great deal of new information.

Active Listening

The key word in the term *active listening* is the adjective *active*. Many think of listening as a "passive" skill: nothing could be further from the truth! Here are a few actions you can take to optimize your listening comprehension.

1. **Create an environment conducive to listening.**
   Sit at the front of the class when participating in class listening exercises, and select a quiet place to complete take-home listening exercises.

2. **Look like you're listening!**
   While listening, make sure your posture is appropriate: laying your head on a desk while listening will facilitate sleep, not concentration.

3. **Think about why you are listening to the passage.**
   Thinking about why the listening passage was assigned will help you focus on the listening passage at hand.

4. **Think about what you already know about the topic of the listening passage.**
   Draw on prior knowledge to put you in the right frame of mind for listening. Try to predict core vocabulary.

5. **Take notes.**
   Write down key terms as you hear them. Use symbols (&), abbreviations (govt.), colours (highlight main ideas in one colour and supporting details in another) and even pictures to summarize what you hear.

6. **Take advantage of nonverbal cues.**
   When watching a video clip, use speakers' body language to help you understand the message.

7. **Read listening instructions and comprehension questions effectively!**
   Listening passages used for class exercises or evaluations come with instructions and/or comprehension questions. Apply effective reading strategies 4 through 7 (see previous section) before listening.

Grammar Guide

Sentence Structure

A sentence is a word or a group of words that has a stated or implied subject, a verb and expresses a complete thought.

> *Go!*
> *Bob is leaving.*

A sentence may be affirmative, negative or interrogative.

> *She studies.*
> *She does not study.*
> *Does she study?*

In this section, we will examine types of sentences that people use when writing down their thoughts.

There are three basic types of sentences:

1. **Simple**
   Mr. Johnson is a teacher.

2. **Compound**
   Kevin is a student, and he works part-time.
   Mary is tired; however, she will finish the work.
   Edith is leaving; she is going home.

3. **Complex**
   Tell Charlie to call me when he gets up.
   Because he works hard, he does well in English.

Simple Sentences

Another term for a simple sentence is an "independent clause."

A simple sentence has only one independent clause, typically comprising one subject and one verb.

Compound Sentences

A compound sentence has two (or more) independent clauses. There are three basic types.

TYPES	DESCRIPTIONS	EXAMPLES
1	Two (or more) independent clauses linked by a *coordinate conjunction*.	Kent eats well, *and* he exercises.
2	Two (or more) independent clauses linked by an *adverbial conjunction*.	Mary bought a new sound system; *furthermore*, she bought a plasma TV.
3	Two (or more) independent clauses linked by a *semicolon*.	I walk fast; she walks slowly.

Note: • The coordinate conjunction is preceded by a comma.
 • The adverbial conjunction is preceded by a semicolon and followed by a comma.

between the two clauses

There are seven coordinate conjunctions.

COORDINATE CONJUNCTIONS	FUNCTIONS	EXAMPLES
and	To add	Sally moved to Toronto, *and* she got a job.
but	To contrast	Jennifer got an A, *but* Anne got a B.
for	To introduce a reason	Christopher did well on his test, *for* he worked hard.
nor	To add an idea after a negative statement	He didn't laugh, *nor* did he cry.
or	To show an alternative	You can do the dishes, *or* you can take out the trash.
so	To show a result	He worked hard, *so* he made a lot of money.
yet	To introduce two opposing ideas	I slept well, *yet* I am still tired.

Note:
- *Nor* is followed directly by an auxiliary + subject + simple form of the verb:
  *She doesn't work, nor **does** she study.*
- As a coordinate conjunction, *for* means "because."

can begin sentence

There are many adverbial conjunctions. Some of the more common are listed below.

ADVERBIAL CONJUNCTIONS	FUNCTIONS	EXAMPLES
accordingly as a result consequently hence therefore thus	To show a result	The instructions said to wash before using; *accordingly*, I put my new set of dishes in the dishwasher and turned it on. My gas gauge wasn't working properly; *as a result*, I ran out of gas on the way to the cottage. They arrived late for work every day last week; *consequently*, they were fired. Julie had a lot of alterations made to her wedding dress; *hence*, it cost twice the original price. Only residents are allowed to park in that lot; *therefore*, you must show your ID at the gate. Our bank account was overdrawn last month; *thus*, we had to pay a bank fee.
also furthermore moreover	To add	Her car insurance covered the repair costs; *also,* it covered the replacement costs of damaged items. Tina's parents bought her a car; *furthermore*, they paid for her studies. Students must register for the trip to Ecuador by Friday; *moreover*, a cheque for $500 must accompany their registration form.
however nevertheless nonetheless	To contrast	Todd does well in school; *however*, he is not enjoying his studies. Derek didn't have time to study very much for his geography exam; *nevertheless*, he passed the mid-term. I can't do a complete revision of your document; *nonetheless*, I will check it for spelling mistakes.

indeed in fact	To emphasize	Jenny did well on her test; *indeed*, she received a perfect grade. Joan won the half-marathon last weekend; *in fact*, she set a new record.
at the same time meanwhile	To show simultaneous actions	Please make the additions I have noted; *at the same time*, check the document for gender-specific vocabulary. Susan was rushing about; *meanwhile*, her husband was taking a nap.
otherwise	To show an alternative consequence	Arrive at work on time; *otherwise*, you will be fired.
for example for instance	To introduce an example	Strong earthquakes can actually move cities; *for example*, Concepción, Chile, was moved at least three metres in the February 2010 quake. Houseplants can remove chemical pollutants from the air; *for instance*, English ivy and rubber plants are very effective in cleaning the air in your house.
likewise similarly	To show similarity	Drivers must wear seat belts; *likewise*, all passengers must buckle up. Teenage boys often perform worse than teenage girls on tests; *similarly*, teenage boys often behave worse than teenage girls at school.

Note: • Coordinate and adverbial conjunctions can express similar functions: to add, to contrast, to show a result and to show an alternative.

Complex Sentences

A complex sentence has two (or more) clauses, at least one of which is a dependent clause.

A dependent clause begins with a subordinate conjunction (or dependent marker) such as *because*: the idea expressed is incomplete. To complete the idea, an independent clause is required.

GRAMMAR TIP

When a dependent clause precedes an independent clause, a comma separates the two clauses.

Because she had run five miles, *Shelly was exhausted.* } complex sentence
      dependent clause   independent clause

Some of the more common subordinate conjunctions are listed below.

SUBORDINATE CONJUNCTIONS	FUNCTIONS	EXAMPLES
after before	To establish a sequence	*After* the police officer had stopped me last night, she asked me to take a Breathalyzer test. *Before* they went to class, they had reviewed their notes.

SUBORDINATE CONJUNCTIONS	FUNCTIONS	EXAMPLES
although even if even though	To present opposing ideas	*Although* she likes mathematics, she is not doing well in his course. *Even if* the condominium is expensive, she is going to have a home of her own. He accepted the invitation *even though* he will have to rent a tuxedo for the occasion.
as just as	To make a comparison	You will do *as* you are told. *Just as* smoking is bad for your health, it is a very expensive habit.
as long as	To introduce a period of time	He will love her *as long as* he lives.
because	To give a reason	*Because* the teachers were on strike, classes were cancelled.
if unless	To set a condition	*If* it rains, she will stay home. *Unless* skateboarders want to run the risk of serious head injuries, they should wear a helmet.
since when	To refer to a point in time	*Since* they got married, they have been fighting like cat and dog. *When* we painted the pool, we repaired the broken tiles as well.
where wherever	To introduce a place	He will go *where* she goes. Special agents are sent *wherever* people report UFO sightings.
whether	To introduce a choice	She does not seem to care *whether* she lives or dies.
while	To show simultaneous actions	They were in chemistry class *while* their friends were in French class.

Note: • Sentences containing relative clauses are also complex sentences. Relative clauses are introduced by relative pronouns such as *who*, *whom*, *that*, *which* and *whose*.
*The student **who ran five miles** was exhausted.*

Pinpoint

CC =	Coordinate Conjunction
AC =	Adverbial Conjunction
SC =	Subordinate Conjunction

Join the two sentences by adding the appropriate conjunction. Make any necessary changes to punctuation, capitalization and sentence order. Write your answers in the space provided.

1. You can cut the grass. You can wash the car. (CC – show an alternative)

   you can cut the grass, or you can wash the car

2. There had been an avalanche. The highway through the mountains was closed. (SC – give a reason)

   Because there had been an avalanche, the highway through the mountain was closed

3. He won the lottery. He quit his job. (CC – show a result)

   He won the lottery, so he quit his job

4. Geoff exercises three times a week. He has not lost any weight. (AC – show a contrast)

   Geoff exercises three times a week; however, he has not lost any weight

5. Robin got an A. Ryland got a B. (CC – show a contrast)

   Robin got an A but Ryland got a B

6. There was a serious accident on the highway. They missed their exam. (AC – show a result)

   There was a serious accident on the highway; thus, they missed their exam.

7. My e-mail account was hacked yesterday. My computer was infected with a virus. (AC – add)

   My e-mail account was hacked yesterday; also, my computer was infected with a virus

8. He lives two blocks from his office. He is often late for work. (SC – present opposing ideas)

   Although he lives two blocks from his office, he is often late for work

9. She doesn't eat red meat. She doesn't drink wine. (CC – add)

   She doesn't eat red meat, and she doesn't drink wine

10. I am finding my chemistry course difficult. I nearly failed my last exam. (AC – emphasize)

    I am finding my chem. course difficult; in fact, I nearly failed my last exam

My eLab 🖉 Now that you have pinpointed your current level of understanding of sentence types, complete related exercises on My eLab for practice and instant feedback.

② Present, Past and Future Tenses

THE PRESENT

The Simple Present Tense

The simple present is used to express

GRAMMAR TIP

Verbs conjugated in the affirmative using the third person singular (*he, she, it*) take an "s"; all other persons (*I, you, we, they*) do not.

- general or repeated actions;
  *Jackson **drives** his children to school **every morning**.*

- facts.
  *We **add** a day to February **every leap year**.*

Key Terms:
in the morning, every morning, every afternoon, every day, often, on the weekend, in general, always, often, as a rule …

Let's examine the following conjugation chart:

AFFIRMATIVE	NEGATIVE	INTERROGATIVE (YES/NO QUESTIONS)
I eat.	I do not eat. (I don't eat.)	Do I eat?
You eat.	You do not eat. (You don't eat.)	Do you eat?
He/She/It eats.	He/She/It does not eat. (He/She/It doesn't eat.)	Does he/she/it eat?
We eat.	We do not eat. (We don't eat.)	Do we eat?
They eat.	They do not eat. (They don't eat.)	Do they eat?

Note:
- In the negative and interrogative forms, the auxiliary *does* is used for the third person singular and *do* is used for all other persons.
- In the negative and interrogative forms, only the auxiliary is conjugated.
- In the negative form, the contractions *don't* and *doesn't* are formed by substituting an apostrophe for the letter "o" and contracting two words into one.
- In the interrogative form, the auxiliary precedes the subject.
- To transform a yes/no question into an information question, place the question word before the auxiliary:
  Does he eat? ➡ ***Why** does he eat?*
  Do they eat? ➡ ***Where** do they eat?*
- Common question words for information questions include *who, what, where, when, why* and *how*. (See Chart A, page 247.)

Spelling Tips:

- Add "s" to most verbs in the third person singular.
  answer ➡ *answers*

- If the verb ends in "ch," "sh," "s" or "x," add "es."
  catch ➡ *catches*   *wash* ➡ *washes*
  miss ➡ *misses*   *fix* ➡ *fixes*

- If the verb ends in "y," change the "y" to "i" and add "es."
  study ➡ *studies*

Pronunciation of Final "S"

There are three ways to pronounce the final "s":

1. As an /s/ sound: *eats, talks, walks …*

2. As a /z/ sound: *lives, loves, moves …*

3. As an /iz/ sound: *kisses, fizzes, washes …*

Pronounce the final "s" as an /s/ sound when the last sound of the verb is voiceless.

Pronounce the final "s" as a /z/ sound when the last sound of the verb is voiced.

Pronounce the final "s" as an /iz/ sound when the simple form of the verb ends in "s," "z," "sh," "ch," "x," "se," "ge" or "ce."

GRAMMAR TIP

Like the verb *be*, the verb *have* is conjugated differently in the third person singular: *he has, she has, it has.*

The Verb *Be*

The verb *be* is conjugated differently from all other verbs.

Take a look at the conjugation chart below:

AFFIRMATIVE	NEGATIVE	INTERROGATIVE (YES/NO QUESTIONS)
I am here. (I'm here.)	I am not here. (I'm not here.)	Am I here?
You are here. (You're here.)	You are not here. (You're not here. You aren't here.)	Are you here?
He/She/It is here. (He's/She's/It's here.)	He/She/It is not here. (He's/She's/It's not here. He/She/It isn't here.)	Is he/she/it here?
We are here. (We're here.)	We are not here. (We're not here. We aren't here.)	Are we here?
They are here. (They're here.)	They are not here. (They're not here. They aren't here.)	Are they here?

Note:
- The first person singular (*I*) and the third person singular (*he, she* or *it*) have different conjugations from the other persons: *am* and *is* are used, not *are*. No auxiliary is required.
- In the negative form, contractions can be formed in two different ways for all persons but the first person singular.
- In the interrogative form, the verb precedes the subject.
- To transform a yes/no question into an information question, place the question word before the verb:
  Is he here? ➡ **Why** *is he here?*

The Present Continuous Tense

GRAMMAR TIP

Use contractions for spoken English and informal writing: *I'm home.*

The present continuous is used to express

- actions occurring now;
  The mayor is speaking with reporters right now.

- planned future actions.
  We are leaving for Europe on Monday.

Key Terms:

at the moment, in an hour, now, right now, at this very minute, in a couple of hours, tomorrow, next week, next month …

The present continuous is composed of an auxiliary (*be* conjugated in the simple present, see above) and a present participle (verb + "ing"). Examine the following conjugation chart:

AFFIRMATIVE	NEGATIVE	INTERROGATIVE (YES/NO QUESTIONS)
I am eating. (I'm eating.)	I am not eating. (I'm not eating.)	Am I eating?
You are eating. (You're eating.)	You are not eating. (You're not eating. You aren't eating.)	Are you eating?
He/She/It is eating. (He's/She's/It's eating.)	He/She/It is not eating. (He's/She's/It's not eating. He/She/It isn't eating.)	Is he/she/it eating?
We are eating. (We're eating.)	We are not eating. (We're not eating. We aren't eating.)	Are we eating?
They are eating. (They're eating.)	They are not eating. (They're not eating. They aren't eating.)	Are they eating?

Note:
- In the negative form, contractions can be formed in two different ways for all persons but the first person singular.
- In the interrogative form, the auxiliary precedes the subject.
- To transform a yes/no question into an information question, place the question word before the auxiliary:
  Are they eating? ➡ *When are they eating?*
- Non-action verbs (stative verbs) such as *know* cannot be used in the continuous form: *I ~~am knowing~~ know you.* Other non-action verbs include *be, believe, belong, exist, forget, hate, hear, like, love, need, own, possess, prefer, remember, see* and *understand*.

THE PAST

The Simple Past Tense

The simple past is used to express

- completed actions.
  She won two gold medals at the 2010 Olympics. (Past tense of irregular verb *win*)
  He moved to Ireland three years ago. (Past tense of regular verb *move*)

Key Terms:
last night, yesterday, last weekend, last month, last year, five years ago ...

Irregular Verbs

Irregular verbs have irregular past forms: eat ➡ *ate.* The only way to know the form is to memorize it—or refer to an irregular verb chart such as the one on pages 248–249. Examine the conjugation chart below:

AFFIRMATIVE	NEGATIVE	INTERROGATIVE (YES/NO QUESTIONS)
I ate.	I did not eat. (I didn't eat.)	Did I eat?
You ate.	You did not eat. (You didn't eat.)	Did you eat?
He/She/It ate.	He/She/It did not eat. (He/She/It didn't eat.)	Did he/she/it eat?
We ate.	We did not eat. (We didn't eat.)	Did we eat?
They ate.	They did not eat. (They didn't eat.)	Did they eat?

Note:
- In the affirmative form, the verb conjugation is always the same.
- In the negative and interrogative forms, only the auxiliary is conjugated and it is always the same: *did.*
- A yes/no question is created by placing the auxiliary before the subject. To transform a yes/no question into an information question, place the question word before the auxiliary: *Did you eat?* ➡ ***What** did you eat?*

The verb *be* is conjugated differently from all other verbs. Take a look at the conjugation chart below:

AFFIRMATIVE	NEGATIVE	INTERROGATIVE (YES/NO QUESTIONS)
I was there.	I was not there. (I wasn't there.)	Was I there?
You were there.	You were not there. (You weren't there.)	Were you there?
He/She/It was there.	He/She/It was not there. (He/She/It wasn't there.)	Was he/she/it there?
We were there.	We were not there. (We weren't there.)	Were we there?
They were there.	They were not there. (They weren't there.)	Were they there?

Note:
- *Be* is an "irregular" irregular verb. There are two simple past forms: *was* for the first and third person singular (I, he/she/it) and *were* for all other persons.
- No auxiliary is required.
- A yes/no question is created by placing the verb before the subject. To transform a yes/no question into an information question, place the question word before the verb: *Was he there?* ➡ ***Why** was he there?*
- Some verbs are both regular and irregular.
  The simple past of the verb *burn* can be either *burnt* (irregular) or *burned*
  The simple past of the verb *learn* can be either *learnt* (irregular) or *learned* (regular).
  Many verbs have two simple past conjugations.

Regular Verbs

Now let's turn our attention to the regular verbs. Examine the following conjugation chart:

AFFIRMATIVE	NEGATIVE	INTERROGATIVE (YES/NO QUESTIONS)
I consumed.	I did not consume. (I didn't consume.)	Did I consume?
You consumed.	You did not consume. (You didn't consume.)	Did you consume?
He/She/It consumed.	He/She/It did not consume. (He/She/It didn't consume.)	Did he/she/it consume?
We consumed.	We did not consume. (We didn't consume.)	Did we consume?
They consumed.	They did not consume. (They didn't consume.)	Did they consume?

Note:
- In the affirmative form, the verb conjugation is always the same (ending with "ed").
- In the negative and interrogative forms, only the auxiliary is conjugated—and it is always the same: *did*.
- A yes/no question is formed by placing the auxiliary before the subject. To transform a yes/no question into an information question, place the question word before the auxiliary:
Did you consume? ➡ **What** *did you consume?*

Spelling Tips:
- Add "ed" to form the simple past of most regular verbs:
visit ➡ *visited*
- Some verbs ending with a "consonant-vowel-consonant" structure require that you double the last consonant before adding "ed":
jog ➡ *jogged*
- If the regular verb ends in "y," change the "y" to "i" before adding "ed":
study ➡ *studied*
- If the regular verb ends in "e," simply add a "d":
place ➡ *placed*

Pronunciation of "ed"

While the endings of regular verbs are quite regular ("ed"), the pronunciation of these endings is not. There are three ways to pronounce the final "ed" of regular verbs:

1. As a /t/ sound: *walked, talked, stopped ...*
2. As a /d/ sound: *planned, exercised, moved ...*
3. As an /id/ sound: *downloaded, landed, planted ...*

Pronounce the final "ed" endings of regular verbs as a /t/ sound when the last sound of the verb is voiceless.

Pronounce the final "ed" endings of regular verbs as a /d/ sound when the last sound of the verb is voiced.

Pronounce the final "ed" endings of regular verbs as an /id/ sound when the last letters of the verb are "t," "te," "d" or "de."

The Past Continuous Tense

The past continuous is used to express

- actions in progress at a specific time in the past;
  *They **were waiting** for the bus **at 8 a.m.***

GRAMMAR TIP

The past continuous is sometimes called the past progressive. Think about the terms *continuous* or *progressive* to remind yourself to use this tense for ongoing actions only.

- interrupted actions;
  *He **was preparing** supper **when** the electricity went off.*

- simultaneous actions;
  ***While** he **was completing** the bibliography, she **was proofreading** the report.*

- background actions.
  *The crew **was preparing** the stage **at the same time as** the band **was practising**.*

Key Terms:
at 8 a.m., when, while, at noon, at midnight, at the same time as …

The past continuous is composed of an auxiliary (*be* conjugated in the simple past) and a present participle (verb + "ing"). Examine the following conjugation chart:

AFFIRMATIVE	NEGATIVE	INTERROGATIVE (YES/NO QUESTIONS)
I was eating.	I was not eating. (I wasn't eating.)	Was I eating?
You were eating.	You were not eating. (You weren't eating.)	Were you eating?
He/She/It was eating.	He/She/It was not eating. (He/She/It wasn't eating.)	Was he/she/it eating?
We were eating.	We were not eating. (We weren't eating.)	Were we eating?
They were eating.	They were not eating. (They weren't eating.)	Were they eating?

Note: • The present participle is always the same—but remember that the verb *be* has two irregular forms: *was* and *were*.

- A yes/no question is created by placing the auxiliary before the subject. To transform a yes/no question into an information question, place the question word before the auxiliary:
  Was he eating? ➡ ***Why** was he eating?*

GRAMMAR TIP

Don't use the past continuous to express past habits; use the simple past instead:
When I was a teenager, I ~~was jogging~~ jogged every day.

THE FUTURE

Both *will* and *be going to* can be used to express

- opinions about the future;
  *I hope he **will** call **today**.*
  *I hope he **is going to** call **today**.*

- predictions.
  *I predict it **will** snow **on the weekend**.*
  *I predict it **is going to** snow **on the weekend**.*

In most situations, *will* and *be going to* are interchangeable when used to express opinions about the future or make predictions.

Exception: When the predicted action is imminent (about to happen), the *be going to* form is used.
*Look at those dark clouds! It ~~will rain~~ **is going to** rain any second.*

However, in some situations, only *will* can be used; in others, only the *be going to* form can be used.

Will

In addition to expressing opinions about the future and making predictions, *will* is used to express

- willingness;
  (A kitchen timer is ringing.)
  Sue: *Barb, **will** you **take** the cookies out of the oven?*
  Barb: *Sure, I**'ll do** that.*

- promises.
  *She promises she **will finish** the marketing plan on time.*

Key Terms:
today, tomorrow, promise, next month, next week, next weekend, next year, soon, tonight …

Let's examine the conjugation chart below:

AFFIRMATIVE	NEGATIVE	INTERROGATIVE (YES/NO QUESTIONS)
I will eat. (I'll eat.)	I will not eat. (I'll not eat. I won't eat.)	Will I eat?
You will eat. (You'll eat.)	You will not eat. (You'll not eat. You won't eat.)	Will you eat?
He/She/It will eat. (He'll/She'll/It'll eat.)	He/She/It will not eat. (He'll/She'll/It'll not eat. He/She/It won't eat.)	Will he/she/it eat?
We will eat. (We'll eat.)	We will not eat. (We'll not eat. We won't eat.)	Will we eat?
They will eat. (They'll eat.)	They will not eat. (They'll not eat. They won't eat.)	Will they eat?

Note:
- The auxiliary *will* is used for all persons.
- In the negative form, contractions can be formed in two different ways.
- In the interrogative form, the auxiliary precedes the subject.
- In the first person singular and plural, *shall* is sometimes used instead of *will* in the interrogative form:
  Shall I eat? Shall we eat?
- To transform a yes/no question into an information question, place the question word before the auxiliary:
  Will you eat? ➡ ***What** will you eat?*
- We use the contracted form of *will* with nouns and interrogative pronouns in spoken English: *Bob'll be on time. What'll he do?*
  Do not use this form in written English.

The *Be Going To* Form

In addition to expressing opinions about the future and making predictions, *be going to* is used to express

- prior plans;
  (Papers, receipts and a calculator are on the desk.)
  He **is going to prepare** his income tax return **this evening**.

  (Suitcases are packed and at the door.)
  Tomorrow morning, they **are going to drive** to PEI to visit their grandparents.

- imminent actions.
  *Hurry up! You **are going to miss** your flight! Don't you know what time it is?*

Key Terms:

in a minute, next week, next month, next weekend, next year, soon, tonight ...

The *be going to* form consists of the present continuous tense of the verb *go* + the full infinitive.
   She is going to eat.

Examine *be going to* conjugations in the chart below:

AFFIRMATIVE	NEGATIVE	INTERROGATIVE (YES/NO QUESTIONS)
I am going to eat. (I'm going to eat.)	I am not going to eat. (I'm not going to eat.)	Am I going to eat?
You are going to eat. (You're going to eat.)	You are not going to eat. (You're not going to eat. You aren't going to eat.)	Are you going to eat?
He/She/It is going to eat. (He's/She's/It's going to eat.)	He/She/It is not going to eat. (He's/She's/It's not going to eat. He/She/It isn't going to eat.)	Is he/she/it going to eat?
We are going to eat. (We're going to eat.)	We are not going to eat. (We're not going to eat. We aren't going to eat.)	Are we going to eat?
They are going to eat. (They're going to eat.)	They are not going to eat. (They're not going to eat. They aren't going to eat.)	Are they going to eat?

Note: • To transform a yes/no question into an information question, place the question word before the auxiliary:

   Is he going to eat? ➡ ***Where** is he going to eat?*

Pinpoint

Part A

Use the correct forms of the verbs in parentheses, choosing the appropriate tense from the two suggested at the end of each question. Do not use the same tense twice in the same question.

1. The city (fill) ___is filling___ potholes today. Workers (fill) ___fill___ more than 30,000 potholes every year. (simple present/present continuous)

2. She (understand) ___understands___ why her business (lose) ___is losing___ money, but she can't do anything to stop the losses. (simple present/present continuous).

3. Is that music you (listen) ___are listening___ to? All I (hear) ___hear___ is noise! (simple present/present continuous)

4. The DVD Depot (have) ___is having___ a sale this weekend. The store (have) ___has___ a great selection of indie movies. (simple present/present continuous)

5. The cashiers (count) ___were counting___ the deposits when a gunman (enter) ___entered___ the bank. (simple past/past continuous)

6. While I (wash) ___was washing___ the dishes last night, I (cut) ___cut___ my finger on a knife. (simple past/past continuous)

7. I (pour) ___was pouring___ coffee when the handle on the coffee pot (break) ___broke___, splattering coffee everywhere. (simple past/past continuous)

8. ___Will___ you (be) ___be___ quiet? You (wake) ___are going to wake___ the baby! (future with *will*/future with *be going to*)

9. I (open) ___will open___ that door for you; I can see your arms are full of groceries. ___Are___ you (make) ___going to make___ supper tonight? (future with *will*/future with *be going to*)

10. I (bring) ___will bring___ the salad if you will bring the dessert. I am sure we (have) ___are going to have___ a fabulous meal! (future with *will*/future with *be going to*)

Part B

Fill in each blank with the correct form of the verb in parentheses using one of the following tenses: the simple present, the present continuous, the simple past, the past continuous, the future with *will* or *be going to*. Do not use contractions. In some cases, more than one answer is possible.

1. Gerry usually (take) ___takes___ the bus to school, but it's really cold today so his father (drive) ___is driving___ him.

2. The students (read) ___read___ three novels for their course last semester. They (tell) ___told___ their teacher that two would have been enough.

3. I (speak) ___spoke___ with my parents last night and (make) ___made___ plans for the holidays. They (pay) ___are___ ___paying___ for my ticket so I can fly home.

4. New furniture (cost) ___costs___ a lot of money. Can you afford to redecorate your office?

5. Ned (change) ___was changing___ in the locker room when the fire alarm (ring) ___rang___ yesterday.

6. I (go) ___will go___ to the store in a few minutes. Do you need anything?

7. The children (sleep) ___are sleeping___. Don't disturb them.

8. Suzanne (travel) ___travels___ a lot for her job. Last week, she (teach) ___taught___ a course in Halifax. Right now, she (give) ___is giving___ a seminar in Quebec City. Next week, she (lead) ___will lead___ a workshop in Whitehorse.

9. We (need) ___will need /are going to need___ more printer paper today. We have only a hundred sheets left.

10. I (get) ___will get___ the manager if you want more information about refunds.

My eLab   Now that you have pinpointed your current level of understanding of the present, past and future tenses, complete related exercises on My eLab for practice and instant feedback.

③ The Perfect Aspect

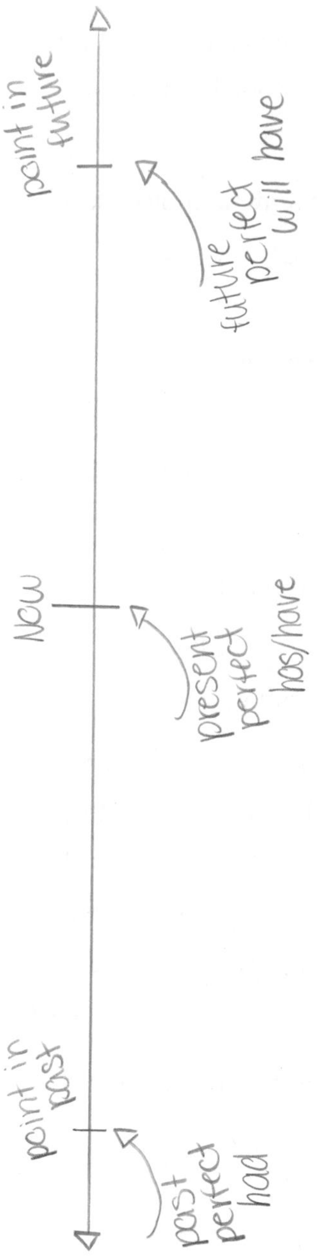

In the previous section, you examined the present, past and future tenses. Here, you will examine a new aspect to these tenses: the perfect aspect.

The perfect aspect is used for a past happening that is seen in relation to a later time or event.[1]

The present perfect is used to express the past as it relates to a present time or event:

*This morning, I **have drunk** three cups of coffee.*

The past perfect is used to express the past as it relates to a past time or event. The past perfect shows a relationship between two past times or events, one of which is "more in the past" than the other:

*By 10 o'clock this morning, I **had drunk** three cups of coffee.*

The future perfect is used to express the past as it relates to a future time or event. The future perfect shows a relationship between two future times or events, one of which is "less in the future" than the other:

*By 10 o'clock tomorrow morning, I **will have drunk** three cups of coffee.*

All three perfect tenses—present, past and future—can be used in the continuous form: *I have been drinking*; *I had been drinking*; and *I will have been drinking*. The continuous form indicates the (limited) duration of an event and that the event may not be complete.

The Simple Present Perfect

The present perfect is used to express

- actions occurring at an indefinite time in the past;
  She has eaten at that restaurant.
  (We don't know *when* she ate there; we just know that she has eaten there.)

- actions occurring in an incomplete period of time;
  *I have done my homework **today**.*
  (*Today* is not finished.)

- incomplete actions (or actions beginning in the past and continuing in the present);
  *They have been in that restaurant **for** two hours (or **since** 8:00 pm).*
  (They arrived at the restaurant two hours ago, and they are still there now.)

- recent actions.
  They have just finished eating.
  (A recent action is a past action close in time to the present moment.)

Key Terms:

today, for, since, just, ever, never, yet, this week, this year, recently …

The present perfect is formed by conjugating *have* in the simple present tense and adding the past participle. The past participle of regular verbs is the same as the simple past form: *walk* ➡ *walked* ➡ *walked*. The past participle of irregular verbs varies (see Chart B, page 248): *eat* ➡ *ate* ➡ *eaten*.

(left margin handwritten timeline labels)
point in future
future perfect will have
now
present perfect has/have
point in past
past perfect had

---

1. Leech, Geoffrey N. *Meaning and the English Verb*. New York: Longman, 1987. 35. Print.

Examine the following conjugation chart:

AFFIRMATIVE	NEGATIVE	INTERROGATIVE (YES/NO QUESTIONS)
I have eaten. (I've eaten.)	I have not eaten. (I've not eaten. I haven't eaten.)	Have I eaten?
You have eaten. (You've eaten.)	You have not eaten. (You've not eaten. You haven't eaten.)	Have you eaten?
He/She/It has eaten. (He's/She's/It's eaten.)	He/She/It has not eaten. (He's/She's/It's not eaten. He/She/It hasn't eaten.)	Has he/she/it eaten?
We have eaten. (We've eaten.)	We have not eaten. (We've not eaten. We haven't eaten.)	Have we eaten?
They have eaten. (They've eaten.)	They have not eaten. (They've not eaten. They haven't eaten.)	Have they eaten?

Note:
- The auxiliary *has* is used for the third person singular and *have* for all other persons.
- In the negative form, contractions can be formed in two different ways.
- In the interrogative form, the auxiliary precedes the subject.
- To transform a yes/no question into an information question, place the question word before the auxiliary:

  Have you eaten? ➡ **What** *have you eaten?*

Questions with *Ever* and *Yet*

Compare the following two questions and answers:

1. *Has Karen **ever** eaten at that restaurant?*
   - ➡ *Yes, Karen has eaten at that restaurant.*
   - ➡ *No, Karen has **never** eaten at that restaurant.*

2. *Has Karen eaten at that restaurant **yet**?*
   - ➡ *Yes, Karen has eaten at that restaurant.*
   - ➡ *No, Karen has not eaten at that restaurant **yet**.*

In the first question, the speaker does not know whether Karen has eaten at the restaurant.

In the second question, the speaker does not know whether Karen has eaten at the restaurant—but thinks she will eat there one day.

GRAMMAR TIP
- The adverb *yet* is placed at the end of interrogative and negative sentences.
- *Ever* is placed before the past participle in interrogative sentences.
- *Never* is placed before the past participle in negative sentences.

Comparing the Simple Past and the Present Perfect

Examine the following two sentences:

Simple past: *I **did** my homework this morning.*
Present perfect: *I **have done** my homework this morning.*

Both of these sentences are correct—in the right contexts! The first sentence is correct *if it is no longer morning,* while the second sentence is correct *if it is still morning.*

GRAMMAR TIP

Conversations often begin in the present perfect but continue in the simple past.

Q: *Have you eaten at any good restaurants lately?*
A: *Yes, yesterday we **ate** at the new bistro on the corner.*

Sometimes, students have difficulty knowing whether to use the simple past or the present perfect.

When unsure which tense to use, ask yourself the following questions:

1. Do I know when the action occurred?
2. Is the period of time in which the action is occurring finished?
3. Is the action finished?
4. Is the action in the distant past?

If the answer to any of these questions is "yes," use the simple past; otherwise, use the present perfect.

The Present Perfect Continuous

Like the simple present perfect, the present perfect continuous is used to express

- actions occurring at an indefinite time in the past;
  She has been sleeping poorly.

- actions occurring in an incomplete period of time;
  *They have been studying hard **this year**.*

- incomplete actions (or actions beginning in the past and continuing in the present).
  *We have been dancing **for** hours.*

When there is no specific reference to time, the present perfect continuous expresses a recent action.

Key Terms:
this year, today, for, since, just, recently …

Unlike the simple present perfect, the present perfect continuous emphasizes the

- duration of an action, answering the question *how long*;
  She has been sleeping poorly (for a couple of weeks now).

- continuation of an action;
  They have been studying hard this year (as they always have).

- temporariness of an action.
  We have been dancing for hours (and will need to stop soon).

The present perfect continuous is formed by conjugating *be* in the simple present perfect and adding the present participle of the verb (verb + "ing"). Examine the following conjugation chart:

AFFIRMATIVE	NEGATIVE	INTERROGATIVE (YES/NO QUESTIONS)
I have been eating. (I've been eating.)	I have not been eating. (I've not been eating. I haven't been eating.)	Have I been eating?
You have been eating. (You've been eating.)	You have not been eating. (You've not been eating. You haven't been eating.)	Have you been eating?
He/She/It has been eating. (He's/She's/It's been eating.)	He/She/It has not been eating. (He's/She's/It's not been eating. He/She/It hasn't been eating.)	Has he/she/it been eating?
We have been eating. (We've been eating.)	We have not been eating. (We've not been eating. We haven't been eating.)	Have we been eating?
They have been eating. (They've been eating.)	They have not been eating. (They've not been eating. They haven't been eating.)	Have they been eating?

Note:
- The auxiliary *has* is used for the third person singular and *have* for all other persons.
- In the negative form, contractions can be formed in two different ways.
- In the interrogative form, the auxiliary precedes the subject.
- Remember that non-action verbs (stative verbs) cannot be used in the continuous form: *I have been knowing known them for decades.*
- To transform a yes/no question into an information question, place the question word before the auxiliary: *Have you been eating?* ➡ ***What** have you been eating?*

The Simple Past Perfect

The simple past perfect is used to express

- an action that occurred before another past time or action.
  ***Before** he started breakfast, he had made a big pot of coffee.*
  ***After** she had corrected her students' exams, she entered the marks on her computer.*
  When Stephanie arrived at the arena, the team had finished its practice.

In the first two examples, the time sequence is clear; it is not necessary to use the past perfect except in formal writing. In these examples, the simple past may be used:

  Before he started breakfast, he made a big pot of coffee.
  After she corrected her students' exams, she entered the marks on her computer.

In the third example, the time sequence is unclear; it is therefore necessary to use the past perfect to indicate that the team finished its practice *before* Stephanie arrived. Changing the past perfect to the simple past would also change the meaning of the sentence, indicating that the team finished its practice *after* Stephanie arrived:

> When Stephanie arrived at the arena, the team finished its practice.

The simple past perfect is formed by conjugating *have* in the simple past and adding the past participle. Examine the following conjugation chart:

AFFIRMATIVE	NEGATIVE	INTERROGATIVE (YES/NO QUESTIONS)
I had eaten. (I'd eaten.)	I had not eaten. (I'd not eaten. I hadn't eaten.)	Had I eaten?
You had eaten. (You'd eaten.)	You had not eaten. (You'd not eaten. You hadn't eaten.)	Had you eaten?
He/She/It had eaten. (He'd/She'd/It'd eaten.)	He/She/It had not eaten. (He'd/She'd/It'd not eaten. He/She/It hadn't eaten.)	Had he/she/it eaten?
We had eaten. (We'd eaten.)	We had not eaten. (We'd not eaten. We hadn't eaten.)	Had we eaten?
They had eaten. (They'd eaten.)	They had not eaten. (They'd not eaten. They hadn't eaten.)	Had they eaten?

Note:
- The auxiliary *had* is used for all persons.
- In the negative form, contractions can be formed in two different ways.
- In the interrogative form, the auxiliary precedes the subject.
- To transform a yes/no question into an information question, place the question word before the auxiliary:
  Had you eaten? ➡ ***What*** *had you eaten?*

The Past Perfect Continuous

The past perfect continuous is used to express

- an ongoing action that occurred before another past time or action.
  It had been snowing heavily for two days when the police finally closed the roads.

The past perfect continuous emphasizes the duration of the ongoing action and may indicate the ongoing action to be a recent one:
  His hands were dirty because he had been gardening.

The past perfect continuous is formed by conjugating *be* in the simple past perfect and adding the present participle of the verb (verb + "ing"). Examine the following conjugation chart:

AFFIRMATIVE	NEGATIVE	INTERROGATIVE (YES/NO QUESTIONS)
I had been eating. (I'd been eating.)	I had not been eating. (I'd not been eating. I hadn't been eating.)	Had I been eating?

You had been eating. (You'd been eating.)	You had not been eating. (You'd not been eating. You hadn't been eating.)	Had you been eating?
He/She/It had been eating. (He'd/She'd/It'd been eating.)	He/She/It had not been eating. (He'd/She'd/It'd not been eating. He/She/It hadn't been eating.)	Had he/she/it been eating?
We had been eating. (We'd been eating.)	We had not been eating. (We'd not been eating. We hadn't been eating.)	Had we been eating?
They had been eating. (They'd been eating.)	They had not been eating. (They'd not been eating. They hadn't been eating.)	Had they been eating?

Note:
- The auxiliary *had* is used for all persons.
- In the negative form, contractions can be formed in two different ways.
- In the interrogative form, the auxiliary precedes the subject.
- Remember that non-action verbs (stative verbs) cannot be used in the continuous form: *I had ~~been knowing~~ known them for decades.*
- To transform a yes/no question into an information question, place the question word before the auxiliary: *Had you been eating?* ➡ ***What** had you been eating?*

The Simple Future Perfect

The simple future perfect is used to express

- an action that will be completed before another future time or action. ***By the time** we next see one another, I will have graduated college.*

The dependent clause refers to the future but uses the simple present and not the future with *will*:

***Before** Steve ~~will return~~ returns home, he will have played golf in many different countries.*

Key Terms:
by the time, before, by next January …

The simple future perfect is formed by conjugating *have* in the simple future (future with *will*) and adding the past participle. Examine the following conjugation chart:

AFFIRMATIVE	NEGATIVE	INTERROGATIVE (YES/NO QUESTIONS)
I will have eaten. (I'll have eaten.)	I will not have eaten. (I'll not have eaten. I won't have eaten.)	Will I have eaten?
You will have eaten. (You'll have eaten.)	You will not have eaten. (You'll not have eaten. You won't have eaten.)	Will you have eaten?

AFFIRMATIVE	NEGATIVE	INTERROGATIVE (YES/NO QUESTIONS)
He/She/It will have eaten. (He'll/She'll/It'll have eaten.)	He/She/It will not have eaten. (He'll/She'll/It'll not have eaten. He/She/It won't have eaten.)	Will he/she/it have eaten?
We will have eaten. (We'll have eaten.)	We will not have eaten. (We'll not have eaten. We won't have eaten.)	Will we have eaten?
They will have eaten. (They'll have eaten.)	They will not have eaten. (They'll not have eaten. They won't have eaten.)	Will they have eaten?

Note:
- The auxiliary *will* is used for all persons.
- In the negative form, contractions can be formed in two different ways.
- In the interrogative form, the auxiliary precedes the subject.
- To transform a yes/no question into an information question, place the question word before the auxiliary:
  Will you have eaten? ➡ ***What*** *will you have eaten?*

The Future Perfect Continuous

The future perfect continuous is used to express

- an ongoing action that will be completed before another future time or action.
  By the time I finish college, I will have been studying for nearly fifteen years.

The future perfect continuous emphasizes the duration of the ongoing action:
  *By next summer, I will have been working at my current job **for more than a decade**!*

Key Terms:
by the time I …, by next summer, by 2055 …

The future perfect continuous is formed by conjugating *be* in the simple future perfect and adding the present participle of the verb (verb + "ing"). Examine the following conjugation chart:

AFFIRMATIVE	NEGATIVE	INTERROGATIVE (YES/NO QUESTIONS)
I will have been eating. (I'll have been eating.)	I will not have been eating. (I'll not have been eating. I won't have been eating.)	Will I have been eating?
You will have been eating. (You'll have been eating.)	You will not have been eating. (You'll not have been eating. You won't have been eating.)	Will you have been eating?
He/She/It will have been eating. (He'll/She'll/It'll have been eating.)	He/She/It will not have been eating. (He'll/She'll/It'll not have been eating. He/She/It won't have been eating.)	Will he/she/it have been eating?

We will have been eating. (We'll have been eating.)	We will not have been eating. (We'll not have been eating. We won't have been eating.)	Will we have been eating?
They will have been eating. (They'll have been eating.)	They will not have been eating. (They'll not have been eating. They won't have been eating.)	Will they have been eating?

Note:
- The auxiliary *will* is used for all persons.
- In the negative form, contractions can be formed in two different ways.
- In the interrogative form, the auxiliary precedes the subject.
- Remember that non-action verbs (stative verbs) cannot be used in the continuous form: *I will have ~~been knowing~~ known them for decades.*
- To transform a yes/no question into an information question, place the question word before the auxiliary:
  Will you have been eating? ➡ ***What** will you have been eating?*

Pinpoint

Fill in each blank with the correct form of the verb in parentheses using one of the following tenses: the simple present perfect, the present perfect continuous, the simple past perfect, the past perfect continuous, the simple future perfect or the future perfect continuous. Do not use contractions. In some cases, more than one answer is possible.

1. I want to travel to Portugal next year. My grandmother (be) _____ _____ there many times, and her favourite city is Lisbon. I (save) _____ money for two years now, and I (accumulated) _____ over $1500. By the time this semester is over, I (add) _____ another $800 to my savings.

2. Last summer, I decided to get a credit card. After I (compare) _____ _____ information from several banks, I chose the GIP Bank. It (serve) _____ me well since then.

3. I wanted to buy a car last year. I checked out deals on the Internet. I (look) _____ for a used Corvette for a couple of weeks when I found one at a good price. However, I (not, check) _____ _____ the fine print: the car needed a new motor!

4. Fraudsters (develop) _____ a lot of telephone and Internet scams. By the time you finish this exercise, people around the world (lose) _____ money.

5. Our family moved from Mexico to Canada back in July, and we (live)

_____ here for five months. When the first

snowstorm hit, we wondered whether we (make) _____

the right move.

6. I (run) _____ for the bus last Saturday evening when I

tripped; I sprained an ankle and fractured a wrist.

7. Sheila (ski) _____ for many years now. She

placed tenth in the last Winter Olympics and is hoping for a gold medal in

the next Games.

8. My uncle drove off the road on the way home last night. It was no surprise.

He (have) _____ too much to drink before he left the party.

9. Our sociology study group is talking to octogenarians for our project on

aging. By the end of the month, we (conduct) _____

_____ interviews for twenty-five days, and we

(speak) _____ with more than one hundred

people over the age of eighty.

10. I (have) _____ a lot of trouble with

my computer lately. I (check) _____ it for viruses

several times this week, but I (find) _____ any.

My eLab ✎ Now that you have pinpointed your current level of understanding of the perfect aspect, complete related exercises on My eLab for practice and instant feedback.

4 Modals and Conditionals

MODALS

In this section, you will examine ways of expressing different moods and various conditions.

Modal auxiliaries, also known as modals, are special verbs used along with other verbs to express a particular *mood*.

> *Alexandre Despatie **can** dive superbly.* (Ability)
> *The government **should** negotiate with its workers.* (Advisability)

Modals can be used to express

- ability;
  *She **can** cook well.*
  *He **could** jog for miles when he was a teenager.* (Past)

- advisability;
  *He **should** apologize to her today.*
  *She **should** have put gas in the car yesterday.* (Past)

- obligation;
  *You **must** be on time.*
  *You **have to** be on time.* (Informal)
  *He **has got to** pass all his exams to stay on the hockey team.* (Informal)
  *You **had to** be on time.* (Past)

- possibility;
  *They **may** study tonight.*
  *He **might** do his homework.*
  *John **could** call tomorrow morning.*
  *She **might** have lost her gloves at the arena last night.* (Past)

- logical conclusion;
  *Someone is at the door. Oh, that **must** be Harold.*
  *It **must** have snowed in the mountains.* (Past)

- preference.
  *I **would rather** have steak than chicken.*
  *I **would rather** have had steak.* (Past)

The simple form of the verb directly follows most modal auxiliaries. In such cases, the modal auxiliary is the same for all persons. To indicate past time with some auxiliaries, use *have* plus the past participle, as seen in the above examples.

Examine the chart below.

FUNCTIONS	MODAL AUXILIARIES	AFFIRMATIVE	NEGATIVE	INTERROGATIVE (YES/NO QUESTIONS)
Ability	can	He can skate.	He cannot skate. (He can't skate.)	Can he skate?
Past	could	He could skate.	He could not skate. (He couldn't skate.)	Could he skate?
Advisability	should	She should pay.	She should not pay. (She shouldn't pay.)	Should she pay?
Past	should	She should have paid.	She should not have paid. (She shouldn't have paid.)	Should she have paid?
Obligation	must	I must pay my bills.		Must I pay my bills?
Informal	have to	I have to pay the fine.	I do not have to pay the fine. (I don't have to pay the fine.)	Do I have to pay the fine?
Past	had to	I had to pay the fine.	I did not have to pay the fine. (I didn't have to pay the fine.)	Did I have to pay the fine?
Possibility	may	It may be sunny.	It may not be sunny.	
	might	It might rain.	It might not rain.	Might it rain?
	could	It could snow.		Could it snow?
Past	may	She may have remembered.	She may not have remembered.	
	might	He might have had an accident.	He might not have had an accident.	
	could	He could have prevented the accident.		Could he have prevented the accident?
Logical conclusion	must	That must be Carole at the door.	That must not be Carole at the door. (That mustn't be Carole at the door.)	Must that be Carole at the door?
Past	must	He must have been sick.	He must not have been sick. (He mustn't have been sick.)	
Preference	would rather	They would rather eat pizza.	They would rather not eat pizza.	Would they rather eat pizza?

Note:
- *Could* can also be used to make suggestions: *You could study harder.* In this case, *could* takes on a function similar to *should* when used as a modal of advisability: *You should study harder.*
- Do not use *must not* to express a lack of obligation: *He ~~must not~~ does not have to speak.* Only *had to* can be used to express a past obligation.
- Do not use *may* in the interrogative form to express possibility: *~~May~~ Might (Could) he speak?*
- Do not use *could not* to express a lack of possibility: *He ~~could~~ may (might) not speak.*
- The contractions *mayn't* and *mightn't* are rarely used.
- The semi-modals *have to* and *have got to* are also followed by the simple form of the verb, but don't forget to conjugate them for he/she/it: *he has, she has, it has*!

I have to leave.	*I can leave.*
You have to leave.	*You can leave.*
He/She/It **has to** *leave.*	*He/She/It can leave.*
We have to leave.	*We can leave.*
They have to leave.	*They can leave.*

- *Have to* is a semi-modal and is conjugated, unlike pure modals:

  (a) Present

  In the negative and interrogative forms, the auxiliary *does* is used for the third person singular, while *do* is used for all other persons.

  (b) Past

  In the negative and interrogative forms, the auxiliary *did* is used for all persons.

- In the interrogative form, the modal auxiliary or the auxiliary *do*, *does* or *did* precedes the subject.
- To transform a yes/no question into an information question, place the question word before the auxiliary:
  Should he apologize? ➡ **Why** *should he apologize?*

GRAMMAR TIP

The semi-modals *have to* and *have got to* are used to express obligation.
I have to study and *I have got to study* both mean *I must study.*
These forms are frequently used in spoken English.

Modals may also be used to make and respond to polite requests.

REQUESTS WITH *I* OR *WE* AS THE SUBJECT	REQUESTS WITH *YOU* AS THE SUBJECT
May I (or we) leave? Yes, you may. No, you may not.	*Would* you explain this to me? Yes, I ~~would~~ will. No, I ~~would~~ will not.
Might I (or we) be excused? Yes, you ~~might~~ may. No, you ~~might~~ may not.	*Will* you show me how to do this? Yes, I will. No, I will not.
Could I (or we) go? Yes, you ~~could~~ may. No, you ~~could~~ may not.	*Could* you repeat that, please? Yes, I ~~could~~ will. No, I ~~could~~ will not.

CONDITIONALS

A conditional has an "if-clause" and a "result clause." The most common conditionals can be classified as follows:

1. **Present real conditional**
   If Sonia listens to the teacher, she will get great marks.
   (Sonia will probably listen to her teacher, so great marks are to be expected.)

   The present real conditional is used to talk about real present/future situations, as the action in the if-clause is quite *probable*.

2. **Present unreal conditional**
   If John listened to the teacher, he would get great marks.
   (John will probably not listen to his teacher, so great marks are not to be expected.)

   The present unreal conditional is used to talk about unreal present/future situations, as the action in the if-clause is *improbable* or *imaginary*.

3. **Past unreal conditional**
   If Adam and Christine had listened to the teacher, they would have gotten great marks.
   (Adam and Christine did not listen to the teacher, so great marks were not obtained.)

   The past unreal conditional is used to talk about unreal past situations, as the action in the if-clause did not occur. The situation is purely *hypothetical*.

GRAMMAR TIP

When conjugating *be* in the if-clause of the present unreal conditional, use *were* for all persons when using formal English:
If Jane ~~was~~ were here, we could start the party.
Were is a subjunctive form.

Examine the chart below:

CONDITIONALS	IF-CLAUSES	RESULT CLAUSES
Present real	If he studies, simple present	he will (he'll) succeed. subject + *will* + simple form of the verb
Present unreal	If he studied, simple past	he would (he'd) succeed. subject + *would* + simple form of the verb
Past unreal	If he had (he'd) studied, past perfect	he would (he'd) have succeeded. subject + *would have* + past participle

Note: • Never use the simple future in an if-clause:
      If he ~~will study~~ studies, he will succeed.
    • Even though the simple past is used in the if-clause of the present unreal conditional, the situation being discussed is in the present/future.
    • The negative form may be used in either—or both—clauses:
      If he does not study hard, he will not succeed.
      If he did not study hard, his father would be upset.
      If he had studied hard, his father would not have been disappointed in him.

To form interrogative sentences, invert the subject and the auxiliary in the result clause.

If he studies, he will succeed. ➡ *If he studies, **will he** succeed?*

If he studied, he would succeed. ➡ *If he studied, **would he** succeed?*

If he had studied, he would have succeeded. ➡ *If he had studied, **would he** have succeeded?*

> **GRAMMAR TIP**
> If you place the result clause before the if-clause, remove the comma.
> *If he studies, he will succeed. Will he succeed if he studies?* ➡ *He will succeed if he studies.*

Conditionals with Modals

The result clause of a conditional can contain a modal. Refer to the chart below for examples:

CONDITIONALS	EXAMPLES WITH MODALS
Present real	• Result clause with *may, can, must* or *should* If she is hungry, she *may* eat my lunch. (Permission) If he burns supper, we *can* eat out. (Possibility) If his stomach is gurgling, he *must* be hungry. (Logical conclusion) If we are served well, we *should* leave a good tip. (Advisability)
Present unreal	• Result clause with *could* or *might* If she knew his name, she *could* call him. (Present ability) If she asked him out, he *might* accept. (Present possibility)
Past unreal	• Result clause with *could have* or *might have* If she had known his name, she *could have* called him. (Past ability) If she had asked him out, he *might have* accepted. (Past possibility)

Pinpoint

Part A

Use an appropriate modal or semi-modal auxiliary with each of the verbs in parentheses, modifying verb forms as required. In some cases, more than one answer is possible. Do not use contractions.

1. My MP3 player isn't working; my brother (forgot) _must have forgotten_ to recharge it.

2. The sky is clouding over. We (get) _might get_ some rain this afternoon.

3. Riding a bike without a helmet is dangerous. You (wear) _should wear_ protective headgear every time you go for a ride.

4. I have an appointment on Delaney Street. _Can_ you (tell) _tell_ me how to get there?

5. I drove into a ditch last night on the way home, but it wasn't my fault.
I (avoid) _was avoiding_ a deer on the highway.

6. Someone is knocking at the door. It (be) _might be_ Steve;
he said he would drop by today.

7. I need some help. I (lift, not) _cannot lift_ this heavy box.

8. He (renew) _should renew_ his lease before the end of
the month, or he will lose the apartment.

9. Dorothy did not go to work yesterday. She (sick) _must be
sick_ .

10. When Josh was in high school, he was in terrible shape. He (run) _could
not run_ more than a mile.

Part B

Complete each of the following conditional sentences using the correct form of the verb in parentheses. In some cases, more than one answer is possible. Do not use contractions.

1. If my parents retire next year, they (sell) _will sell_ their
big house and buy a condo.

2. If he had been over sixty-five years of age, he (receive) _would have
received_ a discount at the cinema.

3. If Margaret worked Friday, she (take) _would take_ the following
Monday off.

4. If seniors (be) _were_ valued for their contribution to society,
they would have more self-esteem.

5. Karl could have been living a life of luxury if he (lose, not) _had not
lost_ so much money in the stock market crash.

6. They (sign) _would've signed_ the contract if the working
conditions had been better.

7. If the storm hadn't damaged our boat, we (leave) _would have
left_ the island.

8. If the weather (be) _is_ good tomorrow, we can go water skiing.

9. You (got) _would've gotten_ a better tip if you had
been polite to the customers.

10. If Mike (be) _were_ here, we could serve the birthday cake.

My eLab ✎ Now that you
have pinpointed your current
level of understanding of
modals and conditionals,
complete related exercises
on My eLab for practice and
instant feedback.

⑤ Passive Voice and Reported Speech

In this section, you will examine two different ways of expressing yourself: using the active or the passive voice and using direct (quoted) or reported (indirect) speech.

The Active and the Passive Voice

There are two voices in English: the active voice and the passive voice. When the subject is doing the action, the active voice is being used. When the subject is being acted upon, the passive voice is being used.

ACTIVE	PASSIVE
Elsie Hambrook *wrote* the article.	The article *was written* by Elsie Hambrook.
You *must submit* the assignment on time.	The assignment *must be submitted* on time.

In the active voice, the subject (Elsie Hambrook/you) "acts": the subject is active.

In the passive voice, the subject (article/assignment) "is acted upon": the subject is passive.

In general, the passive voice is used when the performer of the action is

* unimportant;
  The lawn was mowed.

* unknown.
  The necklace has been stolen.

To make an active sentence passive
1. identify the verb tense of the active verb;
2. conjugate *be* in the same tense as the active verb;
3. add the past participle of the active verb.

*Andrew **is writing** the final report.* (Active)
➡ *The final report **is being written** by Andrew.* (Passive)

> **Note:**
> * The active verb is in the present continuous tense.
> * *Be* in the present continuous tense = *is being*.
> * The past participle of *write* = *written*.

GRAMMAR TIP

For modals in the passive voice, use the base form *be* followed by the past participle:
*They **must** do their work.* ➡
*Their work **must be done**.*

The object of the active sentence (the report) becomes the subject in the passive sentence.

Look at the chart on the next page for examples of the active and passive voices in different verb tenses and modal forms. Each example has the affirmative, negative and interrogative forms.

VERB TENSES/FORMS	ACTIVE VOICE	PASSIVE VOICE
Simple present	She *sends* a cheque every month.	A cheque *is sent* every month.
	He *does not (doesn't) send* a reply.	A reply *is not (isn't) sent*.
	Do they *discuss* the problem?	*Is* the problem *discussed*?
Present continuous	The thief *is hiding* the cash.	The cash *is being hidden*.
	The police *are not (aren't) arresting* the thief.	The thief *is not (isn't) being arrested*.
	Are the police *handcuffing* the thief?	*Is* the thief *being handcuffed*?
Simple past	We *took* the dog for a walk.	The dog *was taken* for a walk.
	We *did not (didn't) leash* the dog.	The dog *was not (wasn't) leashed*.
	Did they *feed* the dog?	*Was* the dog *fed*?
Past continuous	He *was doing* the homework.	The homework *was being done*.
	He *was not (wasn't) writing* a report.	A report *was not (wasn't) being written*.
	Was he *revising* the essay?	*Was* the essay *being revised*?
Past perfect	They *had paid* the bill before the due date.	The bill *had been paid* before the due date.
	They *had not (hadn't) painted* the house for years.	The house *had not (hadn't) been painted* for years.
	Had they cleaned the condo before they left?	*Had* the condo *been cleaned* before they left?
Present perfect	Steven *has paid* the bill.	The bill *has been paid*.
	The chef *has not (hasn't) made* lunch.	Lunch *has not (hasn't) been made*.
	Has someone *washed* the dishes?	*Have* the dishes *been washed*?
Future • With *will* • The *be going to* form	They *will sell* the house. They *are going to sell* the house.	The house *will be sold*. The house *is going to be sold*.
	We *will not (won't) rent* the condo. We *are not (aren't) going to rent* the condo.	The condo *will not (won't) be rented*. The condo *is not (isn't) going to be rented*.
	Will he *give away* the money? *Is* he *going to give away* the money?	*Will* the money *be given away*? *Is* the money *going to be given away*?
Future perfect	They *will have returned* the books.	The books *will have been returned*.
	He *will not (won't) have done* the dishes.	The dishes *will not (won't) have been done*.
	Will they *have left* the door unlocked?	*Will* the door *have been left* unlocked?
Modals	He *might donate* some money.	Some money *might be donated*.
	She *could not (couldn't) answer* the question.	The question *could not (couldn't) be answered*.
	Must they *raise* a lot of money?	*Must* a lot of money *be raised*?

Modals (Past)	She *might have paid* the bill.	The bill *might have been paid.*
	They *could not (couldn't) have recovered* the missing money.	The missing money *could not (couldn't) have been recovered.*
	Should he *have returned* the dog?	*Should* the dog *have been returned*?

Note:
• Form the passive with *be* and the past participle of the verb.
(If you are unsure of the past participle of an irregular verb, refer to Chart B.)
• In the passive interrogative form, the auxiliary precedes the subject.
• To transform a yes/no question into an information question, place the question word before the auxiliary:
Was the dog fed? ➡ **When** *was the dog fed?*

GRAMMAR TIP

The passive voice may be used with *by* to stress the importance of the performer of the action. *The report was completed by Jason—not Andrew!*

GRAMMAR TIP

Only verbs that take direct objects can be used in the passive because the direct object becomes the subject of the passive sentence:
Sylvester walked to the store. ➡ *The store was walked to by Sylvester.*

Direct (Quoted) and Reported (Indirect) Speech

You can directly relate (quote) or indirectly report someone's words:

Albert Einstein said, "The true sign of intelligence is not knowledge but imagination." (Direct speech)

Albert Einstein said (that) the true sign of intelligence is not knowledge but imagination. (Reported speech)

When reporting speech, you usually need to make changes to various parts of speech. Examine the chart below, paying particular attention to any underlined words; then read through the notes at the bottom of the chart.

DIRECT SPEECH	REPORTED SPEECH
1. He says, "I always speak Spanish with my girlfriend."	He says (that) he always speaks Spanish with his girlfriend.
2. Jerry said, "I am always tired."	Jerry said (that) he was always tired.
3. Estelle said, "I am looking for someone to work my Friday shift."	Estelle said (that) she was looking for someone to work her Friday shift.
4. The captain said, "The coach cancelled the afternoon practice."	The captain said (that) the coach had cancelled the afternoon practice.
5. The bystanders said, "We were minding our own business."	The bystanders said (that) they had been minding their own business.
6. Allan said, "I have been to Toronto."	Allan said (that) he had been to Toronto.
7. Harvey and Tanya said, "We will make our own supper today."	Harvey and Tanya said (that) they would make their own supper yesterday.
8. Corinne said, "Victoria is the capital of British Columbia."	Corinne said (that) Victoria is the capital of British Columbia.

DIRECT SPEECH	REPORTED SPEECH
9. She said, "I <u>can</u> drive you to the airport."	She said (that) <u>she</u> <u>could</u> drive me to the airport.
10. She said, "I <u>must</u> drive you to the airport."	She said (that) <u>she</u> <u>had to</u> drive me to the airport.
11. She asked, "When does the meeting <u>start</u>?"	She asked when the meeting <u>started</u>.
12. The instructions say, "<u>Shake</u> the container before opening."	The instructions say <u>to shake</u> the container before opening.

Note:
- When the introductory verb is in the present tense (*say/says*), do not change the tense used in the reported speech (see 1).
- When the introductory verb is in the past tense (*said/stated/asked/replied/…*), change the tense used in the reported speech by moving the tense *one step back into the past*. (This is called "backshifting." See 2 through 7 for examples of backshifting for the simple present, present continuous, simple past, past continuous, present perfect and simple future tenses respectively. Both the simple past and the present perfect are "backshifted" to the past perfect: Geoffrey said, *"I **ate** bison last night, but I **have** never **eaten** moose."* ➡ *Geoffrey said that he **had eaten** bison the night before, but that he **had** never **eaten** moose.*)
- If a general truth is reported, do not change the tense used in the reported speech even if the introductory verb is in the past tense (see 8).
- Modals sometimes require a backshift (see 9 and 10).
- In reported speech, you can often omit *that* after the verb *said*.
- Backshift tenses when changing a direct question into an indirect question, and do not invert the subject and the auxiliary in an indirect question (see 11): *She asked when ~~did the meeting start~~ the meeting started.*
- When reporting instructions or orders, use an infinitive (see 12).
- References to people (pronouns), adjectives and adverbs often need to be changed: *Bob said, "I am sailing away on **my** boat **today**." Bob said that **he** was sailing away on **his** boat **yesterday**.*

Pinpoint

Part A

Rewrite the following sentences in the passive voice. It is not necessary to repeat the subject. The first one has been done for you as an example.

1. The bank will process your loan request tomorrow.

Your loan request will be processed tomorrow.

2. The authorities released the prisoner last Saturday.

the prisoner was released last Saturday

3. They are monitoring access to the Parliament Buildings.

The access to the Parliament Buildings are being monitored

4. Could they repair the dishwasher?

Could the dishwasher be repaired

5. She pays the phone bill by credit card.

the phone bill is paid by credit card

6. The cleaner wasn't washing the floors at 9:00 p.m.

the floors weren't being washed at 9:00 p.m.

7. Are they going to plow the roads tonight?

Are the roads going to be plowed tonight

8. Someone has deleted all my files.

my files have been deleted

9. Something destroyed all my tomato plants.

my tomato plants have been destroyed

10. Will someone mail the letters this afternoon?

will the letters be mailed this afternoon?

Part B

Rewrite the following sentences using reported speech. Make required changes to verb tenses, pronouns, adjectives and adverbs. Maintain contracted forms. The first one has been done for you as an example.

1. Louise said, "I won't call you back."

Louise said (that) she wouldn't call you/me back.

2. Paul said, "I have never read such a clear report."

_____

3. The children said, "We wanted to go to camp this summer."

_____

4. George replied, "I am not interested in going to France."

_____

5. Melissa said, "Supper won't be ready until 7 o'clock."

_____

6. The coach shouted, "I want everyone on the field in five minutes!"

_____

7. The police officer said, "Put your hands up!"

_____

8. Jacob complained, "I don't want to eat sandwiches for lunch."

_____

9. Madison asked, "When will the movie start?"

_____

10. The witness replied, "I have never seen this man in my life!"

_____

My eLab ✎ Now that you have pinpointed your current level of understanding of the active and passive voice, as well as direct and reported speech, complete related exercises on My eLab for practice and instant feedback.

Nouns and Pronouns

NOUNS

A noun is a word or a group of words that names people, places or things.

In this section we will consider kinds of nouns, plural noun forms, non-count nouns, possessive nouns and verbs as nouns.

Kinds of Nouns

There are four kinds of nouns:

1. **common** (general);
   mother, father, baby …

2. **proper** (specific);
   Canada, Montreal, Rufus Wainwright …

3. **abstract** (things that are not concrete);
   love, hate, jealousy …

4. **collective** (group).
   team, group, herd …

GRAMMAR TIP

Collective nouns take a singular verb when considered as a group or a plural verb when considered as individuals in a group.

The other team **is winning** *the match.*

The other team **are wearing** *blue and gold uniforms.*

Plural Noun Forms

Refer to the following table for the rules concerning regular and irregular plurals:

RULES	EXAMPLES	
Most (regular) nouns: The plural is formed by simply adding "s."	mother ➡ mothers	
Nouns that end in "ch," "sh," "s," "x" or "o": Add "es."	match ➡ matches bush ➡ bushes bus ➡ buses	box ➡ boxes hero ➡ heroes
Nouns that end in "y": a) If a vowel precedes the "y," add "s." b) If a consonant precedes the "y," change the "y" to "i" and add "es."	a) boy ➡ boys b) baby ➡ babies	
Most nouns ending in "f" or "fe": Change the "f" or "fe" to "v" and add "es."	half ➡ halves knife ➡ knives leaf ➡ leaves life ➡ lives loaf ➡ loaves	self ➡ selves shelf ➡ shelves thief ➡ thieves wife ➡ wives wolf ➡ wolves
Other nouns ending in "f" or "fe": Simply add "s." (Note: Some of these nouns have two plural forms.)	reef ➡ reefs scarf ➡ scarfs or scarves	

Some nouns: The plural is formed with a vowel change.	fireman ➡ firemen foot ➡ feet goose ➡ geese man ➡ men	policeman ➡ policemen policewoman ➡ policewomen tooth ➡ teeth woman ➡ women
Some other nouns: The singular is the same as the plural.	aircraft ➡ aircraft craft* ➡ craft deer ➡ deer fish ➡ fish offspring ➡ offspring	salmon ➡ salmon series ➡ series sheep ➡ sheep species ➡ species trout ➡ trout
Certain nouns are always plural.	clothes eyeglasses goods pants pliers	police pyjamas scissors stairs surroundings
Many nouns of Greek or Latin origin form their plurals according to the rules of those languages.	axis ➡ axes bacterium ➡ bacteria basis ➡ bases crisis ➡ crises datum ➡ data	diagnosis ➡ diagnoses emphasis ➡ emphases hypothesis ➡ hypotheses nucleus ➡ nuclei ovum ➡ ova

Note: • Abbreviations, decades, letters and numbers can be pluralized: *RRSPs, 1980s, 7s.*
 • The usual plural of *person* is *people*, not *persons*.
 • The plural of *child* is *children*.
 • The correct pronunciation of *women* is /wimmin/.
 • Sometimes nouns that look plural are actually singular: *AIDS, billiards, news.*

* **craft** vessel (boat, ship or airplane)

Non-Count Nouns

Nouns that have a plural form are called count nouns.

Some nouns do not have a plural form: they are called non-count (or mass) nouns because they cannot be counted.

The following chart summarizes common non-count nouns:

KINDS OF NON-COUNT NOUNS	EXAMPLES
No separate parts	coffee, meat, milk, soup, water
Parts too small to count	grass, hair, salt, sand, sugar
Refers to whole categories	clothing, food, furniture, homework, money
Abstract	advice, information, life, love, music
Academic subjects	chemistry, eugenics, history, mathematics, physics

Non-count nouns are not preceded by *a* or *an*. They may be preceded by

some	*any*	*much*	*no*	*a lot of*
a little of	*a piece of*	*a cup of*	*a bottle of*	*a bowl of*

> *They drank ~~a~~ **some coffee***.
> *Did she give you ~~an~~ **any advice**?*
> *He does not have ~~a~~ **much clothing***.

Non-count nouns always take a singular verb.
> *My homework ~~are~~ **is** done.*

Use *there is* with non-count nouns and singular count nouns.
> ***There is** some mail.*
> ***There is** a letter.*

Use *there are* with plural count nouns.
> ***There are** two letters.*

> ### GRAMMAR TIP
> Use *many* with count nouns and *much* with non-count nouns.
> They drank **many bottles** of wine.
> Do you have **much money**?

Possessive Nouns

Nouns referring to people, places, animals and time can "possess":
> *Mr. Anderson's car, Montreal's stadium, the dogs' bones, Tuesday's class, …*

To indicate possession,

- add *'s* to singular nouns and to plural nouns not ending in "s";
  *woman**'s** work   people**'s** lives*

- add an apostrophe only (') to plural nouns ending in "s".
  *two boys**'** bikes*

> ### GRAMMAR TIP
> Proper nouns ending in "s" can take *'s* or an apostrophe alone to indicate possession:
> *Doris' cake, Doris**'s** cake.*

Verbs as Nouns

Verbs are used as nouns when they function as the subject of a sentence or the object of another verb or preposition:

> ***Shovelling** the driveway is good exercise.*
> (*Shovelling* is the subject of the sentence.)

> *I like **to walk** in the park.*
> (*To walk* is the object of the verb *like*.)

> *He did some stretching exercises before **going** for a run.*
> (*Going* is the object of the preposition *before*.)

When verbs function as nouns, they take either the gerund (verb + "ing") or the infinitive (*to* + base form of the verb) form.

The Gerund Form

Gerunds are always used after prepositions.

*They insisted **on** paying for supper.*

Gerunds are always used after certain verbs.

Kevin enjoys ~~to paint~~ painting.

The following chart provides a list of some common verbs that are always followed by gerunds.

COMMON VERBS THAT ARE FOLLOWED BY GERUNDS				
admit	can't see	enjoy	miss	resent
advise	complete	finish	practise	resist
anticipate	consider	imagine	quit	risk
appreciate	deny	keep	recall	suggest
avoid	discuss	mention	recommend	tolerate
can't help	dislike	mind	regret	understand

The Infinitive Form

Infinitives are always used after certain verbs.

Jane hopes ~~spending~~ to spend her summer vacation in South America.

The following chart provides a list of some common verbs that are always followed by infinitives.

COMMON VERBS THAT ARE FOLLOWED BY INFINITIVES				
agree	consent	happen	mean	promise
appear	decide	hesitate	need	refuse
arrange	demand	hope	offer	seem
ask	deserve	intend	plan	threaten
choose	expect	learn	prepare	wait
claim	fail	manage	pretend	want

Some verbs may be followed by either a gerund or an infinitive, often with little or no change in meaning.

It started to rain at midnight.

It started raining at midnight.

Additional examples of such verbs include *begin, like, love, prefer, can't stand, continue* and *hate*.

Some verbs may be followed by either a gerund or an infinitive, but the meaning changes.

I forgot to lock the door. (I didn't lock the door.)

I forgot locking the door. (I locked the door, but I forgot that I had locked it.)

Additional examples of such verbs include *remember, try* and *stop*.

PRONOUNS

A pronoun is a word that stands for or replaces a noun. For example:
Sam *videotaped the recital.* ➡ **He** *videotaped the recital.*

Pronouns are important: without them, sentences would be repetitive and hard to understand.

Compare the following:
Kevin gave Susan a letter Kevin had written, and Susan read the letter.
*Kevin gave Susan a letter **he** had written, and **she** read it.*

There are many different types of pronouns.

- **Personal**
  *He bought a new cellphone, but **he** does not know how to use **it**.*
- **Reflexive**
  *She made **herself** something to eat.*
- **Indefinite**
  ***Everybody** complained about the homework.*
- **Demonstrative**
  ***This** is my textbook.*
- **Possessive**
  *Whose car did you take? We took **theirs**.*
- **Relative**
  *That is the person **who** drove the car.*

Personal Pronouns

A personal pronoun may be singular or plural and act as a subject or object.

	PERSON	SUBJECT	OBJECT	EXAMPLES
Singular	first	I	me	*I told Todd to give me the keys.*
	second	you	you	*You were late even though the teacher had asked you to be on time.*
	third	he/she/it	him/her/it	*She gave him some money.*
Plural	first	we	us	*We insist that the money be given to us.*
	second	you	you	*You failed the exam, but the teacher will give each of you a make-up exam.*
	third	they	them	*They want the teacher to give them an extension.*

Note:
- *You* and *it* have the same subject and object forms.
- Use *it* to refer to a thing or an animal.
- Use *they* to refer to people, things or animals.

Reflexive Pronouns

GRAMMAR TIP

~~Theirself~~, ~~theirselves~~ and ~~hisself~~ do not exist in standard English.

A reflexive pronoun refers back to the doer.

	PERSON	SUBJECT	EXAMPLES
Singular	**first**	myself	I gave *myself* a treat.
	second	yourself	You must behave *yourself*.
	third	himself/herself/itself	He asked *himself* if she loved him.
Plural	**first**	ourselves	We need to discipline *ourselves* to do our homework.
	second	yourselves	You should discipline *yourselves* to work harder.
	third	themselves	They invited *themselves* over for dinner.

Note:
- The subject and the object are the same person.
- The second person singular is *yourself*, and the second person plural is *yourselves*.
- A reflexive pronoun can be used to emphasize a noun or a pronoun: *Karen **herself** made the cake.*

Indefinite Pronouns

An indefinite pronoun does not refer to a specific person or thing.
Some indefinite pronouns are singular, some are plural, and some are both.

INDEFINITE PRONOUNS	SINGULAR	PLURAL	INDEFINITE PRONOUNS	SINGULAR	PLURAL
anybody	X		somebody	X	
anyone	X		someone	X	
each	X		both		X
either	X		few		X
everybody	X		many		X
everyone	X		several		X
everything	X		all	X	X
neither	X		any	X	X
no one	X		most	X	X
nobody	X		none	X	X
one	X		some	X	X

Demonstrative Pronouns

Demonstrative pronouns point to a person or a thing, and they may be singular or plural.

	NEAR	FAR	EXAMPLES
Singular	this	that	*This* is my shirt. *That* is yours.
Plural	these	those	*These* are my books. *Those* are yours.

> Note: • Typically, *this* and *these* refer to what is near and *that* and *those* to what is far.
> • The pronouns *this*, *that*, *these* and *those* may also be used as adjectives: ***This shirt*** *is new.* ***Those shirts*** *are old.*

Possessive Pronouns

Possessive pronouns (and possessive adjectives) indicate ownership.

	PERSON	POSSESSIVE ADJECTIVES	POSSESSIVE PRONOUNS	EXAMPLES
Singular	**first**	my	mine	Whose car is it? It's *my* car. It's *mine*.
	second	your	yours	Whose shirts are they? They're *your* shirts. They're *yours*.
	third	his/her/its	his/hers/its	Whose office is it? It's *her* office. It's *hers*.
Plural	**first**	our	ours	Whose books are they? They're *our* books. They're *ours*.
	second	your	yours	Whose classroom is it? It's *your* classroom. It's *yours*.
	third	their	theirs	Whose keys are they? They're *their* keys. They're *theirs*.

Note: • Do not confuse the contraction of "it is" (*it's*) with the possessive pronoun *its*.

• Do not confuse the contraction of "they are" (*they're*) with the possessive adjective *their* or the adverb *there*:
They're looking for *their* keys over *there*!

• For the third person singular *his* and *its*, the possessive adjective and the possessive pronoun are identical: *his* and *its*.

Relative Pronouns

Relative pronouns introduce relative clauses—dependent clauses that modify nouns and pronouns.

USE	RELATIVE PRONOUNS			EXAMPLES
	SUBJECTIVE	**OBJECTIVE**	**POSSESSIVE**	
People	who (that)	whom/ who (that)	whose	There is the man *who* (or *that*) stole her purse. The man *whom* (or *who*, or *that*) I saw is over there. There is the woman *whose* purse was stolen.
Things	that	that	whose	That is the book *that* caused such uproar. Where is the book *that* I lent you? Here is the book *whose* cover is torn.

Note: • In informal English, *that* is often used to refer to both people and things.

• *Which* is used instead of *that* when relating non-essential information about things:
The documentary, **which** *lasted ninety minutes, won an award.*

• *Whom* is primarily used in formal English.

• The relative pronouns *whom*, *who* and *that* can be omitted when they are objects of verbs in relative clauses: *The teacher (**whom** or **who** or **that**) I wanted to meet was unavailable.*

• When *who* and *that* are used as subjects, make sure that the verb that follows agrees with the noun or pronoun being modified:
Look at the students who ~~is~~ are waiting in line.
A book that ~~have~~ has a red sticker is on sale.

• Do not confuse *whose* with *who's*, which is the contraction of *who is*:
Where is the student ~~whose~~ who's supposed to do her presentation?

Pinpoint

Part A

Write the correct form of each noun in parentheses.

1. We have three small sons. The (boys) _____ toys are all over the house.

2. Jeremy enjoys cross-country (ski) _____.

3. Put all the (knife) _____ in the top drawer.

4. Scientists have suggested several (hypothesis) _____ to explain why stars disappear.

5. We have decided (analyze) _____ all of the (datum) _____ next week.

6. We'll need more (raspberry) _____ for the pie.

7. There are a lot of (hoax) _____ on the Internet.

8. Did you recall (feed) _____ the cat before you left this morning?

9. (Wolf) _____ can't help (chase) _____ (sheep) _____.

10. My nephew refuses (eat) _____ spinach.

Part B

Complete each sentence by circling the correct word in parentheses.

1. I need (an / some) advice about purchasing a used car. Could you help me?

2. There isn't (many / much) information about restaurants in this guidebook.

3. Would you bring (a / some) bread for the picnic?

4. We don't have (many / much) homework in our history class.

5. There (is / are) some food in the cupboard.

6. Your pants (is / are) on the chair beside the bed.

7. News about the accidents (is / are) incomplete at the moment.

8. The Beatles became famous in the (1960's / 1960s).

9. We will need (a / some) new furniture for the baby's room.

10. The police (is / are) investigating the robbery.

Part C

Circle the correct pronoun(s) for each sentence.

1. My secretary can make your appointment. Call (her / him) at his extension: 4561.

2. I'm looking for my other crayon. The box holds twelve, but I only have eleven. Have you seen (them / it)?

3. The teacher and the students all have dictionaries. (Her / Hers) is on her desk and (their / theirs) are in the cupboard.

4. Jim and I are organizing a graduation party. (They / We) are thinking of planning a cruise.

5. Bob, you will have to make supper (yourselves / yourself). I won't be home until midnight.

6. Do you think that truck belongs to me? Sorry. (Its / It's) not (me / mine).

7. You need to contact the supervisor (which / who) signed the evaluation.

8. We finally found (ourselves / ourself) a table in the busy restaurant.

9. The tiger (who / that) escaped from the zoo was captured yesterday.

10. Travellers (who's / whose) luggage is not identified must obtain a name tag from the guide.

My eLab 🖉 Now that you have pinpointed your current level of understanding of nouns and pronouns, complete related exercises on My eLab for practice and instant feedback.

 7 Adjectives and Adverbs

Adjectives describe nouns or pronouns.
> *Vicki has a **new** car; it is **blue**.*

Adverbs describe verbs, adjectives or other adverbs.
> *Vicki drives her **brilliantly** blue car **fairly quickly**.*

There are many different types of adjectives and adverbs.

In this section, we will focus our attention on two of the more common types:

1. Adjectives of quality, and

2. Adverbs of manner

Adjectives of Quality

Adjectives of quality indicate "which kind" of noun or pronoun and may be divided into two broad categories:

1. **opinion**;
   nice, intelligent, beautiful, horrible, delicious, …

2. **fact**.
   big, new, flat, orange, Canadian, …

A fact adjective precedes the noun it modifies.
> *He bought a **new** car.*

Opinion adjectives precede fact adjectives.
> *He married ~~a Canadian intelligent~~ an **intelligent Canadian** doctor.*

Simple, Comparative and Superlative Adjective Forms

Most adjectives of quality have three forms: simple, comparative and superlative.

The comparative form is used to compare two people or things.
> *Joe is **shorter than** Jason.*

The superlative form is used to compare three or more people or things.
> *Joe is 140 pounds, Jason is 150 pounds and Erick is 160 pounds. Of the three, Erick is **the heaviest**.*

Many comparatives and superlatives are formed by adding "er" and "est" endings to the adjective. Other adjectives do not take endings; instead the words *more* or *most* are placed in front of them.

Refer to the following table for the rules to apply when forming the comparative and superlative:

ADJECTIVES	SIMPLE	COMPARATIVE	SUPERLATIVE
One-syllable adjectives: Simply add "er" or "est."	short	shorter (than)	(the) shortest
One-syllable adjectives ending with "consonant + vowel + consonant": Double the last consonant before adding "er" or "est."	hot	hotter (than)	(the) hottest
One-syllable adjectives ending in "e": Simply add "r" or "st."	blue	bluer (than)	(the) bluest
Two-syllable adjectives ending with "consonant + 'y' ": Change the "y" to "i" before adding "er" or "est."	heavy pretty	heavier (than) prettier (than)	(the) heaviest (the) prettiest
Common irregular adjectives: Memorize forms.	good bad little a lot	better (than) worse (than) less (than) more (than)	(the) best (the) worst (the) least (the) most
Other two-syllable adjectives: Place *more* or *most* before the adjective.	splendid	more splendid (than)	(the) most splendid
Three-or-more-syllable adjectives: Place *more* or *most* before the adjective.	elegant	more elegant (than)	(the) most elegant

Note:
- The following one-syllable adjectives use the *more* and *most* forms: *bored* and *tired*. For example: *more tired* and *most tired*.
- The following two-syllable adjectives use the "er" and "est" forms as well as the *more* and *most* forms: *simple, common, handsome, quiet, gentle, narrow, clever, friendly* and *angry*. For example: *handsomer* or *more handsome* and *handsomest* or *most handsome*.
- Only adjectives of quality that are **not absolute** can be used in the comparative or the superlative forms: *Mary's essay was ~~more perfect~~ better than Steve's.*

Adverbs of Manner

Adverbs of manner indicate how something happens.

Spelling Tips: Forming Adverbs
- Many adverbs of manner are formed by simply adding "ly" to the corresponding adjectives:
  nice ➡ nice**ly**
  intelligent ➡ intelligent**ly**
  enormous ➡ enormous**ly**

- If the adjective ends with "consonant + 'y,'" change the final "y" to an "i" before adding "ly":
  merry ➡ merr**i**ly

- If the adjective ends with "consonant + 'le,'" drop the "e" before adding "y": *ample* ➡ *amply*
- If the adjective ends in "ic," add "ally": *basic* ➡ *basically*
- The adjectives *true, due* and *whole* drop the final "e" before adding "ly":
  true ➡ *truly*
  due ➡ *duly*
  whole ➡ *wholly*
- Some adjectives of quality and adverbs of manner have the same form:
  hard ➡ *hard*
  fast ➡ *fast*
  kindly ➡ *kindly*

USAGE TIP

Never place an adverb between the verb and the object: *He eats ~~quickly~~ his meals.*

Adverb Position
Generally, the adverb of manner goes after the verb.
  He **eats quickly**.

If there is an object, the adverb of manner goes after the object.
  He eats **his meals quickly**.

However if the object is long, the adverb of manner goes before the verb.
  He **quickly** eats **the meals that his mother prepares**.

Simple, Comparative and Superlative Adverb Forms

Most adverbs of manner have three forms: simple, comparative and superlative.

ADVERBS	SIMPLE	COMPARATIVE	SUPERLATIVE
One-syllable adverbs	fast	faster (than)	(the) fastest
Adverbs ending in "ly"	bravely	more bravely (than)	(the) most bravely
Common irregular adverbs	well badly	better (than) worse (than)	(the) best (the) worst

Comparisons of Equality
Use the structure "as … as" with adjectives and adverbs to make comparisons of equality.
  *His son is **as tall as** he is.*
  *His mother drives **as quickly as** he does.*

Pinpoint

The sentences below contain errors related to adjectives and adverbs. Underline these errors, and write the corrections in the space provided. In some cases, more than one answer is possible.

1. We enjoyed a Chinese delicious meal last night. _____

2. Let's leave. This is the worse movie I have ever seen. _____

3. Be careful! The security guard told us specificly not to open this door.

   _____

4. Jean's eyes are more green than her twin's. _____

5. Mona jogs more often than her brother, and she is fiter than he.

   _____

6. I was truely amazed by the findings presented in the report. _____

7. My step-brother very much likes maple walnut ice cream. _____

   _____

8. I think Highway 33 was built more recent than Highway 35. _____

9. Of all the players, Oliver skates the better. _____

10. You'll have to work fastly to finish by 5 p.m. _____

My eLab 🖉 Now that you have pinpointed your current level of understanding of adjectives and adverbs, complete related exercises on My eLab for practice and instant feedback.

8 Articles and Prepositions

The articles *a*, *an* and *the* are used with nouns, often to single out a noun from the class named by the noun.

> *For lunch, he ate **a** banana and **an** orange.*
> *I want **the** blue book, not **the** red book.*

As you are working through this section, you may need to refer to section six and review singular and plural nouns and count and non-count nouns.

Articles

There are two kinds of articles: indefinite (*a* and *an*) and definite (*the*). In general, indefinite articles are used with generic singular count nouns while definite articles are used with specific singular and plural nouns and specific count and non-count nouns.

> *Has anyone seen **a** robin this spring?* (Generic)
> *Has anyone seen **the** robin with **a** broken wing?* (Specific)

Examine the following chart:

INDEFINITE	DEFINITE
1. I want to take *a* course next term.	3. *The* book we are reading in our philosophy class is boring.
2. I'm looking for *an* apartment near the college.	4. Where did you put *the* newspapers that were on the table?
	5. Please pass me *the* meat.
	6. She lives in *the* United States, close to *the* Pacific Ocean.

Note:
- When deciding whether to use *a* or *an*, pronounce the word first. If the word begins with a vowel sound (and not simply the vowel *a*, *e*, *i*, *o* or *u*), use *an*; if the word begins with a consonant sound (and not simply a consonant such as *b*, *c*, *d*, ...), use *a*. Be careful of words starting with *e*, *h* or *u* as well as abbreviations such as RCMP (Royal Canadian Mounted Police). For example, *an escape* **but** *a European vacation; a hotel* **but** *an honour; an umbrella* **but** *a university; a recreational vehicle* **but** *an RV* (1 and 2).
- Use *the* with specific singular count nouns (3).
- Use *the* with specific plural count nouns (4).
- Use *the* with specific non-count nouns (5).
- Use *the* with bodies of water, oceans and seas as well as countries in the plural (6).

Do not use an indefinite article before

- plural count nouns;
  I sometimes eat ~~a~~ oranges for breakfast.
- non-count nouns.
  I always eat ~~a~~ fruit for breakfast.

Do not use a definite article before

- generic singular count nouns;
  In general, I prefer reading ~~the~~ a book to watching ~~the~~ a movie.
- generic plural count nouns;
  Everyone knows that ~~the~~ teenagers under sixteen are not allowed to drive cars.
- generic non-count nouns;
  Some believe that ~~the~~ meat is a necessary part of a healthy diet.
- names of cities, provinces, states or singular countries;
  ~~The~~ Ontario is the most populated province in ~~the~~ Canada.
- meals.
  I'm going grocery shopping; what do you want for ~~the~~ breakfast, ~~the~~ lunch and ~~the~~ supper?

Prepositions

Prepositions are used to show a relationship between a noun and other words.
  *The swim team is practising **in** the pool.* (Indicates a relationship of place)
  *Lisa returned to work **after** lunch.* (Indicates a relationship of time)

Prepositions can show a relationship by answering the following questions

- where (static);
  *The books **on** the table belong to Mike.*
  *My dog always sleeps **under** my bed.*

- where (movement);
  *The bear climbed **up** the tree.*
  *Donald hit the baseball **through** the window.*

- when;
  *I'm leaving **in** June, **on** the fifth **at** nine o'clock.*
  *You have to be at the station **by** 7 p.m. or you will miss the bus.*

- how.
  *He speaks Mandarin **with** difficulty.*
  *There was no road, so we approached **on** foot.*

Here are some common prepositions:

Where (static)	above, against, along, among, around, at, behind, below, beneath, beside, between, by, in, in front of, inside, near, next to, on, on top of, outside, over, to the left of, to the right of, under, underneath, within
Where (movement)	across, along, around, away from, down, from, into, off, onto, out of, over, past, through, toward, under, up
When	after, at, before, by, in, on
How	by, in, on, like, with

Pinpoint

Part A

Circle the correct article in parentheses. A "0" indicates no article is required.

1. My daughter is looking for (a / an) used motorcycle. (A / The) motorcycle has to be in (a / 0) good condition and economical on (the / 0) gas.

2. We saw (a / an) horrible movie last night. (An / The) acting was bad and (a / the) music was too loud. It was (a / the) disaster.

3. Everyone knows that (the / 0) cars produce (the / 0) greenhouse gases.

4. I have been waiting here for (a / an) hour! I wonder if (a / the) bus route has been changed.

5. Alex is studying wildlife in (the / 0) Falkland Islands. The islands are found in (the / 0) South Atlantic Ocean. In (a / an) attempt to reclaim this territory, (the / 0) Argentina invaded (the / 0) Falklands in 1982. This attempt was unsuccessful.

6. Jim is usually afraid of (the / 0) dogs, but he likes (the / 0) dogs on his uncle's farm.

7. Investing in (a / an) RRSP is (a / 0) good idea for workers who do not have (a / an) employee pension plan.

8. Could I have (a / an) appointment next week? I am having (a / 0) trouble with (a / the) CD player in my car. I can't eject (the / 0) CDs that are in the player.

9. (An / 0) information about shipping charges is available on our website. (An / The) address can be found on the home page.

10. Do you have (a / an) BA or (a / an) MA? We need someone with (a / an) university degree. For this job, you must have (a / the) degree in (the / 0) psychology.

Part B

Fill in the blanks with the correct preposition. In some cases, more than one answer is possible. Refer to the chart at the bottom of page 235 for examples of common prepositions.

1. I was born _____ Kingston, a city located _____ Ontario. This city is _____ Lake Ontario.

2. As I was walking _____ a path through the park, I heard a noise _____ me. I turned _____ and came face-to-face with a bear.

3. We were sailing _____ the St. Lawrence River _____ October. We were heading _____ the marina when we saw an animal swimming _____ the boat. When we looked closely, we saw it was a seal.

4. When truckers drive _____ an overpass, they must check the height of the overpass to ensure sufficient clearance.

5. With my super powers, I can see _____ walls, climb _____ the outside of buildings and jump _____ skyscrapers.

6. When we have dinner guests, our dog goes _____ the table. She lies _____ the rug, waiting for someone to give her a scrap.

7. You can see the doctor this morning, any time _____ noon. When you come _____ the office, go _____ the side door and wait in the hall.

8. Please place the sofa _____ the two windows, _____ the wall. Then hang my portrait _____ the sofa.

9. My twin brother swims _____ a fish, but I swim _____ a rock. He actually swam _____ the English Channel last year. He went _____ England _____ France.

10. You need to arrive for your job interview _____ 10:45. _____ the interview, you have a questionnaire to answer. Then, the interview starts _____ eleven o'clock sharp. If you pass the first interview, there will be a second one _____ the afternoon _____ lunch.

⑨ Capitalization and Punctuation

Capital letters and punctuation marks make words, groups of words (phrases) and sentences (clauses) easier to understand. Capital letters distinguish the meaning of words like "AIDS" from "aids," and capital letters signal the start of a new sentence. Punctuation marks separate words into groups, clarifying sentence meaning; for example:

Woman, without her man, is nothing.
Woman: without her, man is nothing

In this section, you will examine when and how to capitalize words and punctuate sentences.

Capitalization

The chart below indicates when to use capital letters and provides examples of correct usage.

USE	EXAMPLES
The first word of a sentence	*Interest* rates have declined over the past year.
The first person singular	Mark asked if *I* could help him, and *I* said *I* could.
Direct quotations of complete sentences	Her lawyer said, "*You* will win your case." "*Please* give John my message," said Evelyn.
The first word of each item in a numbered or bulleted list	You will need these items for your art project: • *Coloured* pencils • *Graph* paper • *Scissors*
Job and courtesy titles, first and last names	Have you met *Dr.* and *Mrs. Abernathy*? Our next contestant is *Ms. Michelle Potter.* *Captain Edward John Smith* was the captain of a famous ship.
All important words in a title	Sky Wilson wrote the trilogy composed of *The Dome, Under the Dome* and *When the Dome Breaks.* Have you read *To Live or to Die*?
Holidays, weekdays, months	*Labour Day* falls on the first *Monday* in *September.*
Countries, languages, nationalities, races and religions	In three days, I am leaving for *Cuba,* where the people speak *Spanish.* Many *Cubans* are *Christians* or *Santerians.* The *Santeria* religion was introduced to *Cuba* by *African* slaves.
Specific place names and vehicles	According to people living in *Toronto, Yonge Street* is the longest street in the world. Who was the captain of the *Titanic*? I believe it was Edward John Smith.
Acronyms and abbreviations	*AIDS* is caused by *HIV*, a virus that attacks the human immune system. *UNESCO* is a *UN* organization that deals with education, social and natural science, culture and communication.

Note:
- Some acronyms that have entered the language as words do not have capitals. You can rent *scuba* (**s**elf-**c**ontained **u**nderwater **b**reathing **a**pparatus) diving equipment at the beach. You can have *laser* (**l**ight **a**mplification by **s**timulated **e**mission of **r**adiation) treatments to remove unwanted tattoos.

Punctuation

The chart below indicates when to use various punctuation marks and provides examples of correct usage.

PUNCTUATION	USE	EXAMPLES
Periods	After sentences	Don't speak on your cellphone while driving.
	With abbreviations	The meeting will finish at 4:30 p.m. You must declare cats, dogs, birds, etc., when you cross the border.
Question marks	After direct questions	Would you like to go to a movie this evening?
	After question tags	You have seen *Avatar*, haven't you?
Exclamation marks	To express strong emotion	Look out for that falling rock!
Commas	Between independent clauses joined by a coordinate conjunction	Jorge speaks Spanish, but he can't write it very well. I was having money problems, so I sold my car.
	After dependent clauses	If you need assistance, go to the Customer Service Department. Whenever it rains, our roof leaks.
	In a series	I put mushrooms, onion and red pepper in my omelette.
	Between coordinate adjectives	We can expect hot, humid, sticky weather at the end of July.
	After introductory words	Initially, Cindy wanted a big dog, but she changed her mind and bought a miniature poodle.
	After introductory phrases	First of all, we need to organize our work. Every once in a while, you need to "defrag" your computer.
	Before direct quotations	She asked, "Where do our fears come from?" As the saying goes, "All is fair in love and war."
	Between two consecutive numbers	In 2008, 162 heart transplants were performed in Canada.
Semicolons	Between independent clauses	Jane found a summer job; her friend Kelly didn't find one.

PUNCTUATION	USE	EXAMPLES
Colons	Before a list	Bring the following for the camping trip: a tent, a sleeping bag and warm clothes.
	After "note"	Note: Applications must be received before March 15. Note: Post-dated cheques will not be accepted.
	Between hours and minutes	The flight leaves at 8:23 p.m. The 11:30 train is late.
Quotation marks	For direct quotations	"Up with your hands," he shouted. The sign reads, "Do not touch. Wet paint."
	For titles of works contained in another work (articles, book chapters, TV episodes, etc.)	Did you read the article "Life after Death" in *Newsmonth*? Do you watch *The Mentalist*? Did you see "Red Hair and Silver Tape"?
Apostrophes	With contractions	He doesn't know if he'll return or not. Jason can't swim.
	With possessive nouns	The Wilsons' house is up for sale. Have you seen Sheila's new car and her husband's new motorcycle?
Parentheses	With references to pages, units, appendices, etc., or to add a clarification or personal thought	You should review the BNA Act (Chapter 5) before the exam. A good red wine (my personal favourite) is Norman Hardie's Pinot Noir.
Hyphens	To join a prefix to some words	Self-esteem is important for happiness and success. My math teacher is my sister's ex-boyfriend.
	To join two or more words to create a compound word	Use an up-to-date dictionary to check spelling. My neighbour has an eight-foot fence around his property.
	When writing numbers as words	Cheques will be deposited on the twenty-fifth of the month. Seventy-six poems were submitted for the poetry prize.

Note:
- Adjectives are coordinate when they modify the same noun equally, can be used in any order and can be written with *and* between them: *We are having a **warm**, **dry** spring.*
- In a website address, the "period" is called a dot.
- In decimal numbers, the "period" is called a point: *thirty-three **point** five* (33.5).

© PEARSON LONGMAN • REPRODUCTION PROHIBITED

Pinpoint

Rewrite each sentence, adding capital letters and punctuation marks as required.

1. the taxi driver asked when does your plane leave

   _____

   _____

2. our son in law speaks portuguese and a little english

   _____

   _____

3. the shining is such a scary book

   _____

   _____

4. costumes inc hasnt changed its address on its website

   _____

   _____

5. which organization has their headquarters in geneva

   _____

   _____

6. you can contact mr lombardi if you want an italian translation of the contract

   _____

   _____

7. steve didnt remember his wifes birthday but he did buy her chocolates for valentines day

   _____

   _____

8. the secretaries offices are being renovated next week new furniture has been ordered it will arrive tomorrow

   _____

   _____

   _____

9. mr and mrs smiths cottage was destroyed by fire on may 15 2010 arson is suspected the police have no leads

   _____

   _____

   _____

10. my wife and i decided to go south for a little vacation in january originally we planned to fly but i enjoy driving so we took the car we stopped in washington to see the white house and have lunch with president and mrs obama once we had crossed floridas sunshine skyway bridge it was only a short drive to silver beach and the beachmere condos our condo had a fantastic view of the gulf of mexico we didnt want to return to snow and ice but we had to leave on january 22

_____

_____

_____

_____

_____

_____

_____

_____

_____

_____

_____

My eLab 🖊 Now that you have pinpointed your current level of understanding of capitalization and punctuation, complete related exercises on My eLab for practice and instant feedback

🔟 Common Sentence Errors

Before submitting a writing assignment for evaluation, you should revise your work. An important part of revising is proofreading, a process in which you isolate and correct any errors you might have made. In this section, you will examine some of the more common types of sentence errors in order to assist you in the proofreading process. (For more information on proofreading, see Appendix A, page 181.)

Run-on Sentences

If you have two (or more) independent clauses, they must be joined by a comma followed by a coordinate conjunction, a semicolon followed by an adverbial conjunction or a semicolon (see page 185).

A run-on sentence error is committed when you omit the required punctuation.

Ken wanted an SUV his wife wanted a convertible.

This error can be corrected in a number of ways:

Ken wanted an SUV, but his wife wanted a convertible.
Ken wanted an SUV; however, his wife wanted a convertible.
Ken wanted an SUV; his wife wanted a convertible.

Sentence Fragments

A sentence must have a subject and a verb and must express a complete thought (see page 185). A sentence fragment error occurs when you omit a subject, a verb and/or a complete thought.

In the garage. There is a racoon.

"In the garage" has neither a subject nor a verb but is followed by a period; as such, it constitutes a sentence fragment.

One possible correction would be:

There is a racoon in the garage.

The following is an example of a sentence fragment resulting from the expression of an incomplete thought.

Because she tripped a player. She was given a two-minute penalty.

"Because she tripped a player" is a dependent clause and as such, the thought expressed is incomplete (see page 187).

One possible correction would be.

Because she tripped a player, she was given a two-minute penalty.

(For more information on sentence structure, see section one.)

Misplaced or Dangling Modifiers

A modifier is a word or group of words that describes, explains or limits another word or group of words. Errors occur when the modifier is misplaced (not close enough to the word or group of words it describes, explains or limits) or dangling (does not describe, explain or limit any word or group of words in the sentence).

In the following example, the modifier "easily" is misplaced.

*We can't understand the French spoken by our Parisian visitors **easily**.*

To correct a misplaced modifier, you must determine which word or group of words the modifier describes, explains or limits and then reposition the modifier closer to that word or group of words.

*We can't **easily** understand the French spoken by our Parisian visitors.*

In the following example, the modifier "being completely blind" is dangling.

***Being completely blind**, Aunt Mary read the newspaper to Uncle Fred.*

A dangling modifier can be corrected by changing

* the subject of the sentence;
Being completely blind, Uncle Fred had Aunt Mary read him the newspaper.
* the modifier into a dependent clause.
Because he was blind, Aunt Mary read the newspaper to Uncle Fred.

Faulty Parallelism

Items in a series should be written in the same grammatical form: they should respect parallelism. Faulty parallelism occurs when the items are of different forms.

*Campers like swimming, canoeing and **to hike**.*

"Swimming" and "canoeing" are both gerunds while "to hike" is an infinitive. (For more information on gerunds and infinitives, see page 223.) To correct errors in parallelism, give each of the items the same form.

*Campers like swimming, canoeing and **hiking**.*

Subject-Verb Agreement

Subjects and verbs need to agree; in other words, a singular verb takes a singular verb, and a plural verb takes a plural verb. When a subject and a verb don't agree, an error occurs.

*Each of the employees **have** a private office.*

"Each" is the subject of the sentence and is singular.

*Each of the employees **has** a private office.*

Some nouns have the same singular and plural forms, and some nouns are always plural. (See page 220 for examples.) Some indefinite pronouns are singular, some are plural and some can be either singular or plural. (See page 225 for examples.)

Noun-Pronoun Agreement

A pronoun must agree in gender and number with the noun it replaces, and a possessive adjective must agree in gender with the person to whom it refers. When a noun and pronoun don't agree, or when a possessive adjective and a person don't agree, an error occurs.

Where was the 2007 World Series? **They** *were in Boston.*
James is my mother's personal assistant. **Her** *office is beside my mother's.*

In the above examples, "series" is a singular noun and "James" is a male.

Where was the 2007 World Series? **It** *was in Boston.*
James is my mother's personal assistant. **His** *office is beside my mother's.*

In formal writing, a possessive adjective must agree in gender with the person (or persons) to whom it refers.

A student should submit ~~their~~ *his or her assignments on time.*

Verb Tense and Voice Shifts

Be consistent in your writing, avoiding unnecessary shifts in tense and voice.

In winter, birds **eat** *the seeds that I* **bought***.*
The lights **were turned off***, and he* **locked** *the door.*

In the first example, "eat" is in the simple present tense and "bought" is in the simple past tense. In the second example, "were turned off" is in the passive voice and "locked" is in the active voice. To correct these errors, make sure the tenses and the voices are the same.

In winter, birds **eat** *the seeds that I* **buy***.*
He **turned off** *the lights, and he* **locked** *the door.*

(For more information on the active and the passive voice, see section five.)

Pinpoint

Rewrite each of the following sentences, correcting sentence errors.
In some cases, more than one correction is possible.

1. The Jacksons aren't members they have to pay full price to see the exhibit.

_____

_____

2. Please wash the dishes. As soon as you clear the table.

_____

_____

3. They realized the danger of neglecting car maintenance quickly.

_____

_____

4. Working out keeps me in shape regularly.

_____

5. I was tired out it was difficult for me to finish the race.

_____

_____

6. Carter is punctual, generous and a lot of fun.

_____

_____

7. Every spectator in the stadium have a great view of the playing field.

_____

_____

8. Julian is looking for her wife's passport.

_____

_____

9. If there is a storm tonight, you need to close the windows, unplug the computer and you will get out a flashlight.

_____

_____

10. The tests were finished, so Carrie left the classroom.

_____

_____

My eLab 🖉 Now that you have pinpointed your current level of understanding of common sentence errors, complete related exercises on My eLab for practice and instant feedback.

Chart **A** Common Information Question Words

INFORMATION QUESTION WORDS	EXAMPLES
Who	*Who* did Mary ask to the prom? Mary asked *Jason.* *Who* saw Jason at the prom? *Jason's brother* saw him.
What	*What* do you want for lunch? I want *chicken.* *What* was happening out there? *Two men were fighting.*
Where	*Where* do they live? They live *in Ottawa.*
When	*When* do you leave for South America? We leave *at the end of the month.*
Why	*Why* do you study so often? Because *I want to get good marks.*
Whose	*Whose book* is that? That's *Anna's book.*
Which	*Which* shirt will you buy? I will buy *the brown shirt*, not the green shirt.
How	*How* does she get such good marks? *She studies every day.*
How far	*How far* is Montreal from Toronto? It is *about 600 km.*
How much/many	*How much* money do you have with you? I have *about twenty dollars.* *How many* books did he buy? He bought *eleven books.*
How long	*How long* is the movie? It is *about two hours.*
How often	*How often* do you go to the supermarket? *About once a week.*

Note:
- *Who* and *what* can be used as subjects or objects.
  Who did you see? (Object) *Who* saw you? (Subject)
  What do you want? (Object) *What* is that? (Subject)
- *Whom* is used as an object in formal English.
  Whom did you see?
- *How much* is used with uncountable nouns and *how many* is used with countable nouns.
  How much coffee is left? (Coffee, a liquid, is uncountable.)
  How many cups of coffee have you had today? (Cups are countable.)

Chart B Common Irregular Verbs

The verb chart below lists 100 common irregular verbs.

BASE FORM	SIMPLE PAST	PAST PARTICIPLE	BASE FORM	SIMPLE PAST	PAST PARTICIPLE
be	was, were	been	fall	fell	fallen
become	became	become	feed	fed	fed
begin	began	begun	feel	felt	felt
bend	bent	bent	fight	fought	fought
bet	bet	bet	find	found	found
bite	bit	bitten	fit	fit	fit
bleed	bled	bled	fly	flew	flown
blow	blew	blown	forbid	forbade	forbidden
break	broke	broken	forget	forgot	forgotten
bring	brought	brought	forgive	forgave	forgiven
build	built	built	freeze	froze	frozen
burst	burst	burst	get	got	gotten
buy	bought	bought	give	gave	given
catch	caught	caught	go	went	gone
choose	chose	chosen	grow	grew	grown
come	came	come	hang	hung	hung
cost	cost	cost	have	had	had
cut	cut	cut	hear	heard	heard
deal	dealt	dealt	hide	hid	hidden
dig	dug	dug	hit	hit	hit
do	did	done	hold	held	held
draw	drew	drawn	hurt	hurt	hurt
drink	drank	drunk	keep	kept	kept
drive	drove	driven	know	knew	known
eat	ate	eaten	lay	laid	laid

BASE FORM	SIMPLE PAST	PAST PARTICIPLE	BASE FORM	SIMPLE PAST	PAST PARTICIPLE
lead	led	led	show	showed	shown
leave	left	left	shut	shut	shut
lend	lent	lent	sing	sang	sung
let	let	let	sit	sat	sat
lie	lay	lain	sleep	slept	slept
light	lit	lit	slide	slid	slid
lose	lost	lost	speak	spoke	spoken
make	made	made	spend	spent	spent
mean	meant	meant	stand	stood	stood
meet	met	met	steal	stole	stolen
pay	paid	paid	swim	swam	swum
put	put	put	swing	swung	swung
quit	quit	quit	take	took	taken
read	read	read	teach	taught	taught
ride	rode	ridden	tear	tore	torn
ring	rang	rung	tell	told	told
rise	rose	risen	think	thought	thought
run	ran	run	throw	threw	thrown
say	said	said	understand	understood	understood
see	saw	seen	wake	woke	woken
seek	sought	sought	wear	wore	worn
sell	sold	sold	win	won	won
send	sent	sent	wind	wound	wound
shake	shook	shaken	withdraw	withdrew	withdrawn
shoot	shot	shot	write	wrote	written

Notes